MATHEMATICS REVISION
FOR LEAVING CERTIFICATE
HIGHER LEVEL
PAPER 1

Third Edition

GEORGE HUMPHREY

Gill & Macmillan

Gill & Macmillan Ltd
Hume Avenue
Park West
Dublin 12
with associated companies throughout the world
www.gillmacmillan.ie

© George Humphrey 1996, 2000, 2007, 2008, 2010

978 0 7171 4149 4

Typeset by Replika Press Pvt Ltd, India

*The paper used in this book is made from the wood pulp of managed forests.
For every tree felled, at least one tree is planted, thereby renewing
natural resources.*

Contents

Preface

This book was written to help you revise for the Leaving Certificate Higher Level Mathematics Examination, Paper 1. It has been developed to help you to achieve the best result you can in the examination. Unlike a textbook, this book has been organised to make your revision easier.

Throughout your course you can use the book to:

- remind you of what you have been taught
- help you with your homework
- do some extra practice at the kinds of question you will meet in the examination
- sort out things you did not quite follow in class
- focus on the essential points in each topic
- organise your revision and preparation for the actual examination.

To make the best use of this book, attempt to solve the problems yourself before looking at the solutions given. Re-do any questions you answer incorrectly. Get into the habit of making your own notes as you work throughout the book and use these notes in later revision sessions.

I would like to thank Michael Dunne, Maryfield College, who read the entire manuscript and made many valuable suggestions which I have included in the final text. I would also like to thank Jane Finucane, first-year student, Trinity College, Dublin, who also read the entire manuscript and greatly reduced my errors!

I also wish to express my thanks to the staff at Gill & Macmillan for their advice, guidance and untiring assistance in the preparation and presentation of the text.

George Humphrey
St Andrew's College
Booterstown Avenue
Blackrock
Co. Dublin

Guidelines on Doing the Exam

Each question carries a total of 50 marks. Therefore, you should not spend more than 25 minutes answering any one question. Attempt each part of each question as there is an **'attempt mark'** given for each part which is normally worth one-third of the marks. Marks may be lost if all your work is not shown. If you use a calculator, show the results of each stage of the calculation. Do what the question asks and always write any formula that you use. Give clear reasons for your answers if asked. Make sure you understand the words *solve, verify, evaluate, show, prove, plot, investigate, hence, calculate.* Be familiar with the relevant pages of the mathematical tables, in particular pages 6, 7, 9, 41 and 42. Drawing diagrams can help you in obtaining a solution, but do not answer questions from the diagram where the use of a formula would be expected. It is good practice to make the units on both axes the same and it is essential when drawing circles.

Marking Scheme

There is an attempt to divide each question into 3 parts:

(a) Straightforward, testing only one or two basic concepts and carrying a total of 10 marks.
(b) More difficult but still straightforward and carrying a total of 20 marks.
(c) Much more challenging and may have several parts, all related to the one situation and carrying a total of 20 marks.

Structure of the examination

Paper 1

Time: $2\frac{1}{2}$ hours   Marks: 300

Attempt any 6 questions from a choice of 8

Q1, 2	Algebra
Q3	Matrices and Complex Numbers
Q4, 5	Sequences and Series, Induction, Logs and Inequalities
Q6, 7	Differentiation
Q8	Integration

Chapter **1**
Algebra

Simplifying Algebraic Expressions

Special Factors

1. $x^2 - y^2 = (x + y)(x - y)$
2. $x^3 + y^3 = (x + y)(x^2 - xy + y^2)$
3. $x^3 - y^3 = (x - y)(x^2 + xy + y^2)$

These factors occur frequently and should be memorised.

Example

Simplify $\dfrac{x - \dfrac{16}{x}}{1 + \dfrac{4}{x}}$.

Solution:

$$\dfrac{x - \dfrac{16}{x}}{1 + \dfrac{4}{x}}$$

$$= \frac{x^2 - 16}{x + 4} \qquad \text{[multiply each part of the fraction by } x]$$

$$= \frac{(x - 4)(x + 4)}{(x + 4)} \qquad \text{[factorise the top]}$$

$$= x - 4 \qquad \text{[divide top and bottom by } (x + 4)]$$

Example

Show that $\dfrac{\dfrac{x + 1}{x - 1} - \dfrac{x - 1}{x + 1}}{\dfrac{1}{x + 1} + \dfrac{1}{x - 1}}$

simplifies to a constant for $x \neq \pm 1$.

1

Solution:

$$\frac{\dfrac{x+1}{x-1} - \dfrac{x-1}{x+1}}{\dfrac{1}{x+1} + \dfrac{1}{x-1}}$$

$$= \frac{(x+1)(x+1) - (x-1)(x-1)}{(x-1)+(x+1)} \quad \left[\begin{array}{l}\text{multiply each fraction on the top and bottom} \\ \text{by } (x-1)(x+1)\end{array}\right]$$

$$= \frac{x^2 + 2x + 1 - x^2 + 2x - 1}{x - 1 + x + 1} \qquad \text{[remove brackets]}$$

$$= \frac{4x}{2x} \qquad\qquad\qquad\qquad \text{[simplify top and bottom]}$$

$$= 2 \quad \text{(a constant)} \qquad\qquad \text{[divide top and bottom by } 2x]$$

Example

If $x = \dfrac{6t}{1+t^2}$ and $y = \dfrac{2(1-t^2)}{1+t^2}$, evaluate $\dfrac{x^2}{3^2} + \dfrac{y^2}{2^2}$.

Solution:

$$\frac{x^2}{3^2} + \frac{y^2}{2^2} = \frac{\left(\dfrac{6t}{1+t^2}\right)^2}{9} + \frac{\left(\dfrac{2(1-t^2)}{1+t^2}\right)^2}{4}$$

$$= \frac{36t^2}{9(1+t^2)^2} + \frac{4(1 - 2t^2 + t^4)}{4(1+t^2)^2}$$

$$= \frac{4t^2}{(1+t^2)^2} + \frac{1 - 2t^2 + t^4}{(1+t^2)^2}$$

$$= \frac{1 + 2t^2 + t^4}{(1+t^2)^2} \qquad \text{[both fractions have the same denominator]}$$

$$= \frac{1 + 2t^2 + t^4}{1 + 2t^2 + t^4}$$

$$= 1$$

Note: It is not an acceptable method to substitute a particular value for t before evaluating.

Example

$f(x) = \dfrac{x^3 + 8}{x^2 - 4}, x \neq \pm 2, \quad g(x) = \dfrac{x^2 - 2x + 4}{x^2 - x - 2}, x \neq -1, 2.$

If $f(x) \div g(x) = ax + b$, find the value of a and the value of b.

Solution:

$f(x) \div g(x)$

$= \dfrac{x^3 + 8}{x^2 - 4} \div \dfrac{x^2 - 2x + 4}{x^2 - x - 2}$

$= \dfrac{x^3 + 8}{x^2 - 4} \times \dfrac{x^2 - x - 2}{x^2 - 2x + 4}$ $\qquad \left[\begin{array}{l}\text{turn the fraction we divide by} \\ \text{upside down and multiply}\end{array}\right]$

$= \dfrac{(x + 2)(x^2 - 2x + 4)}{(x - 2)(x + 2)} \times \dfrac{(x + 1)(x - 2)}{(x^2 - 2x + 4)}$ $\qquad$ [factorise top and bottom]

$= x + 1$ $\qquad \left[\begin{array}{l}\text{divide top and bottom by the common} \\ \text{factors } (x - 2), (x + 2) \text{ and } (x^2 - 2x + 4)\end{array}\right]$

Comparing:

$x + 1 = ax + b$

$\therefore \quad a = 1 \quad \text{and} \quad b = 1$

Example

For a fixed $k > 0$, let $f(x) = x^3 - k^2x, x \in \mathbf{R}$.
For $p \neq q$, divide $f(p) - f(q)$ by $(p - q)$.

Solution:

$f(x) = x^3 - k^2x$

$\therefore \quad f(p) = p^3 - k^2p \quad \text{and} \quad f(q) = q^3 - k^2q$

Thus,

$\dfrac{f(p) - f(q)}{(p - q)}$

$= \dfrac{(p^3 - k^2p) - (q^3 - k^2q)}{(p - q)}$

$= \dfrac{p^3 - k^2p - q^3 + k^2q}{(p - q)}$ $\qquad$ [remove brackets on top]

$= \dfrac{p^3 - q^3 - k^2p + k^2q}{(p - q)}$

$= \dfrac{(p - q)(p^2 + pq + q^2) - k^2(p - q)}{(p - q)}$ $\qquad$ [factorise the top]

$= p^2 + pq + q^2 - k^2$ $\qquad$ [divide top and bottom by $(p - q)$]

Changing the Subject of a Formula

When we rearrange a formula so that one of the variables is given in terms of the others, we are said to be 'changing the subject of the formula'. The rules in changing the subject of a formula are the same as when solving an equation; that is, we can:

> 1. Add or subtract the same quantity to or from both sides.
>
>   (In practice this involves moving a term from one side to another and changing its sign.)
>
> 2. Multiply or divide both sides by the same quantity.
>
> 3. Square both sides, cube both sides, etc.
>
> 4. Take the square root, cube root, etc. of both sides.

Example

If $\dfrac{8 - q^2}{2a^2} = m$, express a in terms of m and q.

Find the values of a when $q = 2$ and $m = 4.5$.

Solution:

$$\frac{8 - q^2}{2a^2} = m$$

$$8 - q^2 = 2a^2m \qquad\qquad \text{[multiply both sides by } 2a^2\text{]}$$

$$2a^2m = 8 - q^2 \qquad\qquad \text{[swap sides to have '}a\text{' on the left-hand side]}$$

$$a^2 = \frac{8 - q^2}{2m} \qquad\qquad \text{[divide both sides by } 2m\text{]}$$

$$a = \pm\sqrt{\frac{8 - q^2}{2m}} \qquad\qquad \text{[take the square root of both sides]}$$

$$q = 2, \quad m = 4.5$$

$$a = \pm\sqrt{\frac{8 - q^2}{2m}} = \pm\sqrt{\frac{8 - 2^2}{2(4.5)}} = \pm\sqrt{\frac{8 - 4}{9}} = \pm\sqrt{\frac{4}{9}} = \pm\frac{\sqrt{4}}{\sqrt{9}} = \pm\frac{2}{3}$$

Note: If $x^2 = k$, then $x = \pm k$. Always include both the positive and negative solutions.

Example

If $\sqrt[3]{\dfrac{3x-1}{2x+1}} = y$, express x in terms of y.

Solution:

$$\sqrt[3]{\dfrac{3x-1}{2x+1}} = y$$

$$\left(\dfrac{3x-1}{2x+1}\right)^{\frac{1}{3}} = y \qquad\qquad \text{[replace } \sqrt[3]{\ } \text{ with } (\ )^{\frac{1}{3}}\text{]}$$

$$\left[\left(\dfrac{3x-1}{2x+1}\right)^{\frac{1}{3}}\right]^{3} = y^3 \qquad\qquad \text{[cube both sides]}$$

$$\dfrac{3x-1}{2x+1} = y^3$$

$$3x - 1 = (2x+1)y^3 \qquad \text{[multiply both sides by } (2x+1)\text{]}$$

$$3x - 1 = 2xy^3 + y^3$$

$$3x - 2xy^3 = y^3 + 1 \qquad\qquad \text{[terms with } x \text{ on the left-hand side]}$$

$$x(3 - 2y^3) = y^3 + 1 \qquad\qquad \text{[take out common factor } x \text{ on the left-hand side]}$$

$$x = \dfrac{y^3 + 1}{3 - 2y^3} \qquad\qquad \text{[divide both sides by } (3 - 2y^3)\text{]}$$

Surds

Properties of surds:

$$\textbf{1.} \quad \sqrt{ab} = \sqrt{a}\,\sqrt{b} \qquad \textbf{2.} \quad \sqrt{\dfrac{a}{b}} = \dfrac{\sqrt{a}}{\sqrt{b}} \qquad \textbf{3.} \quad \sqrt{a}\,\sqrt{a} = a$$

Simplification of Surds

The key idea is to find the largest possible perfect square that will divide evenly into the number under the square root and use property **1**.

The perfect squares are 1, 4, 9, 16, 25, 36, 49, 64, 81, 100, ..., etc.

Example

Write each of the following in the form $a\sqrt{b}$, where b is prime:

(i) $\sqrt{8}$ (ii) $\sqrt{45}$ (iii) $\sqrt{75}$ (iv) $\sqrt{80}$ (v) $\sqrt{200}$ (vi) $\frac{1}{3}\sqrt{108}$

Solutions:

(i) $\sqrt{8} = \sqrt{4 \times 2} = \sqrt{4}\,\sqrt{2} = 2\sqrt{2}$

(ii) $\sqrt{45} = \sqrt{9 \times 5} = \sqrt{9}\,\sqrt{5} = 3\sqrt{5}$

(iii) $\sqrt{75} = \sqrt{25 \times 3} = \sqrt{25}\,\sqrt{3} = 5\sqrt{3}$

(iv) $\sqrt{80} = \sqrt{16 \times 5} = \sqrt{16}\,\sqrt{5} = 4\sqrt{5}$

(v) $\sqrt{200} = \sqrt{100 \times 2} = \sqrt{100}\,\sqrt{2} = 10\sqrt{2}$

(vi) $\frac{1}{3}\sqrt{108} = \frac{1}{3}\sqrt{36 \times 3} = \frac{1}{3}\sqrt{36}\,\sqrt{3} = \frac{1}{3}6\sqrt{3} = 2\sqrt{3}$

Rationalising the Denominator

To rationalise the denominator, multiply top and bottom by the conjugate surd of the bottom.

$a + \sqrt{b}$ is a compound surd. Its conjugate is $a - \sqrt{b}$.

$\sqrt{a} - \sqrt{b}$ is a compound surd. Its conjugate is $\sqrt{a} + \sqrt{b}$.

Example

Express $\dfrac{1 - \sqrt{3}}{1 + \sqrt{3}}$ in the form $\sqrt{a} - b$.

Solution:

$$\frac{1 - \sqrt{3}}{1 + \sqrt{3}} = \frac{1 - \sqrt{3}}{1 + \sqrt{3}} \cdot \frac{1 - \sqrt{3}}{1 - \sqrt{3}} \qquad \text{[multiply top and bottom by } (1 - \sqrt{3})\text{]}$$

$$= \frac{1 - \sqrt{3} - \sqrt{3} + 3}{1 - \sqrt{3} + \sqrt{3} - 3} \qquad \left[\begin{array}{l}\text{multiply top by the top and}\\ \text{bottom by the bottom}\end{array}\right]$$

$$= \frac{4 - 2\sqrt{3}}{-2}$$

$$= \frac{2\sqrt{3} - 4}{2} \qquad \text{[multiply each part by } -1\text{]}$$

$$= \sqrt{3} - 2 \qquad \text{[divide each part by 2]}$$

Example

(i) If $k(5 - \sqrt{2})(5 + \sqrt{2}) = 46$, find k.

(ii) Simplify $(\sqrt{p + q} - \sqrt{p})(\sqrt{p + q} + \sqrt{p})$.

Solution:

(i)
$$k(5 - \sqrt{2})(5 + \sqrt{2}) = 46$$
$$k(25 + 5\sqrt{2} - 5\sqrt{2} - 2) = 46$$
$$k(23) = 46$$
$$23k = 46$$
$$k = 2$$

(ii) $(\sqrt{p + q} - \sqrt{p})(\sqrt{p + q} + \sqrt{p})$

$= p + q + \sqrt{p}\sqrt{p + q} - \sqrt{p}\sqrt{p + q} - p$

$= q$

Example

If $\dfrac{\sqrt{5} - 2}{\sqrt{5} + 2} + \dfrac{\sqrt{5} + 2}{\sqrt{5} - 2} = k$, express $\sqrt{k}$ in the form $a\sqrt{b}$, where b is prime.

Solution:

$$\frac{\sqrt{5} - 2}{\sqrt{5} + 2} + \frac{\sqrt{5} + 2}{\sqrt{5} - 2}$$

$$= \frac{(\sqrt{5} - 2)(\sqrt{5} - 2) + (\sqrt{5} + 2)(\sqrt{5} + 2)}{(\sqrt{5} + 2)(\sqrt{5} - 2)} \qquad \left[\text{we use the fact that } \frac{a}{b} + \frac{c}{d} = \frac{ad + bc}{bd} \right]$$

$$= \frac{5 - 4\sqrt{5} + 4 + 5 + 4\sqrt{5} + 4}{5 - 2\sqrt{5} + 2\sqrt{5} - 4}$$

$$= \frac{18}{1}$$

$$= 18 = k$$

$$\sqrt{k} = \sqrt{18} = \sqrt{9 \times 2} = \sqrt{9}\sqrt{2} = 3\sqrt{2}$$

Quadratic Equations

Any equation of the form $ax^2 + bx + c = 0$, $a \neq 0$, is called a quadratic equation. To solve a quadratic equation we either:

1. Factorise and let each factor $= 0$; or
2. Use the formula $x = \dfrac{-b \pm \sqrt{b^2 - 4ac}}{2a}$.

Example

Solve $x^2 - 9x + 20 = 0$ and, hence, solve $\left(t + \dfrac{4}{t}\right)^2 - 9\left(t + \dfrac{4}{t}\right) + 20 = 0$.

Solution:

$$x^2 - 9x + 20 = 0$$

$$\Rightarrow \quad (x - 5)(x - 4) = 0$$

$$\Rightarrow \quad x - 5 = 0 \quad \text{or} \quad x - 4 = 0$$

$$\Rightarrow \quad x = 5 \quad \text{or} \quad x = 4$$

$$\text{Let}\left(t + \dfrac{4}{t}\right) = x$$

$\Rightarrow \qquad t + \dfrac{4}{t} = 5$ or $\Rightarrow \qquad t + \dfrac{4}{t} = 4$

$\Rightarrow \qquad t^2 + 4 = 5t$ $\Rightarrow \qquad t^2 + 4 = 4t$

[multiply across by t]   [multiply across by t]

$\Rightarrow \qquad t^2 - 5t + 4 = 0$ $\Rightarrow \qquad t^2 - 4t + 4 = 0$

$\Rightarrow \qquad (t - 4)(t - 1) = 0$ $\Rightarrow \qquad (t - 2)(t - 2) = 0$

$\Rightarrow \qquad t - 4 = 0 \quad \text{or} \quad t - 1 = 0$ $\Rightarrow \qquad t - 2 = 0$

$\Rightarrow \qquad t = 4 \quad \text{or} \quad t = 1$ $\Rightarrow \qquad t = 2$

$$\therefore \quad t = 4,\ t = 1 \text{ or } t = 2$$

Example

Express in surd form the roots x_1 and x_2 of the quadratic equaion $x^2 - 6x + 1 = 0$ and evaluate $x_1 + x_2$.

Solution:

$x^2 - 6x + 1 = 0$ [surd form $\therefore$ use formula]

$a = 1, \quad b = -6, \quad c = 1$

$$x = \frac{-b \pm \sqrt{b^2 - 4ac}}{2a}$$

$$= \frac{6 \pm \sqrt{(-6)^2 - 4(1)(1)}}{2(1)}$$

$$= \frac{6 \pm \sqrt{36 - 4}}{2}$$

$$= \frac{6 \pm \sqrt{32}}{2}$$

$$= \frac{6 \pm 4\sqrt{2}}{2}$$

$$= 3 \pm 2\sqrt{2} \qquad \text{[divide both parts on top by 2]}$$

$\sqrt{32}$

$= \sqrt{16 \times 2}$

$= \sqrt{16}\sqrt{2}$

$= 4\sqrt{2}$

$$\therefore \quad x_1 = 3 + 2\sqrt{2} \quad \text{and} \quad x_2 = 3 - 2\sqrt{2}$$

$$x_1 + x_2 = 3 + 2\sqrt{2} + 3 - 2\sqrt{2} = 6$$

Quadratic Equations in Fractional Form

When fractions are involved, do the following:

1. Factorise denominators (if necessary).
2. Find the L.C.M. of the denominators.
3. Express each part of the equation with its denominator equal to this L.C.M.
4. Remove the L.C.M.
5. Solve as before (using factors or formula).
6. Any answer that makes one of the original denominators = 0 must be rejected.

Example

Solve the equation $\dfrac{x}{x - 1} + \dfrac{1}{x^2 - 3x + 2} = \dfrac{3x}{x - 2}$, $x \neq 1, 2$.

Solution:

$$\frac{x}{x - 1} + \frac{1}{x^2 - 3x + 2} = \frac{3x}{x - 2}$$

$$\Rightarrow \quad \frac{x}{(x - 1)} + \frac{1}{(x - 1)(x - 2)} = \frac{3x}{(x - 2)} \qquad \text{[factorise denominators]}$$

9

The L.C.M. is $(x - 1)(x - 2)$

$\Rightarrow \quad \dfrac{x(x - 2) + 1 = 3x(x - 1)}{(x - 1)(x - 2)}$ [each part in terms of the L.C.M.]

$\Rightarrow \quad x(x - 2) + 1 = 3x(x - 1)$ [remove L.C.M.]

$\Rightarrow \quad x^2 - 2x + 1 = 3x^2 - 3x$ [remove brackets]

$\Rightarrow \quad x^2 - 2x + 1 - 3x^2 + 3x = 0$ [every term to the left]

$\Rightarrow \quad -2x^2 + x + 1 = 0$ [clear up left-hand side]

$\Rightarrow \quad 2x^2 - x - 1 = 0$ [make coefficient of x^2 positive]

$\Rightarrow \quad (2x + 1)(x - 1) = 0$ [factorise]

$\Rightarrow \quad 2x + 1 = 0 \quad$ or $\quad x - 1 = 0$ [let each factor = 0]

$\Rightarrow \quad 2x = -1 \quad$ or $\quad x = 1$

$\Rightarrow \quad x = -\tfrac{1}{2} \quad$ or $\quad x = 1$

$x = -\tfrac{1}{2}$ will satisfy the original equation and is a solution.

$x = 1$ will make $\dfrac{x}{x - 1} = \dfrac{1}{0}$, which is undefined.

Hence, $x = 1$ is rejected as a solution

$\therefore \quad$ the solution is $x = -\tfrac{1}{2}$.

So when solving an equation given in fractional form, reject any solution that would make any expression on the bottom equal to zero in the original equation.

Simultaneous Linear Equations

Simultaneous linear equations are solved with the following steps:

1. Write both equations in the form $ax + by = k$.

2. Make the coefficients of one of the variables the same in both equations.

3. Add or subtract (depending on signs) one equation from the other to form a new equation in one variable.

4. Solve the new equation obtained in step **3**.

5. Put the value obtained in step **4** into one of the given equations to find the corresponding value of the other variable.

Example

Solve the simultaneous equations $2x - 5y = 19$ and $\dfrac{3x}{2} + \dfrac{4y}{3} = -1$.

Solution:

First clear the second equation of fractions.

$$\frac{3x}{2} + \frac{4y}{3} = -1$$

$\Rightarrow \qquad 9x + 8y = -6$ [multiply each part by 6]

Write the equation thus:

$2x - 5y = 19$	①
$9x + 8y = -6$	②

Step 1: Make coefficients of x the same.

Multiply ① by 9 and – by 2

$18x - 45y = 171$	① × 9
$18x + 16y = -12$	② × 2

Step 2: Subtract the second equation from the first. $\qquad -61y = 183$

Step 3: Solve this new equation $\qquad\qquad \Rightarrow 61y = -183$

$$\Rightarrow \quad y = -3$$

Step 4: Put $y = -3$ into equation ① or ②. $\qquad 2x - 5y = 19 \qquad$ ①

$\Rightarrow \qquad 2x - 5(-3) = 19$

$\Rightarrow \qquad 2x + 15 = 19$

$\Rightarrow \qquad 2x = 19 - 15$

$\Rightarrow \qquad 2x = 4$

$\Rightarrow \qquad x = 2$

Thus, the solution is $x = 2$, $y = -3$.

Sometimes a substitution is required, as in the next example.

Example

Solve the simultaneous equations

$$\frac{3}{x-3} + \frac{4}{y+1} = -5 \quad \text{and} \quad \frac{2}{x-3} - \frac{3}{y+1} = 8.$$

Solution:

Let $p = \dfrac{1}{x-3}$ and $q = \dfrac{1}{y+1}$.

Then the equations become $3p + 4q = -5$ and $2p - 3q = 8$.

$3p + 4q = -5$	①	
$2p - 3q = 8$	②	

$6p + 8q = -10$ ① × 2
$6p - 9q = 24$ ② × 3

$17q = -34$ (subtract)
$q = -2$

$$p = \frac{1}{x - 3} = 1$$

$\Rightarrow \qquad 1 = x - 3$
$\Rightarrow \qquad x = 4$

$3p + 4q = -5$
$\downarrow$

$3p + 4(-2) = -5$
$3p - 8 = -5$

$3p = 3$
$p = 1$

$$q = \frac{1}{y + 1} = -2$$

$\Rightarrow \qquad 1 = -2y - 2$
$\Rightarrow \qquad 2y = -3$
$\Rightarrow \qquad y = -\frac{3}{2}$

Solutions containing fractions or unknown coefficients

If the solution contains fractions, or unknown coefficients, the substitution can be difficult. In such situations the following method is useful:

> **Step 1:** Eliminate y and solve the new equation to find x.
>
> **Step 2:** Eliminate x and solve the new equation to find y.

Example

Solve the equations $2x + 3y = -2$ and $3x + 7y = -6$.

Solution:

Step 1: Eliminate y

$2x + 3y = -2$ ①
$3x + 7y = -6$ ②

$14x + 21y = -14$ ① × 7
$9x + 21y = -18$ ② × 3

$5x = 4$ [subtract]
$\Rightarrow \qquad x = \frac{4}{5}$

Step 2: Eliminate x

$2x + 3y = -2$ ①
$3x + 7y = -6$ ②

$6x + 9y = -6$ ① × 3
$6x + 14y = -12$ ① × 2

$-5y = 6$ [subtract]
$\Rightarrow \qquad 5y = -6$
$\Rightarrow \qquad y = -\frac{6}{5}$

Thus, the solution is $x = \frac{4}{5}$ and $y = -\frac{6}{5}$.

Note: This method can also be used if the solution does not contain fractions.

Example

Solve, for x and y, the simultaneous equations

$ax + by = c$ and $px + qy = r$.

Solution:

Eliminate y

$ax + by = c$	①
$px + qy = r$	②
$aqx + bqy = cq$	① × q
$bpx + bqy = br$	② × b
$aqx - bpx = cq - br$	[subtract]
$(aq - bp)x = cq - br$	

$$x = \frac{cq - br}{aq - bp}$$

Eliminate x

$ax + by = c$	①
$px + qy = r$	②
$apx + bpy = cp$	① × p
$apx + aqy = ar$	② × a
$bpy - aqy = cp - ar$	[subtract]
$(bp - aq)y = cp - ar$	

$$y = \frac{cp - ar}{bp - aq}$$

Simultaneous Linear Equations in Three Variables

Simultaneous linear equations in three variable are solved with the following steps:

We are given three equations, ①, ② and ③.

1. Select one pair of equations and eliminate one of the variables; call this equation ④.

2. Select another pair of equations and eliminate the **same** variable; call this equation ⑤.

3. Solve the equations ④ and ⑤.

4. Put the answers from step 3 into ①, ②, or ③ to find the value of the third variable.

Example

Solve $\quad x - 3y + z = 2$

$\qquad 2x + 5y - z = 21$

$\qquad 4x + 3y + 3z = 25$

Hence, solve $\quad \dfrac{1}{a + 1} - \dfrac{3}{b - 1} + \dfrac{1}{c} = 2$

$$\dfrac{2}{a + 1} + \dfrac{5}{b - 1} - \dfrac{1}{c} = 21$$

$$\dfrac{4}{a + 1} + \dfrac{3}{b - 1} + \dfrac{3}{c} = 25$$

Solution:

$$x - 3y + z = 2 \qquad ①$$
$$2x + 5y - z = 21 \qquad ②$$
$$4x + 3y + 3z = 25 \qquad ③$$

$x - 3y + z = 2 \qquad ①$	$3x - 9y + 3z = 6 \qquad ① \times 3$
$\underline{2x + 5y - z = 21 \qquad ②}$	$\underline{4x + 3y + 3z = 25 \qquad ③}$
$3x + 2y = 23 \qquad ④ \text{ [add]}$	$-x - 12y = -19 \qquad ⑤ \text{ [subtract]}$

Now solve between equations ④ and ⑤:

$3x + 2y = 23 \qquad ④$	$-x - 12y = -19 \qquad ④$
$\underline{-3x - 36y = -57 \qquad ⑤ \times 3}$	$-x - 12(1) = -19$
$-34y = -34 \qquad \text{[add]}$	$-x - 12 = -19$
$34y = 34$	$-x = -7$
$y = 1$	$x = 7$

$$x - 3y + z = 2 \qquad\qquad ①$$
$$7 - 3(1) + z = 2 \qquad\qquad [\text{put in } x = 7, y = 1]$$
$$7 - 3 + z = 2$$
$$z = 2 - 7 + 3$$
$$z = -2$$

Thus, $x = 7$, $y = 1$ and $z = -2$.
By comparison:

$\dfrac{1}{a + 1} = x$	$\dfrac{1}{b - 1} = y$	$\dfrac{1}{c} = z$
$\dfrac{1}{a + 1} = 7$	$\dfrac{1}{b - 1} = 1$	$\dfrac{1}{c} = -2$
$7a + 7 = 1$	$b - 1 = 1$	$-2c = 1$
$7a = -6$	$b = 1 + 1$	$2c = -1$
$a = -\frac{6}{7}$	$b = 2$	$c = -\frac{1}{2}$

Note: If one equation contains only two unknowns, then the other two equations should be used to obtain a second equation in the same two unknowns; e.g. solve:

$$3x + 2y - z = 3 \quad ① \qquad 5x - 3y + 2z = 3 \quad ② \qquad \text{and} \quad 5x + 3z = 14 \quad ③$$

Here, from equations ① and ②, y should be eliminated to obtain an equation in x and z, which should then be taken with equation ③.

The next example illustrates the case where one equation contains one unknown, the next equation contains two unknowns and the third equation contains three unknowns.

Example

Solve the simultaneous equations:

$$\frac{1}{x} = 1\tfrac{1}{4}, \qquad \frac{1}{x} + \frac{1}{y} = 2\tfrac{1}{3}, \qquad \frac{1}{x} + \frac{1}{y} + \frac{1}{z} = 3\tfrac{1}{2}.$$

Solution:

$$\frac{1}{x} = 1\tfrac{1}{4}$$

$$\frac{1}{x} = \frac{5}{4}$$

$$x = \frac{4}{5}$$

[invert both sides]

$$\frac{1}{x} + \frac{1}{y} = 2\tfrac{1}{3}$$

$$\frac{5}{4} + \frac{1}{y} = \frac{7}{3}$$

$$\frac{1}{y} = \frac{7}{3} - \frac{5}{4}$$

$$\frac{1}{y} = \frac{13}{12}$$

$$y = \frac{12}{13} \qquad \text{[invert both sides]}$$

$$\frac{1}{x} + \frac{1}{y} + \frac{1}{z} = 3\tfrac{1}{2}$$

$$\frac{5}{4} + \frac{13}{12} + \frac{1}{z} = \frac{7}{2}$$

$$\frac{1}{z} = \frac{7}{2} - \frac{5}{4} - \frac{13}{12}$$

$$\frac{1}{z} = \frac{7}{6}$$

$$z = \frac{6}{7} \qquad \text{[invert both sides]}$$

Linear–Quadratic Systems

The **method of substitution** is used to solve between a linear equation and a quadratic equation.

The method involves three steps:

1. From the linear equation, express one variable in terms of the other.
2. Substitute this into the quadratic equation and solve.
3. Substitute separately the value(s) obtained in step 2 into the linear equation in step 1 to find the corresponding value(s) of the other variable.

Example

Solve the simultaneous equations:
$2x - y - 1 = 0$ and $3x^2 - 2xy + y^2 = 9$.

Solution:

Step 1: $2x - y - 1 = 0$ [get y on its own from the linear equation.

$$-y = -2x + 1$$

It is easier to get y on its own rather than x,
because it avoids fractions.]

$$y = (2x - 1)$$

Step 2:
$$3x^2 - 2xy + y^2 = 9$$
$$3x^2 - 2x(2x - 1) + (2x - 1)^2 = 9 \quad \text{[put in } (2x - 1) \text{ for } y]$$
$$3x^2 - 4x^2 + 2x + 4x^2 - 4x + 1 = 9 \quad \text{[remove brackets]}$$
$$3x^2 - 2x - 8 = 0$$
$$(3x + 4)(x - 2) = 0$$
$$3x + 4 = 0 \quad \text{or} \quad x - 2 = 0$$
$$3x = -4 \quad \text{or} \quad x = 2$$
$$x = -\frac{4}{3} \quad \text{or} \quad x = 2$$

Step 3: Substitute separately $x = -\frac{4}{3}$ and $x = 2$ into the linear equation.

$x = -\frac{4}{3}$: $y = 2x - 1 = 2\left(-\frac{4}{3}\right) - 1 = -\frac{8}{3} - I = -\frac{11}{3}$

$x = 2$: $y = 2x - 1 = 2(2) - 1 = 4 - 1 = 3$

Thus, the solutions are $x = -\frac{4}{3}, y = -\frac{11}{3}$ or $x = 2, y = 3$.

Example

Solve the simultaneous equations:
$2x - 3y - 1 = 0$ and $x^2 - 2xy - 3y^2 + 3 = 0$.

Solution:

Step 1: $2x - 3y - 1 = 0$ [get x, or y, on its own from the linear equation]

$$2x = 3y + 1$$

$$x = \left(\frac{3y + 1}{2}\right) \quad \text{[}x \text{ on its own]}$$

Step 2:
$$x^2 - 2xy - 3y^2 + 3 = 0$$

$$\left(\frac{3y + 1}{2}\right)^2 - 2\left(\frac{3y + 1}{2}\right)y - 3y^2 + 3 = 0 \qquad \left[\text{put in}\left(\frac{3y + 1}{2}\right)\text{for } x\right]$$

$$\frac{(1 + 6y + 9y^2)}{4} - 3y^2 - y - 3y^2 + 3 = 0$$

$$1 + 6y + 9y^2 - 12y^2 - 4y - 12y^2 + 12 = 0 \qquad \text{[multiply across by 4]}$$

$$-15y^2 + 2y + 13 = 0$$

$$15y^2 - 2y - 13 = 0 \qquad \text{[change all signs]}$$

$$(15y + 13)(y - 1) = 0$$

$$15y + 13 = 0 \qquad \text{or} \qquad y - 1 = 0$$

$$15y = -13 \qquad \text{or} \qquad y = 1$$

$$y = -\tfrac{13}{15} \qquad \text{or} \qquad y = 1$$

Step 3: Substitute separately $y = -\frac{13}{15}$ and $y = 1$ into the linear equation.

$$y = -\tfrac{13}{15}: \quad x = \frac{3y + 1}{2} = \frac{3(-\frac{13}{15}) + 1}{2} = \frac{-\frac{13}{5} + 1}{2} = \frac{-13 + 5}{10} = -\frac{8}{10} = -\frac{4}{5}$$

$$y = 1: \quad x = \frac{3y + 1}{2} = \frac{3(1) + 1}{2} = \frac{3 + 1}{2} = \frac{4}{2} = 2$$

Thus, the solutions are $x = -\frac{4}{5}, y = -\frac{13}{15}$ or $x = 2, y = 1$.

Note: Sometimes it is not so obvious which equation is of the 1st degree and which equation is of the 2nd degree. Consider the equations:

(i) $\quad \dfrac{1}{x} + \dfrac{y}{x} = 25 \qquad$ and $\qquad$ (ii) $\quad \dfrac{x}{y} + x = \dfrac{9}{y}$

(i) $\quad \dfrac{1}{x} + \dfrac{y}{x} = 25 \qquad\qquad\qquad$ (ii) $\quad \dfrac{x}{y} + x = \dfrac{9}{y}$

$\Rightarrow 1 + y = 25x \qquad\qquad\qquad\qquad \Rightarrow x + xy = 9$

[multiply across by x] $\qquad\qquad\qquad$ [multiply across by y]

This is a 1st degree equation. $\qquad\qquad$ This is a 2nd degree equation.

This solution is now similar to the previous example,

giving $x = \frac{3}{5}, y = 14$ or $x = -\frac{3}{5}, y = -16$.

Surd Equations

Surd equations are solved with the following steps:

1. **(a)** When the equation contains one surd, arrange to have this surd on one side on its own and then square both sides.

   (b) When there are two surd parts in the equation it is advisable to have one surd on either side before squaring both sides. After squaring there will be only one surd part. Arrange to have this surd on its own on one side and then square both sides again.

2. Solve the resultant equation

3. Test every root in the **original** equation.

Example

Solve $x = \sqrt{14 - x} + 2$.

Solution:

$$x = \sqrt{14 - x} + 2.$$

$(x - 2) = \sqrt{14 - x}$ [rearrange with surd expression on its own]

$(x - 2)^2 = (\sqrt{14 - x})^2$ [square both sides]

$x^2 - 4x + 4 = 14 - x$ [remove brackets]

$x^2 - 4x + 4 - 14 + x = 0$ [everything to the left]

$x^2 - 3x - 10 = 0$ [clear up]

$(x - 5)(x + 2) = 0$ [factorise]

$x - 5 = 0$ or $x + 2 = 0$

$x = 5$ or $x = -2$

$$x = \sqrt{14 - x} + 2$$

$x =$	5		$x =$	-2
x	$\sqrt{14 - x} + 2$		x	$\sqrt{14 - x} + 2$
5	$\sqrt{14 - 5} + 2$		-2	$\sqrt{14 - (-2)} + 2$
	$= \sqrt{9} + 2$			$= \sqrt{16} + 2$
	$= 3 + 2$			$= 4 + 2$
	$= 5$			$= 6$

$5 = 5$ $-2 \neq 6$

$\therefore x = 5$ is a solution $\therefore x = -2$ is not a solution

$\therefore$ solution is $x = 5$.

Example

Solve $\sqrt{3x-2} - \sqrt{x-2} = 2$.

Solution:

$$\sqrt{3x-2} - \sqrt{x-2} = 2$$

$$\sqrt{3x-2} = 2 + \sqrt{x-2} \qquad \text{[one surd on each side]}$$

$$(\sqrt{3x-2})^2 = (2 + \sqrt{x-2})^2 \qquad \text{[square both sides]}$$

$$3x - 2 = 4 + 4\sqrt{x-2} + x - 2 \qquad \text{[remove brackets]}$$

$$3x - 2 - 4 - x + 2 = 4\sqrt{x-2} \qquad \text{[surd on its own]}$$

$$2x - 4 = 4\sqrt{x-2} \qquad \text{[clear up left-hand side]}$$

$$x - 2 = 2\sqrt{x-2} \qquad \text{[divide both sides by 2]}$$

$$(x-2)^2 = (2\sqrt{x-2})^2 \qquad \text{[square both sides]}$$

$$x^2 - 4x + 4 = 4(x-2)$$

$$x^2 - 4x + 4 = 4x - 8$$

$$x^2 - 8x + 12 = 0$$

$$(x-6)(x-2) = 0$$

$$x - 6 = 0 \quad \text{or} \quad x - 2 = 0$$

$$x = 6 \quad \text{or} \quad x = 2$$

Both $x = 6$ and $x = 2$ will satisfy the original equation and, hence, are solutions.

Modulus Equations

Modulus equations are solved with the following steps:

1. Arrange to have the modulus part by itself on one side of the equation.
2. Square both sides (this removes the modulus bars).
3. Solve the resultant equation.

Note: If there are two modulus parts, arrange to have one modulus part on each side.

19

Example

Solve $|2x + 3| - |x + 7| = 0$.

Solution:

$$|2x + 3| - |x + 7| = 0$$

$\Rightarrow \qquad |2x + 3| = |x + 7| \qquad$ [one modulus on each side]

$\Rightarrow \qquad (2x + 3)^2 = (x + 7)^2 \qquad$ [square both sides]

$\Rightarrow \qquad 4x^2 + 12x + 9 = x^2 + 14x + 49$

$\Rightarrow \qquad 3x^2 - 2x - 40 = 0$

$\Rightarrow \qquad (3x + 10)(x - 4) = 0$

$\Rightarrow \qquad 3x + 10 = 0 \qquad$ or $\qquad x - 4 = 0$

$\Rightarrow \qquad 3x = -10 \qquad$ or $\qquad x = 4$

$\Rightarrow \qquad x = -\frac{10}{3} \qquad$ or $\qquad x = 4$

Example

Find the values of k for which $\dfrac{5|k - 1|}{\sqrt{k^2 + 1}} = \sqrt{10}$.

Solution:

Squaring both sides removes both the modulus bars and the square roots.

$$\frac{5|k - 1|}{\sqrt{k^2 + 1}} = \sqrt{10}$$

$\Rightarrow \qquad \dfrac{25(k^2 - 2k + 1)}{k^2 + 1} = 10 \qquad$ [square both sides]

$\Rightarrow \qquad 25k^2 - 50k + 25 = 10k^2 + 10 \qquad$ [multiply both sides by $(k^2 + 1)$]

$\Rightarrow \qquad 15k^2 - 50k + 15 = 0$

$\Rightarrow \qquad 3k^2 - 10k + 3 = 0$

$\Rightarrow \qquad (3k - 1)(k - 3) = 0$

$\Rightarrow \qquad 3k - 1 = 0 \quad$ or $\quad k - 3 = 0$

$\Rightarrow \qquad 3k = 1 \quad$ or $\qquad k = 3$

$\Rightarrow \qquad k = \frac{1}{3} \quad$ or $\qquad k = 3$

Simple Inequalities

Solving inequalities is exactly the same as solving equations, with the following exception:

> If we multiply or divide both sides of an inequality by a negative number, we must reverse the direction of the inequality.
>
> '>' becomes '<'   or   '<' becomes '>'

Example

Solve (i) $3(x - 4) \geq 5(2x - 3) + 17$ (ii) $\frac{1}{2}x - 2 < x - \frac{1}{2}$.

Solution:

(i)

	$3(x - 4) \geq 5(2x - 3) + 17$	
$\Rightarrow$	$3x - 12 \geq 10x - 15 + 17$	[remove the brackets]
$\Rightarrow$	$3x - 10x \geq -15 + 17 + 12$	[letters to the left, numbers to the right]
$\Rightarrow$	$-7x \geq 14$	[clear up both sides]
$\Rightarrow$	$7x \leq -14$	[change signs and reverse inequality sign]
$\Rightarrow$	$x \leq -2$	[divide both sides by 7]

(ii)

	$\frac{1}{2}x - 2 < x - \frac{1}{2}$	
$\Rightarrow$	$x - 4 < 2x - 1$	[multiply each part by 2]
$\Rightarrow$	$x - 2x < -1 + 4$	[letters to the left, numbers to the right]
$\Rightarrow$	$-x < 3$	[clear up both sides]
$\Rightarrow$	$x > -3$	[change signs and reverse inequality sign]

Quadratic Inequalities

Quadratic inequalities are solved with the following steps:

1. Replace $\geq, \leq, >$ or $<$ with $=$ (make it an equation).
2. Solve the equation to find the roots.
3. Test a number between the roots in the **original** inequality (usually 0).
4. Two possibilities arise:

   (a) If the inequality holds, then the solution lies between the roots.

   (b) If the inequality does not hold, then the solution does not lie between the roots.

Note: We can also test a number **outside** the roots.

21

Example

Solve $4 - 3x - x^2 \le 0$

Solution:

$$4 - 3x - x^2 \le 0$$

1. $4 - 3x - x^2 = 0$ [replace $\le$ with $=$]

2. $x^2 + 3x - 4 = 0$ [change all signs]

        $(x + 4)(x - 1) = 0$

        $x + 4 = 0$ or $x - 1 = 0$

           $x = -4$ or $x = 1$

3.   Test 0 (between the roots) in the original inequality.

        $4 - 3\,(0) - (0)^2 \le 0$

               $4 \le 0$ false

4. $\therefore$ solution does not lie between -4 and 1

      $\therefore$ solution is $x \le -4 \cup x \ge 1$.

Example

Solve $x + 3 > 2x^2$.

Solution:

$$x + 3 > 2x^2$$

1. $x + 3 = 2x^2$ [replace $>$ with $=$]

2. $-2x^2 + x + 3 = 0$

       $2x^2 - x - 3 = 0$

    $(2x - 3)(x + 1) = 0$

      $2x - 3 = 0$ or $x + 1 = 0$

        $2x = 3$ or $x = -1$

         $x = \frac{3}{2}$ or $x = -1$

3.   Test 0 (between the roots) in the original inequality.

           $0 + 3 > 2(0)^2$

             $3 > 0$ true

4. $\therefore$ solution lies between -1 and $\frac{3}{2}$

        $\therefore$ solution is $-1 < x < \frac{3}{2}$.

Modulus Inequalities

Method:

Square both sides. This reduces the problem to that of solving a quadratic inequality.

Example

Solve $|\,3x - 1\,| \le 10$.

Solution:

$$|\,3x - 1\,| \le 10$$
$$\Rightarrow \qquad (3x - 1)^2 \le (10)^2 \qquad \text{[square both sides]}$$
$$\Rightarrow \qquad 9x^2 - 6x + 1 \le 100$$
$$\Rightarrow \qquad 9x^2 - 6x - 99 \le 0$$
$$\Rightarrow \qquad 3x^2 - 2x - 33 \le 0$$

Let $\qquad 3x^2 - 2x - 33 = 0 \qquad \text{[replace} \le \text{with =]}$
$$\Rightarrow (3x - 11)(x + 3) = 0$$
$$\Rightarrow \qquad x = \tfrac{11}{3} \quad \text{or} \quad x = -3$$

Test 0 (inside the roots) in the original inequality.
$$|\,3(0) - 1\,| \le 10$$
$$|-1\,| \le 10$$
$$1 \le 10 \quad \text{true} \qquad\qquad \therefore \quad \text{solution is between } -3 \text{ and } \tfrac{11}{3}$$

$\therefore$ solution is $-3 \le x \le \tfrac{11}{3}$.

If two moduli appear on the same side of the inequality, arrange to have one modulus on each side before squaring both sides.

Example

Solve $2\,|\,x - 2\,| - |\,x - 1\,| > 0$.

Solution:

$$2\,|\,x - 2\,| - |\,x - 1\,| > 0$$
$$\Rightarrow \qquad 2\,|\,x - 2\,| > |\,x - 1\,| \qquad \text{[one modulus on each side]}$$
$$\Rightarrow \qquad 2^2(x - 2)^2 > (x - 1)^2 \qquad \text{[square both sides]}$$
$$\Rightarrow \qquad 4(x^2 - 4x + 4) > x^2 - 2x + 1$$
$$\Rightarrow \qquad 4x^2 - 16x + 16 > x^2 - 2x + 1$$
$$\Rightarrow \qquad 3x^2 - 14x + 15 > 0$$

Let $\qquad 3x^2 - 14x + 15 = 0 \qquad \text{[replace} > \text{with =]}$
$$\Rightarrow \qquad (3x - 5)(x - 3) = 0$$
$$\Rightarrow \qquad x = \tfrac{5}{3} \quad \text{or} \quad x = 3$$

23

Test 0 (outside the roots) in the original inequality.

$$2\,|\,0-2\,|-|\,0-1\,|>0$$

$$2\,|-2\,|-|-1\,|>0$$

$$2(2)-(1)>0$$

$$3>0 \quad \text{true} \quad \therefore \quad \text{solution is not between } \tfrac{5}{3} \text{ and } 3$$

$\therefore$ solution is $x < \tfrac{5}{3} \cup x > 3$.

Example

Solve $1 > \left| \dfrac{1}{2x+1} \right|$.

Solution:

$$1 > \left| \dfrac{1}{2x+1} \right|$$

$$1 > \dfrac{1}{(2x+1)^2} \qquad \text{[square both sides]}$$

$$(2x+1)^2 > 1 \qquad \text{[multiply both sides by } (2x+1)^2, \text{ which is positive]}$$

$$4x^2 + 4x + 1 > 1$$

$$4x^2 + 4x > 0$$

$$x^2 + x > 0$$

Let $\qquad x^2 + x = 0 \qquad\qquad$ [replace > with =]

$$x(x+1) = 0$$

$$x = 0 \quad \text{or} \quad x = -1$$

Test 1 (outside the roots) in the original inequality.

$$1 > \left| \dfrac{1}{2(1)+1} \right|$$

$1 > \tfrac{1}{3}$ true $\qquad\qquad \therefore$ solution is not between -1 and 0

$\therefore$ solution is $x < -1 \cup x > 0$.

Rational Inequalities

Method:

Turn the rational inequality into a quadratic inequality by multiplying both sides by a positive expression.

Example

Solve the inequality $\dfrac{x}{2x-1} < -2$.

Solution:

As $(2x-1)$ could be positive or negative, we multiply both sides by $(2x-1)^2$, which is positive.

$$\frac{x}{2x-1} < -2$$

$\Rightarrow \quad \dfrac{(2x-1)^2\, x}{(2x-1)} < -2(2x-1)^2 \qquad$ [multiply both sides by $(2x-1)^2$]

$\Rightarrow \quad (2x-1)x < -2(4x^2-4x+1)$

$\Rightarrow \quad 2x^2 - x < -8x^2 + 8x - 2$

$\Rightarrow \quad 10x^2 - 9x + 2 < 0$

Let $\quad 10x^2 - 9x + 2 = 0 \qquad$ [replace $<$ with $=$]

$\Rightarrow \quad (5x-2)(2x-1) = 0$

$\Rightarrow x = \frac{2}{5}$ or $x = \frac{1}{2}$

Test 0 (outside the roots) in the original inequality.

$$\frac{0}{2(0)-1} < -2$$

$\qquad 0 < -2$, false $\quad \therefore \quad$ solution lies between $\frac{2}{5}$ and $\frac{1}{2}$

$\therefore \quad$ solution is $\frac{2}{5} < x < \frac{1}{2}$.

Example

Find the set of values of $x \in \mathbf{R}$ for which $\dfrac{2x - 1}{x + 3} < \dfrac{1}{4}$.

Solution:

$$\frac{2x - 1}{x + 3} < \frac{1}{4}$$

$\Rightarrow \quad \dfrac{4(x + 3)^2 \, (2x - 1)}{(x + 3)} < \dfrac{4(x + 3)^2 \cdot 1}{4}$ [multiply both sides by $4(x + 3)^2$]

$\Rightarrow \qquad 4(x + 3)(2x - 1) < (x + 3)^2$

$\Rightarrow \qquad 8x^2 + 20x - 12 < x^2 + 6x + 9$

$\Rightarrow \qquad 7x^2 + 14x - 21 < 0$

$\Rightarrow \qquad x^2 + 2x - 3 < 0$

Let $\qquad x^2 + 2x - 3 = 0$

$\qquad (x + 3)(x - 1) = 0$

$\qquad x = -3 \quad \text{or} \quad x = 1$

Test 0 (between the roots) in the original inequality.

$$\frac{2(0) - 1}{0 + 3} < \frac{1}{4}$$

$-\dfrac{1}{3} < \dfrac{1}{4}$, true $\quad \therefore \quad$ solution lies between -3 and 1

$\therefore \qquad$ solution is $-3 < x < 1$.

Further Inequalities

Many basic inequalities are based on the following fact:

$$\boxed{\text{(any real number)}^2 \geq 0 \quad \text{or} \quad -\text{(any real number)}^2 \leq 0}$$

Example

If $p > 0$ and $q > 0$, prove $\dfrac{p+q}{2} > \sqrt{pq}$, $p \neq q$.

Solution:

$$\frac{p+q}{2} > \sqrt{pq}$$

$$\left(\frac{p+q}{2}\right)^2 > (\sqrt{pq})^2 \qquad \text{[square both sides as we know both sides are positive]}$$

$$\frac{p^2 + 2pq + q^2}{4} > pq$$

$$p^2 + 2pq + q^2 > 4pq \qquad \text{[multiply both sides by 4]}$$

$$p^2 - 2pq + q^2 > 0$$

$$(p-q)^2 > 0 \qquad \text{[true]}$$

$\therefore \dfrac{p+q}{2} > \sqrt{pq}$ is true for all $p, q > 0$ and $p \neq q$.

Example

Prove that   **(i)** $a^2 + b^2 \geq 2ab$ for all real values of a and b

and   **(ii)** hence, prove that $a^2 + b^2 + c^2 \geq ab + bc + ca$ for all real values of a, b and c.

Solution:

(i) Method 1

$\qquad$(any real number)$^2 \geq 0$

$\qquad\quad$Thus, $(a-b)^2 \geq 0$

$\qquad\therefore \quad a^2 - 2ab + b^2 \geq 0$

$\qquad\therefore \qquad\qquad a^2 + b^2 \geq 2ab$

Method 2

$\qquad\qquad\qquad\quad a^2 + b^2 \geq 2ab$

$\Rightarrow \quad a^2 - 2ab + b^2 \geq 0$

$\Rightarrow \qquad (a-b)^2 \geq 0, \quad$ [true]

$\therefore \qquad\quad a^2 + b^2 \geq 2ab$

(ii) From (i)

$\qquad a^2 + b^2 \geq 2ab, \quad b^2 + c^2 \geq 2bc \quad$ and $\quad c^2 + a^2 \geq 2ca$

Adding: $\quad a^2 + b^2 + b^2 + c^2 + c^2 + a^2 \geq 2ab + 2bc + 2ca$

$$2(a^2 + b^2 + c^2) \geq 2(ab + bc + ca)$$

Hence: $\qquad\qquad a^2 + b^2 + c^2 \geq ab + bc + ca$

Example

If $a, b > 0$, prove that $\dfrac{1}{b} + \dfrac{1}{a} \geq \dfrac{4}{a + b}$.

Solution:

$$\frac{1}{b} + \frac{1}{a} \geq \frac{4}{a + b}$$

$\Rightarrow \quad ab \cdot \dfrac{1}{b} + ab \cdot \dfrac{1}{a} \geq \ ab \cdot \dfrac{4}{a + b}$ [multiply each part by ab, which is positive]

$\Rightarrow \qquad\qquad a + b \geq \dfrac{4ab}{a + b}$

$\Rightarrow \qquad (a + b)(a + b) \geq (a + b) \cdot \dfrac{4ab}{a + b}$ [multiply both sides by $(a + b)$, which is positive]

$\Rightarrow \qquad a^2 + 2ab + b^2 \geq 4ab$

$\Rightarrow \qquad a^2 - 2ab + b^2 \geq 0$

$\Rightarrow \qquad\quad (a - b)^2 \geq 0$ [true]

Thus, $\dfrac{1}{b} + \dfrac{1}{a} \geq \dfrac{4}{a + b}$ for $a, b > 0$.

Example

Prove that if $x, y \in R$, then $x^4 + y^4 \geq 2x^2y^2$.
By expanding $(xy - zt)^2$ deduce that if x, y, z and $t \in R$, then:

$$x^4 + y^4 + z^4 + t^4 \geq 4xyzt$$

Solution:

$$x^4 + y^4 \geq 2x^2y^2$$

$$x^4 - 2x^2y^2 + y^4 \geq 0$$

$$(x^2 - y^2)^2 \geq 0 \qquad \text{[true]}$$

$\therefore \qquad\quad x^4 + y^4 \geq 2x^2y^2 \qquad ①$

$\therefore \qquad\qquad z^4 + t^4 \geq 2z^2t^2$

Thus, $x^4 + y^4 + z^4 + t^4 \geq 2x^2y^2 + 2z^2t^2 \qquad ①$

$$(xy - zt)^2 \geq 0$$

$\Rightarrow \quad x^2y^2 - 2xyzt + z^2t^2 \geq 0$

$\Rightarrow \qquad\quad x^2y^2 + z^2t^2 \geq 2xyzt$

$\Rightarrow \qquad 2x^2y^2 + 2z^2t^2 \geq 4xyzt \qquad ②$

[If $a > b$ and $b > c$, then $a > c$.]

So we have:

$$x^4 + y^4 + z^4 + t^4 \overset{①}{\geq} 2x^2y^2 + 2z^2t^2 \overset{②}{\geq} 4xyzt$$

$$\therefore x^4 + y^4 + z^4 + t^4 \geq 4xyzt$$

Example

If $p > 0$ and $q > 0$, prove that $\dfrac{p^3 - q^3}{p^2q - pq^2} > 3$.

Solution:

$$\frac{p^3 - q^3}{p^2q - pq^2} > 3$$

$$\Rightarrow \quad \frac{(p - q)(p^2 + pq + q^2)}{pq(p - q)} > 3 \qquad \text{[factorise top and bottom on left-hand side]}$$

$$\Rightarrow \quad \frac{p^2 + pq + q^2}{pq} > 3 \qquad \text{[divide top and bottom by } (p - q)]$$

$$\Rightarrow \quad p^2 + pq + q^2 > 3pq \qquad \text{[multiply both sides by } pq, \text{ which}$$
$$\Rightarrow \quad p^2 - 2pq + q^2 > 0 \qquad \text{is positive]}$$

$$\Rightarrow \quad (p - q)^2 > 0 \qquad \text{[true]}$$

$$\therefore \quad \frac{p^3 - q^3}{p^2q - pq^2} > 3$$

The Nature of the Roots of a Quadratic Equation

$ax^2 + bx + c = 0$, $a \neq 0$ is a quadratic equation.

The roots of the equation are given by: $\boxed{x = \dfrac{-b \pm \sqrt{b^2 - 4ac}}{2a}}$

The value of the expression $(b^2 - 4ac)$ will determine the nature of the roots of the equation and is called the **discriminant** of the equation. The three diagrams below of the curve $y = ax^2 + bx + c$ $(a > 0)$ show the three possible cases.

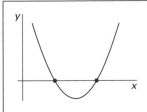

Two distinct real roots
$b^2 - 4ac > 0$

Two equal real roots
$b^2 - 4ac = 0$

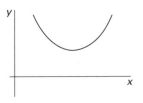

No real roots
$b^2 - 4ac > 0$

Note: For real roots we combine the first two conditions:

If $b^2 - 4ac \geq 0$, the roots are real.

Example

Determine the nature of the roots of the equations:

(i) $2x^2 + 3x + 5 = 0$ (ii) $5x^2 - 13x + 7 = 0$

(iii) $x^2 + 2px + p^2 = 0$ (iv) $x^2 - qx - q^2 = 0$

Solution:

(i) $2x^2 + 3x + 5 = 0$

$a = 2, \quad b = 3, \quad c = 5$

$b^2 - 4ac$

$= (3)^2 - 4(2)(5)$

$= 9 - 40$

$= -31 < 0$

∴   non-real roots (complex)

(ii) $5x^2 - 13x + 7 = 0$

$a = 5, \quad b = -13, \quad c = 7$

$b^2 - 4ac$

$= (-13)^2 - 4(5)(7)$

$= 169 - 140$

$= 29 > 0$

∴   two distinct real roots

(iii) $x^2 + 2px + p^2 = 0$

$a = 1, \quad b = 2p, \quad c = p^2$

$b^2 - 4ac$

$= (2p)^2 - 4(1)\,(p^2)$

$= 4p^2 - 4p^2$

$= 0$

∴   two equal real roots

(iv) $x^2 - qx - q^2 = 0$

$a = 1, \quad b = -q, \quad c = -q^2$

$b^2 - 4ac$

$= (-q)^2 - 4(1)\,(-q^2)$

$= q^2 + 4q^2$

$= 5q^2 \geq 0$

∴   real roots

(as $5q^2$ cannot be negative)

Example

$f(x) = (k-2)x^2 + 2x - k.$

Prove that $f(x) = 0$ has real roots for all values of $k \in \mathbf{R}$.

Solution:

$$f(x) = 0$$
$$\Rightarrow \quad (k-2)x^2 + 2x - k = 0$$
$$a = (k-2), \quad b = 2, \quad c = -k$$
$$b^2 - 4ac = (2)^2 - 4(k-2)(-k)$$
$$= 4 + 4k^2 - 8k$$
$$= 4k^2 - 8k + 4$$
$$= 4(k^2 - 2k + 1)$$
$$= 4(k-1)^2$$

$(k-1)^2$ cannot be negative for any value of $k \in \mathbf{R}$, so $b^2 - 4ac$ cannot be negative.
∴ the roots are always real.

Example

(i) If the roots of the equation $2x^2 - kx + 8 = 0$ are equal, find the values of k.

(ii) If $px^2 - 4x + 1 = 0$ has equal roots, find the value of p.

Solution:

(i) $2x^2 - kx + 8 = 0$

$a = 2, b = -k, c = 8$

Equal roots; $b^2 - 4ac = 0$

$\Rightarrow (-k)^2 - 4(2)(8) = 0$

$\Rightarrow \qquad k^2 - 64 = 0$

$\Rightarrow \qquad k^2 = 64$

$\therefore \qquad k = \pm 8$

(ii) $px^2 - 4x + 1 = 0$

$a = p, b = -4, c = 1$

Equal roots: $b^2 - 4ac = 0$

$\Rightarrow \qquad (-4)^2 - 4(p)(1) = 0$

$\Rightarrow \qquad 16 - 4p = 0$

$\Rightarrow \qquad 4p = 16$

$\therefore \qquad p = 4$

Example

A quadratic function is defined as follows:

$\qquad f(x) = 2mx^2 - 4(m+3)x + 25, \ x \in \mathbf{R}.$

(i) Find the values of m for which the equation $f(x) = 0$ has equal roots.

(ii) Find a value of m such that $f(2) = f(6)$.

Solution:

(i)
$$f(x) = 0$$
$$\Rightarrow \quad 2mx^2 - 4(m + 3)x + 25 = 0$$
$$a = 2m, \quad b = -4(m + 3), \quad c = 25$$

Equal roots: $\quad b^2 - 4ac = 0$

$$\Rightarrow \quad [-4(m + 3)]^2 - 4(2m)(25) = 0$$
$$\Rightarrow \quad 16(m^2 + 6m + 9) - 200m = 0$$
$$\Rightarrow \quad 16m^2 + 96m + 144 - 200m = 0$$
$$\Rightarrow \quad 16m^2 - 104m + 144 = 0$$
$$\Rightarrow \quad 2m^2 - 13m + 18 = 0 \quad \text{[divide across by 8]}$$
$$\Rightarrow \quad (2m - 9)(m - 2) = 0$$
$$\Rightarrow \quad 2m - 9 = 0 \quad \text{or} \quad m - 2 = 0$$
$$\Rightarrow \quad 2m = 9 \quad \text{or} \quad m = 2$$
$$\Rightarrow \quad m = \tfrac{9}{2} \quad \text{or} \quad m = 2$$

(ii) $\qquad\qquad f(x) = 2mx^2 - 4(m + 3)x + 25$

Given: $\qquad\qquad f(2) = f(6)$

$$2m(2)^2 - 4(m + 3)(2) + 25 = 2m(6)^2 - 4(m + 3)(6) + 25$$
$$2m(4) - 8(m + 3) = 2m(36) - 24(m + 3)$$
$$8m - 8m - 24 = 72m - 24m - 72$$
$$-24 = 48m - 72$$
$$-48m = -72 + 24$$
$$-48m = -48$$
$$m = 1$$

Example

Find the range of values of $k \in \mathbf{R}$ for which the equation
$$(k + 3)x^2 + (6 - 2k)x + k - 1 = 0$$
has non-real roots.

Solution:

$$(k + 3)x^2 + (6 - 2k)x + (k - 1) = 0$$
$$a = (k + 3), \quad b = (6 - 2k), \quad c = (k - 1)$$

Non-real roots:
$$b^2 - 4ac < 0$$
$$(6 - 2k)^2 - 4(k + 3)(k - 1) < 0$$
$$36 - 24k + 4k^2 - 4(k^2 + 2k - 3) < 0$$
$$36 - 24k + 4k^2 - 4k^2 - 8k + 12 < 0$$
$$-32k < -48$$
$$32k > 48 \qquad \text{[change sign, reverse inequality]}$$
$$k > \tfrac{3}{2}$$

Example

Find the range of values of $a \in \mathbf{R}$ for which

$$4x^2 + 2(a + 1)x + a^2 = 0 \quad \text{has real roots.}$$

Solution:

$$4x^2 + 2(a + 1)x + a^2 = 0$$
$$a = 4, \quad b = 2(a + 1), \quad c = a^2$$
$$\text{Real roots for} \quad b^2 - 4ac \geq 0$$
$$\Rightarrow \qquad [2(a + 1)]^2 - 4(4)\,(a^2) \geq 0$$
$$\Rightarrow \qquad 4(a^2 + 2a + 1) - 16a^2 \geq 0$$
$$\Rightarrow \qquad 4a^2 + 8a + 4 - 16a^2 \geq 0$$
$$\Rightarrow \qquad -12a^2 + 8a + 4 \geq 0$$
$$\Rightarrow \qquad 12a^2 - 8a - 4 \leq 0 \quad \text{[change signs, reverse inequality]}$$
$$\Rightarrow \qquad 3a^2 - 2a - 1 \leq 0 \quad \text{[divide across by 4]}$$

Let $\quad 3a^2 - 2a - 1 = 0$
$$\Rightarrow \qquad (3a + 1)(a - 1) = 0$$
$$\Rightarrow \qquad 3a + 1 = 0 \quad \text{or} \quad a - 1 = 0$$
$$\Rightarrow \qquad a = -\tfrac{1}{3} \quad \text{or} \quad a = 1$$

Test 0: $3(0)^2 - 2(0) - 1 \leq 0$

$-1 \leq 0 \quad$ (true)

(inside roots)

∴ solution lies between $-\tfrac{1}{3}$ and 1.

Thus, the solution is: $-\tfrac{1}{3} \leq a \leq 1$.

Example

Show that the quadratic equation

$$(1 + a - b)x^2 + 2x + (1 - a + b) = 0$$

has real roots, one of which is independent of a and b while the other is not.

Solution:

$$(1 + a - b)x^2 + 2x + (1 - a + b) = 0$$

$$a = (1 + a - b), \quad b = 2, \quad c = (1 - a + b)$$

Real roots if $b^2 - 4ac \geq 0$

$$(2)^2 - 4(1 + a - b)(1 - a + b)$$

$$= 4 - 4(1 - a + b + a - a^2 + ab - b + ab - b^2)$$

$$= 4 - 4(-a^2 + 2ab - b^2 + 1)$$

$$= 4 + 4a^2 - 8ab + 4b^2 - 4$$

$$= 4a^2 - 8ab + 4b^2$$

$$= 4(a^2 - 2ab + b^2)$$

$$= 4(a - b)^2 \geq 0$$

As $(a - b)^2$ cannot be negative, $b^2 - 4ac \geq 0$, $\therefore$ roots are always real.

Roots are given by $x = \dfrac{-b \pm \sqrt{b^2 - 4ac}}{2a}$

$$x = \frac{-2 \pm \sqrt{2^2 - 4(1 + a - b)(1 - a + b)}}{2(1 + a - b)}$$

$$= \frac{-2 \pm \sqrt{4(a - b)^2}}{2(1 + a - b)} = \frac{-2 \pm 2(a - b)}{2(1 + a - b)} = \frac{-1 \pm (a - b)}{(1 + a - b)}$$

$$= \frac{-1 - a + b}{(1 + a - b)} \quad \text{or} \quad \frac{-1 + a - b}{1 + a - b}$$

$$= \frac{-1(1 + a - b)}{(1 + a - b)} \quad \text{or} \quad \frac{-1 + a - b}{1 + a - b}$$

$$= -1 \quad \text{or} \quad \frac{-1 + a - b}{1 + a - b}$$

$\therefore$ one root, -1, is independent of a and b.

Sum and Product of the Roots of a Quadratic Equation

The quadratic equation $ax^2 + bx + c = 0$ can be written $x^2 + \dfrac{b}{a}x + \dfrac{c}{a} = 0$.

If α and β are the roots of $x^2 + \dfrac{b}{a}x + \dfrac{c}{a} = 0$, then:

$$\alpha + \beta = -\dfrac{b}{a} \quad \text{and} \quad \alpha\beta = \dfrac{c}{a}$$

The quadratic equation can be written:

$$x^2 - (\alpha + \beta)x + \alpha\beta = 0$$

or

$$x^2 - (\text{sum of the roots})\, x + (\text{product of the roots}) = 0$$

This can be used to obtain a new quadratic equation whose roots are known or are given as functions of α and β.

Example

If α and β are the roots of the equation $2x^2 - x - 3 = 0$, find, in simplest form, the value of:

(i) $\alpha + \beta$ (ii) $\alpha\beta$ (iii) $\alpha^2 + \beta^2$

(iv) $\dfrac{\alpha}{\beta} + \dfrac{\beta}{\alpha}$ (v) $\alpha^3 + \beta^3$ (vi) $\dfrac{\alpha}{\alpha + 2} + \dfrac{\beta}{\beta + 2}$

Solution:

$2x^2 - x - 3 = 0$

$\Rightarrow x^2 - \tfrac{1}{2}x - \tfrac{3}{2} = 0$ [divide across by 2 to make coefficient of x^2 equal to 1]

(i) $\alpha + \beta = \tfrac{1}{2}$ (ii) $\alpha\beta = -\tfrac{3}{2}$

We write each of the other expressions in terms of $(\alpha + \beta)$ and $\alpha\beta$ and evaluate.

(iii) $\alpha + \beta = \tfrac{1}{2}$

$\Rightarrow \quad (\alpha + \beta)^2 = (\tfrac{1}{2})^2$

$\Rightarrow \quad \alpha^2 + 2\alpha\beta + \beta^2 = \tfrac{1}{4}$

$\Rightarrow \qquad \alpha^2 + \beta^2 = \tfrac{1}{4} - 2\alpha\beta$

$= \tfrac{1}{4} - 2(-\tfrac{3}{2})$

$= \tfrac{1}{4} + 3$

$= 3\tfrac{1}{4}$

(iv) $\dfrac{\alpha}{\beta} + \dfrac{\beta}{\alpha}$

$= \dfrac{\alpha^2 + \beta^2}{\alpha\beta}$

$= \dfrac{3\tfrac{1}{4}}{-\tfrac{3}{2}}$

$= -\tfrac{13}{6}$

(v) $\alpha^3 + \beta^3 = (\alpha + \beta)(\alpha^2 - \alpha\beta + \beta^2)$

$$= (\alpha + \beta)[(\alpha^2 + \beta^2) - \alpha\beta]$$

$$= (\tfrac{1}{2})(3\tfrac{1}{4} + \tfrac{3}{2}) = (\tfrac{1}{2})(4\tfrac{3}{4}) = 2\tfrac{3}{8}$$

(vi) $\dfrac{\alpha}{\alpha + 2} + \dfrac{\beta}{\beta + 2} = \dfrac{\alpha(\beta + 2) + \beta(\alpha + 2)}{(\alpha + 2)(\beta + 2)}$

$$= \dfrac{\alpha\beta + 2\alpha + \alpha\beta + 2\beta}{\alpha\beta + 2\alpha + 2\beta + 4}$$

$$= \dfrac{2\alpha\beta + 2(\alpha + \beta)}{\alpha\beta + 2(\alpha + \beta) + 4}$$

$$= \dfrac{2(-\tfrac{3}{2}) + 2(\tfrac{1}{2})}{-\tfrac{3}{2} + 2(\tfrac{1}{2}) + 4}$$

$$= \dfrac{-2}{3\tfrac{1}{2}} = -\tfrac{4}{7}$$

Example

If α and β are the roots of $x^2 - px + q = 0$,

(i)   write $\alpha^2 + \beta^2$ in terms of p and q

(ii)   show that $(\alpha^2 + 1)(\beta^2 + 1) = p^2 + (q - 1)^2$.

Solution:

$$x^2 - px + q = 0$$
$$\alpha + \beta = p \quad \text{and} \quad \alpha\beta = q$$

(i)
$$\alpha + \beta = p$$
$$\Rightarrow \quad (\alpha + \beta)^2 = p^2$$
$$\Rightarrow \quad \alpha^2 + 2\alpha\beta + \beta^2 = p^2$$
$$\Rightarrow \quad \alpha^2 + \beta^2 = p^2 - 2\alpha\beta$$
$$\Rightarrow \quad \alpha^2 + \beta^2 = p^2 - 2q$$

(ii)
$$(\alpha^2 + 1)(\beta^2 + 1$$
$$= \alpha^2\beta^2 + \alpha^2 + \beta^2 + 1$$
$$= (\alpha\beta)^2 + (\alpha^2 + \beta^2) + 1$$
$$= q^2 + p^2 - 2q + 1$$
$$= p^2 + q^2 - 2q + 1$$
$$= p^2 + (q - 1)^2$$

Example

If $3x^2 - 6x + 7 = 0$ has roots α and β, find the equation whose roots are:

(i) 3α and 3β

(ii) $\dfrac{1}{\alpha}$ and $\dfrac{1}{\beta}$

(iii) $\dfrac{\alpha}{\beta}$ and $\dfrac{\beta}{\alpha}$

Solution:

$$3x^2 - 6x + 7 = 0$$

$$\Rightarrow x^2 - 2x + \tfrac{7}{3} = 0$$

$\therefore \quad \alpha + \beta = 2 \text{ and } \alpha\beta = \tfrac{7}{3}$

(i) $3\alpha \quad$ and $\quad 3\beta$

$x^2 - (\text{sum of the roots})x + (\text{product of the roots}) = 0$

$x^2 - (3\alpha + 3\beta)x + (3\alpha)(3\beta) = 0$

$x^2 - 3(\alpha + \beta)x + 9\alpha\beta = 0$

$x^2 - 3(2)x + 9\left(\tfrac{7}{3}\right) = 0$

$x^2 - 6x + 21 = 0$

(ii) $\dfrac{1}{\alpha}$ and $\dfrac{1}{\beta}$

$x^2 - (\text{sum of the roots})x + (\text{product of the roots}) = 0$

$$x^2 - \left(\frac{1}{\alpha} + \frac{1}{\beta}\right)x + \left(\frac{1}{\alpha}\right)\left(\frac{1}{\beta}\right) = 0$$

$$x^2 - \left(\frac{\alpha + \beta}{\alpha\beta}\right)x + \frac{1}{\alpha\beta} = 0$$

$$x^2 - \left(\frac{2}{\frac{7}{3}}\right)x + \frac{1}{\frac{7}{3}} = 0$$

$$x^2 - \tfrac{6}{7}x + \tfrac{3}{7} = 0$$

$$7x^2 - 6x + 3 = 0$$

(iii) $\dfrac{\alpha}{\beta}$ and $\dfrac{\beta}{\alpha}$

$x^2 - (\text{sum of the roots})x + (\text{product of the roots}) = 0$

$$x^2 - \left(\frac{\alpha}{\beta} + \frac{\beta}{\alpha}\right)x + \left(\frac{\alpha}{\beta}\right)\left(\frac{\beta}{\alpha}\right) = 0$$

$$x^2 - \left(\frac{\alpha^2 + \beta^2}{\alpha\beta}\right)x + 1 = 0$$

$$x^2 - \left(\frac{-\frac{2}{3}}{\frac{7}{3}}\right)x + 1 = 0$$

$$x^2 + \tfrac{2}{7}x + 1 = 0$$

$$7x^2 + 2x + 7 = 0$$

$\alpha + \beta = 2$

$(\alpha + \beta)^2 = 2^2$

$\alpha^2 + 2\alpha\beta + \beta^2 = 4$

$\alpha^2 + \beta^2 = 4 - 2\alpha\beta$

$\qquad = 4 - 2(\tfrac{7}{3})$

$\qquad = 4 - \tfrac{14}{3}$

$\qquad = -\tfrac{2}{3}$

Example

If $a \neq 0$ and one of the roots of the equation $ax^2 + bx + c = 0$ is three times the other, show that $3b^2 = 16ac$.

Solution:

Let α and 3α be the roots of $ax^2 + bx + c = 0$.

$\therefore \quad \alpha + 3\alpha = -\dfrac{b}{a} \qquad$ and $\qquad (\alpha)(3\alpha) = \dfrac{c}{a}$

i.e. $\quad 4\alpha = -\dfrac{b}{a} \quad$ ① $\quad$ i.e. $\quad 3\alpha^2 = \dfrac{c}{a} \quad$ ②

Get α on its own from ① and put this into ②.

$4\alpha = -\dfrac{b}{a} \quad$ ①

$\Rightarrow \quad \alpha = \left(-\dfrac{b}{4a}\right)$

Put this into ②.

$3\alpha^2 = \dfrac{c}{a} \quad$ ②

$\Rightarrow \quad 3\left(-\dfrac{b}{4a}\right)^2 = \dfrac{c}{a}$

$\Rightarrow \quad \dfrac{3b^2}{16a^2} = \dfrac{c}{a}$

$\Rightarrow \quad 3ab^2 = 16a^2c$

$\Rightarrow \quad 3b^2 = 16ac$

Example

Find the values of k if the roots of $4x^2 + kx + 1 = 0$ are in the ratio $1 : 4$.

Solution:

Let α and 4α be the roots of $4x^2 + kx + 1 = 0$.

$$\therefore \quad \alpha + 4\alpha = -\frac{k}{4} \qquad \text{and} \qquad (\alpha)(4\alpha) = \frac{1}{4}$$

$$5\alpha = -\frac{k}{4} \quad \text{①} \qquad\qquad 4\alpha^2 = \frac{1}{4} \quad \text{②}$$

From ② get two values of α and put these into ①.

$$4\alpha^2 = \tfrac{1}{4} \quad \text{②}$$
$$\alpha^2 = \tfrac{1}{16}$$
$$\alpha = \pm \tfrac{1}{4}$$

$$5\alpha = -\frac{k}{4} \quad \text{①}$$
$$\Rightarrow \quad 20\alpha = -k$$
$$\therefore k = -20\alpha$$

$$\alpha = \tfrac{1}{4}, \qquad k = -20(\tfrac{1}{4}) = -5$$

$$\alpha = -\tfrac{1}{4}, \qquad k = -20(-\tfrac{1}{4}) = 5$$

Thus, $k = \pm 5$.

Cubic Expressions and Cubic Equations

Factor Theorem

> If $f(a) = 0$ for a polynomial $f(x)$, then:
> $(x - a)$ is a factor of $f(x)$
> It follows $x = a$ is a root (solution) of $f(x) = 0$.

Note: The Factor Theorem can be extended: if $f\left(\frac{b}{a}\right) = 0$, then $(ax - b)$ is a factor of $f(x)$.

Example

If $(2x - 1)$ is a factor of $2x^3 + kx^2 - 11x + 6$, find the value of k and, hence, find the three linear factors of $2x^3 + kx^2 - 11x + 6$.

Solution:

Let $f(x) = 2x^3 + kx^2 - 11x + 6$.

If $(2x - 1)$ is a factor, then $x = \frac{1}{2}$ is a root and $f(\frac{1}{2}) = 0$.

$$f(\tfrac{1}{2}) = 0$$

$\Rightarrow \quad 2(\frac{1}{2})^3 + k(\frac{1}{2})^2 - 11(\frac{1}{2}) + 6 = 0 \qquad$ [replace x with $\frac{1}{2}$]

$\Rightarrow \quad 2(\frac{1}{8}) + k(\frac{1}{4}) - 11(\frac{1}{2}) + 6 = 0$

$\Rightarrow \quad \frac{1}{4} + \frac{1}{4}k - 5\frac{1}{2} + 6 = 0$

$\Rightarrow \quad 1 + k - 22 + 24 = 0 \qquad$ [multiply across by 4]

$\Rightarrow \quad k + 3 = 0$

$\Rightarrow \quad k = -3$

Now divide $2x^3 - 3x^2 - 11x + 6$ by $2x - 1$

$$
\begin{array}{r}
x^2 - x - 6 \\
2x - 1\overline{)2x^3 - 3x^2 - 11x + 6} \\
\underline{2x^3 - x^2} \\
-2x^2 - 11x \\
\underline{-2x^2 + x} \\
-12x + 6 \\
\underline{-12x + 6} \\
0
\end{array}
$$

Now factorise $x^2 - x - 6$

$x^2 - x - 6$

$= (x - 3)(x + 2)$

Thus, the three linear factors of $2x^3 - 3x^2 - 11x + 6$ are $(2x - 1)$, $(x - 3)$ and $(x + 2)$.

Example

If $(x + 1)$ and $(x - 2)$ are factors of $x^3 + 2x^2 + ax + b$, find the values of $a, b \in \mathbf{R}$.

Solution:

Let $f(x) = x^3 + 2x^2 + ax + b$.
If $(x + 1)$ is a factor, then $x = -1$ is a root and $f(-1) = 0$.
If $(x - 2)$ is a factor, then $x = 2$ is a root and $f(2) = 0$.

$$f(-1) = 0$$

$(-1)^3 + 2(-1)^2 + a(-1) + b = 0$

$-1 + 2 - a + b = 0$

$-a + b = 1 - 2$

$-a + b = -1 \quad \textcircled{1}$

$$f(2) = 0$$

$(2)^3 + 2(2)^2 + a(2) + b = 0$

$8 + 8 + 2a + b = 0$

$2a + b = -8 - 8$

$2a + b = -16 \quad \textcircled{2}$

We now solve the simultaneous equations ① and ②

$$-a + b = -1 \qquad ①$$
$$\underline{2a + b = -16 \qquad ②}$$
$$-3a = 15 \qquad \text{(subtract)}$$
$$\Rightarrow \qquad 3a = -15$$
$$\Rightarrow \qquad a = -5$$

Put in $a = -5$ into ① or ②

Thus, $a = -5$ and $b = -6$.

$$-a + b = -1 \qquad ①$$
$$-(-5) + b = -1$$
$$\Rightarrow \qquad 5 + b = -1$$
$$\Rightarrow \qquad b = -1 - 5$$
$$\Rightarrow \qquad b = -6$$

Example

$x^2 + ax + b$ is a factor of $x^3 + qx^2 + rx + s$.

Prove that $r - b = a(q - a)$ and $s = b(q - a)$.

Solution:

Method 1: Use long division

$$
\begin{array}{r}
x + (q - a) \\
x^2 + ax + b \overline{\smash{)}x^3 + qx^2 + rx + s}
\end{array}
$$

$$x^3 + ax^2 + bx$$
$$\overline{(q - a)x^2 + (r - b)x + s}$$
$$(q - a)x^2 + (q - a)ax + (q - a)b$$
$$\overline{[r - b - a(q - a)]x + [s - b(q - a)]}$$

As $x^2 + ax + b$ is a factor, the remainder must $= 0$

$$\therefore \qquad r - b - a(q - a) = 0 \qquad \text{and} \qquad s - b(q - a) = 0$$
$$\Rightarrow \qquad r - b = a(q - a) \qquad \text{and} \qquad s = b(q - a)$$

Method 2: Equating coefficients

Let $(x + k)$ be the third factor.

Thus, $\quad x^3 + qx^2 + rx + s = (x + k)(x^2 + ax + b)$

$$x^3 + qx^2 + rx + s = x^3 + ax^2 + xb + kx^2 + kax + kb$$
$$x^3 + qx^2 + rx + s = x^3 + (a + k)x^2 + (b + ka)x + kb$$

$\Rightarrow \quad q = a + k \quad ① \qquad r = b + ka \quad ② \qquad s = kb \quad ③$

From ① $k = q - a$, and put this into ② and ③

$$r = b + ka \qquad ②$$
$$r = b + (q - a)a$$
$$r - b = a(q - a)$$

$$s = kb \qquad ③$$
$$s = (q - a)b$$
$$s = b(q - a)$$

41

Example

$f(x) = x^3 - (a + 2)x + 2b$ and $g(x) = 2x^3 + ax^2 - 4x - b$.

If $f(x)$ and $g(x)$ have a common factor $x + 3$, find the values of a and b.

Solution:

As $x + 3$ is a factor of both $f(x)$ and $g(x)$, then $f(-3) = 0$ and $g(-3) = 0$.

$f(-3) = 0$	$g(-3) = 0$
$(-3)^3 - (a + 2)(-3) + 2b = 0$	$2(-3)^3 + a(-3)^2 - 4(-3) - b = 0$
$-27 + 3(a + 2) + 2b = 0$	$2(-27) + a(9) - 4(-3) - b = 0$
$-27 + 3a + 6 + 2b = 0$	$-54 + 9a + 12 - b = 0$
$3a + 2b = 21$ ①	$9a - b = 42$ ②

Solving the simultaneous equations ① and ② gives $a = 5$ and $b = 3$.

Example

(i)   Show that $(x - k)$ is a factor of $x^n - k^n$.

(ii)   Show that $(x - a)$ is a factor of $x^3 - (a + b + c)x^2 + (ab + bc + ca)x - abc$.

Solution:

(i)   Let $f(x) = x^n - k^n$.

To show that $(x - k)$ is a factor, we need to show that $f(k) = 0$.

$$f(k) = k^n - k^n = 0$$

Thus, $(x - k)$ is a factor of $f(x)$.

(ii)   Let $f(x) = x^3 - (a + b + c)x^2 + (ab + bc + ca)x - abc$.

To show that $(x - a)$ is a factor we need to show that $f(a) = 0$.

$$\begin{aligned} f(a) &= a^3 - (a + b + c)(a^2) + (ab + bc + ca)(a) - abc \\ &= a^3 - (a^3 + a^2b + a^2c) + a^2b + abc + a^2c - abc \\ &= a^3 - a^3 - a^2b - a^2c + a^2b + abc + a^2c - abc \\ &= 0 \end{aligned}$$

Thus, $(x - a)$ is a factor of $f(x)$.

Example

Find the values of a if $(x - 2)$ is a factor of $a^2x^3 - 3ax^2 - 10x + 24$.

Solution:

Let $f(x) = a^2x^3 - 3ax^2 - 10x + 24$.
If $(x - 2)$ is a factor, then $f(2) = 0$.

$$f(2) = 0$$

$\Rightarrow \quad a^2(2)^3 - 3a(2)^2 - 10(2) + 24 = 0 \quad$ [replace x with 2]

$\Rightarrow \qquad\qquad 8a^2 - 12a - 20 + 24 = 0$

$\Rightarrow \qquad\qquad\quad 8a^2 - 12a + 4 = 0$

$\Rightarrow \qquad\qquad\quad\; 2a^2 - 3a + 1 = 0$

$\Rightarrow \qquad\qquad\; (2a - 1)(a - 1) = 0$

$\Rightarrow \qquad\qquad 2a - 1 = 0 \quad$ or $\quad a - 1 = 0$

$\Rightarrow \qquad\qquad\quad a = \frac{1}{2} \quad$ or $\qquad a = 1$

Solving Cubic Equations

A cubic equation is solved with the following steps:

1. Find the first root a by trial and error, i.e. try $(f(1), f(-1), f(2), f(-2)$, etc. (Only try numbers that divided evenly into the constant in the equation.)

2. If $x = a$ is a root, then $(x - a)$ is a factor.

3. Divide $f(x)$ by $(x - a)$, which always gives a quadratic expression.

4. Let this quadratic $= 0$ and solve.

Example

Solve the equation $2x^3 - 9x^2 + 7x + 6 = 0$.

Solution:

Let $f(x) = 2x^3 - 9x^2 + 7x + 6$.

1. The first root will be a factor of 6

$\therefore$ We need try only those values which are factors of 6, i.e. $\pm 1, \pm 2, \pm 3, \pm 6$.

$f(1) = 2(1)^3 - 9(1)^2 + 7(1) + 6 = 2 - 9 + 7 + 6 = 6 \neq 0$

$f(-1) = 2(-1)^3 - 9(-1)^2 + 7(-1) + 6 = -2 - 9 - 7 + 6 = -12 \neq 0$

$f(2) = 2(2)^3 - 9(2)^2 + 7(2) + 6 = 16 - 36 + 14 + 6 = 0$

$\therefore \qquad x = 2$ is a root

2. $\therefore$ $x - 2$ is a factor.

3. Divide $2x^3 - 9x^2 + 7x + 6$ by $(x - 2)$

$$
\begin{array}{r}
2x^2 - 5x - 3 \\
x - 2 \overline{)2x^3 - 9x^2 + 7x + 6} \\
\underline{2x^3 - 4x^2} \\
-5x^2 + 7x \\
\underline{-5x^2 + 10x} \\
-3x + 6 \\
\underline{-3x + 6} \\
0
\end{array}
$$

4. Let $2x^2 - 5x - 3 = 0$

$\Rightarrow \quad (2x + 1)(x - 3) = 0 \qquad$ [factorise]

$\Rightarrow \quad 2x + 1 = 0 \quad$ or $\quad x - 3 = 0 \quad$ [let each factor = 0]

$\quad 2x = -1 \quad$ or $\quad x = 3$

$\quad x = -\frac{1}{2} \quad$ or $\quad x = 3$

Thus, the roots of the equation are $-\frac{1}{2}$, 2 and 3.

Example

Let $g(x)$ be a cubic polynomial such that

$$g(-1) = 0 = g(1) \quad \text{and} \quad g(2) = 5g(0).$$

Find the three roots of the equation $g(x) = 0$.

Solution:

Method 1:

Given: $g(-1) = 0 \quad \Rightarrow \quad (x + 1)$ is a factor of $g(x)$

Given: $g(1) = 0 \quad \Rightarrow \quad (x - 1)$ is a factor of $g(x)$

Let the third factor be $(x + k)$.

Thus, $\quad g(x) = (x + 1)(x - 1)(x + k)$

$\quad g(x) = (x^2 - 1)(x + k)$

$\quad g(x) = x^3 + kx^2 - x - k$

Given: $\qquad\qquad\qquad g(2) = 5g(0)$

$\Rightarrow \quad (2)^3 + k(2)^2 - (2) - k = 5[(0)^3 + k(0)^2 - (0) - k]$

$\Rightarrow \qquad 8 + 4k - 2 - k = 5(-k)$

$\Rightarrow \qquad\qquad 3k + 6 = -5k$

$\Rightarrow \qquad\qquad\qquad 8k = -6$

$\Rightarrow \qquad\qquad\qquad k = -\frac{6}{8} = -\frac{3}{4}$

Thus, $(x + k) = (x - \frac{3}{4})$ and is a factor of $g(x)$

$\therefore$ $x = \frac{3}{4}$ is a root of $g(x) = 0$.

Thus, the three roots of $g(x) = 0$ are 1, –1 and $\frac{3}{4}$.

Method 2:

Let $g(x) = x^3 + ax^2 + bx + c = 0$.

Given: $g(1) = 0$

$(1)^3 + a(1)^2 + b(1) + c = 0$

$1 + a + b + c = 0$

$a + b + c = -1$ ①

Given: $g(-1) = 0$

$(-1)^3 + a(-1)^2 + b(-1) + c = 0$

$-1 + a - b + c = 0$

$a - b + c = 1$ ②

Given: $g(2) = 5g(0)$

$(2)^3 + a(2)^2 + b(2) + c = 5(c)$

$8 + 4a + 2b + c = 5c$

$4a + 2b - 4c = -8$

$2a + b - 2c = -4$ ③

Solving the simultaneous equations ①, ② and ③ gives $a = -\frac{3}{4}$, $b = -1$ and $c = \frac{3}{4}$.

Thus, $g(x) = x^3 - \frac{3}{4}x^2 - x + \frac{3}{4}$

$$g(x) = 0$$

$\Rightarrow$ $x^3 - \frac{3}{4}x^2 - x + \frac{3}{4} = 0$

$\Rightarrow$ $4x^3 - 3x^2 - 4x + 3 = 0$ [multiply across by 4]

As $g(-1) = 0 = g(1)$, then $(x + 1)$ and $(x - 1)$ are factors.

If $(x + 1)$ and $(x - 1)$ are factors, then $(x + 1)(x - 1) = x^2 - 1$ is also a factor.

Dividing $4x^3 - 3x^2 - 4x + 3$ by $x^2 - 1$ gives $4x - 3$, the third factor.

If $4x - 3$ is a factor, then $x = \frac{3}{4}$ is a root.

Thus, the three roots of $g(x) = 0$ are 1, –1 and $\frac{3}{4}$.

Example

Show that $x = 1$ is a root of $x^3 + (2p - 1)x^2 + (q - 2p)x - q = 0$.
Given that the other two roots are equal, prove that $p^2 = q$.

Solution:

$$x^3 + (2p - 1)x^2 + (q - 2p)x - q = 0$$

Let $x = 1$

$$(1)^3 + (2p - 1)(1)^2 + (q - 2p)(1) - q$$
$$= 1 + (2p - 1)(1) + (q - 2p)(1) - q$$
$$= 1 + 2p - 1 + q - 2p - q$$
$$= 2p - 2p + q - q + 1 - 1 = 0$$
$$\therefore \quad x = 1 \text{ is a solution.}$$

Other two roots are equal; prove that $p^2 = q$.

Method 1: Use long division

$$
\begin{array}{r}
x^2 + 2px + q \\
x - 1 \overline{) x^3 + (2p - 1)x^2 + (q - 2p)x - q}
\end{array}
$$

$$
\begin{array}{l}
x^3 \quad - \qquad\qquad x^2 \\
\overline{} \\
\qquad\qquad 2px^2 + (q - 2p)x \\
\qquad\qquad 2px^2 - \qquad 2px \\
\qquad\qquad \overline{} \\
\qquad\qquad\qquad\quad qx - q \\
\qquad\qquad\qquad\quad qx - q \\
\qquad\qquad\qquad\quad \overline{} \\
\qquad\qquad\qquad\qquad\quad 0
\end{array}
$$

$x^2 + 2px + q \qquad a = 1,\ b = 2p,\ c = q$

$b^2 = 4ac \quad$ [roots are equal]

$(2p)^2 = 4(1)\,(q)$

$4p^2 = 4q$

$\boxed{p^2 = q}$

Method 2: Let the roots be 1, a and a (two equal)

$\therefore \quad$ the factors are $(x - 1)(x - a)(x - a)$.

$(x - 1)(x - a)(x - a)$
$= (x - 1)(x^2 - 2ax + a^2)$
$= x^3 - 2ax^2 + a^2x - x^2 + 2ax - a^2$
$= x^3 + (-2a - 1)x^2 + (a^2 + 2a)x - a^2$

$x^3 + (2p - 1)x^2 + (q - 2p)x - q$ [original expression]

By comparing coefficients of both:

① $\quad 2p - 1 = -2a - 1$ $\qquad$ ② $\quad -q = -a^2$

$\Rightarrow \qquad 2p = -2a$ $\qquad\qquad \Rightarrow \quad q = a^2$

$\Rightarrow \qquad p = -a$

$\Rightarrow \qquad p^2 = a^2$

$\therefore \; p^2 = q \quad$ [i.e. both equal a^2]

Indices

Rules of indices

1.	$a^m \cdot a^n = a^{m+n}$		**5.**	$\left(\dfrac{a}{b}\right)^m = \dfrac{a^m}{b^m}$
2.	$\dfrac{a^m}{a^n} = a^{m-n}$		**6.**	$a^0 = 1$
3.	$(a^m)^n = a^{mm}$		**7.**	$a^{-m} = \dfrac{1}{a^m}$
4.	$(ab)^m = a^m b^m$		**8.**	$a^{\frac{m}{n}} = (a^{\frac{1}{n}})^m$

Note: An index can be moved from one side of an equation to the other side if it is inverted.

$$\text{If } a^{\frac{m}{n}} = b, \text{ then } a = b^{\frac{n}{m}}$$

Note: $\quad \sqrt[n]{a} = a^{\frac{1}{n}}$ and $\sqrt[n]{a^m} = a^{\frac{m}{n}}$.

Example

Evaluate each of the following, expressing your answers as rational numbers:

(i) $32^{\frac{4}{5}}$ (ii) $64^{-\frac{2}{3}}$ (iii) $16^{\frac{3}{4}} \cdot 27^{-\frac{2}{3}}$ (iv) $(2\frac{1}{4})^{1\frac{1}{2}}$ (v) $\left(\dfrac{25}{16}\right)^{-\frac{3}{2}}$ (vi) $\left(\dfrac{1}{27}\right)^{\frac{2}{3}}$

Solution:

(i) $\quad 32^{\frac{4}{5}} = (32^{\frac{1}{5}})^4 = (2)^4 = 16$

(ii) $\quad 64^{-\frac{2}{3}} = \dfrac{1}{64^{\frac{2}{3}}} = \dfrac{1}{(64^{\frac{1}{3}})^2} = \dfrac{1}{(4)^2} = \dfrac{1}{16}$

(iii) $\quad 16^{\frac{3}{4}} \cdot 27^{-\frac{2}{3}} = \dfrac{16^{\frac{3}{4}}}{27^{\frac{2}{3}}} = \dfrac{(16^{\frac{1}{4}})^3}{(27^{\frac{1}{3}})^2} = \dfrac{(2)^3}{(3)^2} = \dfrac{8}{9}$

(iv) $\quad (2\frac{1}{4})^{1\frac{1}{2}} = \left(\dfrac{9}{4}\right)^{\frac{3}{2}} = \dfrac{9^{\frac{3}{2}}}{4^{\frac{3}{2}}} = \dfrac{(9^{\frac{1}{2}})^3}{(4^{\frac{1}{2}})^3} = \dfrac{(3)^3}{(2)^3} = \dfrac{27}{8}$

(v) $\quad \left(\dfrac{25}{16}\right)^{-\frac{3}{2}} = \dfrac{25^{-\frac{3}{2}}}{16^{-\frac{3}{2}}} = \dfrac{16^{\frac{3}{2}}}{25^{\frac{3}{2}}} = \dfrac{(16^{\frac{1}{2}})^3}{(25^{\frac{1}{2}})^3} = \dfrac{(4)^3}{(5)^3} = \dfrac{64}{125}$

(vi) $\quad \left(\dfrac{1}{27}\right)^{\frac{2}{3}} = \dfrac{1^{\frac{2}{3}}}{27^{\frac{2}{3}}} = \dfrac{1}{(27^{\frac{1}{3}})^2} = \dfrac{1}{(3)^2} = \dfrac{1}{9}$

Example

If (i) $x^{\frac{2}{3}} = 16$, (ii) $y^{\frac{3}{4}} = 27$, (iii) $z^{\frac{3}{2}} = 16^{\frac{3}{4}}$, find the values of x, y and z.

Solution:

(i) $\quad x^{\frac{2}{3}} = 16$

$\Rightarrow \quad x = 16^{\frac{3}{2}}$

$\Rightarrow \quad x = (16^{\frac{1}{2}})^3$

$\Rightarrow \quad x = (4)^3$

$\Rightarrow \quad x = 64$

(ii) $\quad y^{\frac{3}{4}} = 27$

$\Rightarrow \quad y = 27^{\frac{4}{3}}$

$\Rightarrow \quad y = (27^{\frac{1}{3}})^4$

$\Rightarrow \quad y = (3)^4$

$\Rightarrow \quad y = 81$

(iii) $\quad z^{\frac{3}{2}} = 16^{\frac{3}{4}}$

$\Rightarrow \quad z = (16^{\frac{3}{4}})^{\frac{2}{3}}$

$\Rightarrow \quad z = 16^{\frac{3}{4} \times \frac{2}{3}}$

$\Rightarrow \quad z = 16^{\frac{1}{2}}$

$\Rightarrow \quad z = 4$

Example

Simplify $\dfrac{27^{n+3} - 6 \cdot 3^{3n+6}}{3^{n+1} \cdot 9^{n+3}}$

Solution:

Write every term as a power of 3.

$$\frac{27^{n+3} - 6 \cdot 3^{3n+6}}{3^{n+1} \cdot 9^{n+3}} = \frac{(3^3)^{n+3} - 2 \cdot 3^1 \cdot 3^{3n+6}}{3^{n+1} \cdot (3^2)^{n+3}}$$

$$= \frac{3^{3n+9} - 2 \cdot 3^{3n+7}}{3^{n+1} \cdot 3^{2n+6}}$$

$$= \frac{3^{3n+9} - 2 \cdot 3^{3n+7}}{3^{3n+7}}$$

$$= \frac{3^2 - 2(1)}{1} \qquad \text{[divide each term by } 3^{3n+7}\text{]}$$

$$= 9 - 2$$

$$= 7$$

Example

Simplify (i) $\dfrac{x^{\frac{3}{2}} - x^{-\frac{1}{2}}}{x^{\frac{1}{2}} - x^{-\frac{1}{2}}}$ (ii) $\dfrac{(x-1)^{\frac{1}{2}} + (x-1)^{-\frac{1}{2}}}{(x-1)^{\frac{1}{2}}}$

Solution:

(i) $\dfrac{x^{\frac{3}{2}} - x^{-\frac{1}{2}}}{x^{\frac{1}{2}} - x^{-\frac{1}{2}}}$

$= \dfrac{x^2 - 1}{x - 1}$

[multiply each term by $x^{\frac{1}{2}}$]

$= \dfrac{(x - 1)(x + 1)}{(x - 1)}$

$= x + 1$

(ii) $\dfrac{(x-1)^{\frac{1}{2}} + (x-1)^{-\frac{1}{2}}}{(x-1)^{\frac{1}{2}}}$

$= \dfrac{(x - 1)^1 + (x - 1)^0}{(x - 1)^1}$

[multiply each term by $(x - 1)^{\frac{1}{2}}$]

$= \dfrac{x - 1 + 1}{x - 1}$

$= \dfrac{x}{x - 1}$

Index Equations

Example

Solve (i) $27.9^{x-1} = 3.3^{x-2}$

(ii) $2^x = 8^{\frac{1}{5}}$

Solution:

We express both sides as powers of the same number, equate the powers and solve.

(i) $\qquad 27.9^{x-1} = 3.3^{x-2}$

$\qquad 3^3.(3^2)^{x-1} = 3^1.3^{x-2}$

$\qquad 3^3.3^{2x-2} = 3^{1+x-2}$

$\qquad\qquad 3^{2x+1} = 3^{x-1}$

$\Rightarrow \qquad 2x + 1 = x - 1$

$\Rightarrow \qquad\qquad x = -2$

(ii) $\qquad 2^x = 8^{\frac{1}{5}}$

$\qquad 2^x = (2^3)^{\frac{1}{5}}$

$\qquad 2^x = 2^{\frac{3}{5}}$

$\Rightarrow \qquad x = \frac{3}{5}$

Sometimes index equations lead to simultaneous equations.

Example

Solve for x and y if $2^x = 8^{y+1}$ and $9^y = 3^{x-9}$.

Solution:

$2^x = 8^{y+1}$

$2^x = (2^3)^{y+1}$

$2^x = 2^{3y+3}$

$x = 3y + 3$

$x - 3y = 3 \qquad ①$

$9^y = 3^{x-9}$

$(3^2)^y = 3^{x-9}$

$3^{2y} = 3^{x-9}$

$2y = x - 9$

$x - 2y = 9 \qquad ②$

By solving the simultaneous equations ① and ②, we get $x = 21$ and $y = 6$.

Sometimes index equations lead to quadratic equations.

Example

Solve $\dfrac{(8^x)^x}{32^x} = 4$

Solution:

$$\frac{(8^x)^x}{32^x} = 4$$

$$\frac{(2^{3x})^x}{(2^5)^x} = 2^2$$

$$\frac{2^{3x^2}}{2^{5x}} = 2^2$$

$$2^{3x^2 - 5x} = 2^2$$

$$\Rightarrow \quad 3x^2 - 5x = 2$$

$$3x^2 - 5x = 2$$

$$3x^2 - 5x - 2 = 0$$

$$(3x + 1)(x - 2) = 0$$

$$3x + 1 = 0 \quad \text{or} \quad x - 2 = 0$$

$$x = -\tfrac{1}{3} \quad \text{or} \quad x = 2$$

Often a substitution of the form $y = a^x$ is required to obtain an equation in y.

Note: $a^{2x} = (a^x)^2 = y^2$.

Example

Solve **(i)** $3^{2x} - 10 \cdot 3^x + 9 = 0$ **(ii)** $2^{2x+1} - 15 \cdot 2^x - 8 = 0$

Solution:

(i)

$$3^{2x} - 10 \cdot 3^x + 9 = 0$$

$$3^{2x} = (3^x)^2$$

$$\therefore \quad (3^x)^2 - 10 \cdot 3^x + 9 = 0$$

$$\text{let } y = 3^x$$

$$\Rightarrow \quad y^2 - 10y + 9 = 0$$

$$\Rightarrow \quad (y - 9)(y - 1) = 0$$

$$\Rightarrow \quad y - 9 = 0 \quad \text{or} \quad y - 1 = 0$$

$$\Rightarrow \quad y = 9 \quad \text{or} \quad y = 1$$

$$\Rightarrow \quad 3^x = 9 \quad \text{or} \quad 3^x = 1$$

$$\Rightarrow \quad 3^x = 3^2 \quad \text{or} \quad 3^x = 3^0$$

$$\Rightarrow \quad x = 2 \quad \text{or} \quad x = 0$$

(ii)

$$2^{2x+1} - 15 \cdot 2^x - 8 = 0$$

$$2^{2x+1} = 2^{2x} \cdot 2^1 = 2 \cdot 2^{2x} = 2(2^x)^2$$

$$\therefore \quad 2(2^x)^2 - 15 \cdot 2^x - 8 = 0$$

$$\text{let } y = 2^x$$

$$\Rightarrow \quad 2y^2 - 15y - 8 = 0$$

$$\Rightarrow \quad (2y + 1)(y - 8) = 0$$

$$\Rightarrow \quad 2y + 1 = 0 \quad \text{or} \quad y - 8 = 0$$

$$\Rightarrow \quad y = -\tfrac{1}{2} \quad \text{or} \quad y = 8$$

$$\Rightarrow \quad 2^x = -\tfrac{1}{2} \quad \text{or} \quad 2^x = 8$$

$$\Rightarrow \quad 2^x = 2^3$$

$$\Rightarrow \quad x = 3$$

(There is no solution to $2^x = -\tfrac{1}{2}$.)

Example

Let $f(x) = \left(\dfrac{b^n - a^n}{b - a} \right) x + ab \left(\dfrac{a^{n-1} - b^{n-1}}{b - a} \right)$ for $a \neq b$.

Show that $f(a) = a^n$.

Solution:

$$f(x) = \left(\frac{b^n - a^n}{b - a} \right) x + ab \left(\frac{a^{n-1} - b^{n-1}}{b - a} \right)$$

$$f(a) = \left(\frac{b^n - a^n}{b - a} \right) a^1 + a^1 b^1 \left(\frac{a^{n-1} - b^{n-1}}{b - a} \right) \qquad \text{[replace } x \text{ with } a\text{]}$$

$$= \frac{ab^n - a^{n+1}}{b - a} + \frac{a^n b - ab^n}{b - a}$$

$$= \frac{ab^n - a^{n+1} + a^n b - ab^n}{b - a} \qquad \text{[both with the same denominator } (b - a)\text{]}$$

$$= \frac{a^n b - a^{n+1}}{b - a}$$

$$= \frac{a^n (b - a)}{(b - a)}$$

$$= a^n$$

Example

If for all integers n, $u_n = (n - 20)2^n$, verify that $u_{n+2} - 4u_{n+1} + 4u_n = 0$.

Find the values of n for which $u_{n+1} > 3u_n$.

Solution:

$$u_n = (n - 20)2^n$$

$$u_{n+1} = (n + 1 - 20)2^{n+1} = (n - 19)2 \cdot 2^n = 2(n - 19)2^n$$

$$u_{n+2} = (n + 2 - 20)2^{n+2} = (n - 18)2^2 \cdot 2^n = 4(n - 18)2^n$$

$$\underset{u_{n+2}}{\searrow} \quad - \quad \underset{4u_{n+1}}{\searrow} \quad + \quad \underset{4u_n}{\searrow}$$

$$= [4(n - 18)2^n] - 4[2(n - 19)2^n] + 4[(n - 20)2^n]$$

$$= 4(n - 18)2^n - 8(n - 19)2^n + 4(n - 20)2^n$$

$$= 2^n[4(n - 18) - 8(n - 19) + 4(n - 20)] \qquad \text{[factor out } 2^n\text{]}$$

$$= 2^n[4n - 72 - 8n + 152 + 4n - 80]$$

$$= 2^n[8n - 8n + 152 - 152]$$

$$= 2[0]$$

$$= 0$$

$$u_{n+1} > 3u_n$$

$\Rightarrow \quad 2(n-19)2^n > 3(n-20)2^n$

$\Rightarrow \quad 2(n-19) > 3(n-20)$ [divide both sides by 2^n, which is positive]

$\Rightarrow \quad 2n - 38 > 3n - 60$

$\Rightarrow \quad -n > -22$

$\Rightarrow \quad n < 22$ [change signs, reverse inequality]

Logs

The basis laws of logs are as follows:

L1. $\log_a mn = \log_a m + \log_a n$

L2. $\log_a \dfrac{m}{n} = \log_a m - \log_a n$

L3. $\log_a m^n = n \log_a m$

L4. $\log_n m = \dfrac{\log_a m}{\log_a n}$ (change of base)

L5. $\log_a a = 1$

L6. $\log_a 1 = 0$

Notation:

$a = b^c$ (index form)

$\log_b a = c$ (log form)

e.g.

$9 = 3^2$ (index form)

$\log_3 9 = 2$ (log form)

Example

Evaluate each of the following:

(i) $\log_3 81$ (ii) $\log_8 64$ (iii) $\log_4 2$ (iv) $\log_3 \frac{1}{3}$

(v) $\log_2 16$ (vi) $\log_2 8$ (vii) $\log_8 16$ (viii) $\dfrac{\log_5 49}{\log_5 7}$

Solution:

(i) $\log_3 81$

$= \log_3 3^4$

$= 4 \log_3 3$ (L3)

$= 4 (1)$ (L5)

$= 4$

(ii) $\log_8 64$

$= \log_8 8^2$

$= 2 \log_8 8$ (L3)

$= 2 (1)$ (L5)

$= 2$

(iii) $\log_4 2$

$= \log_4 4^{\frac{1}{2}}$ ($2 = 4^{\frac{1}{2}}$)

$= \frac{1}{2} \log_4 4$ (L3)

$= \frac{1}{2} (1)$ (L5)

$= \frac{1}{2}$

53

(iv) $\log_3 \frac{1}{3}$

$\quad = \log_3 1 - \log_3 3$ (L2)

$\quad = 0 - 1$ (L5 and L6)

$\quad = -1$

(v) $\log_2 16$

$\quad = \log_2 2^4$

$\quad = 4 \log_2 2$ (L3)

$\quad = 4\,(1)$ (L5)

$\quad = 4$

(vi) $\log_2 8$

$\quad = \log_2 2^3$

$\quad = 3 \log_2 2$ (L3)

$\quad = 3(1)$ (L5)

$\quad = 3$

(vii) $\log_8 16$

$\quad = \dfrac{\log_2 16}{\log_2 8}$ (L4, change of base)

(as 16 and 8 can be written as powers of 2)

$\quad = \frac{4}{3}$ [from **(v)** and **(vi)**]

(viii) $\dfrac{\log_5 49}{\log_5 7}$

$\quad = \log_7 49$ (L4, change of base)

$\quad = \log_7 7^2$

$\quad = 2 \log_7 7 = 2(1) = 2$

Example

If $p = \log_{10} 2$ and $q = \log_{10} 3$, express in terms of p and/or q:

(i) $\log_{10} 6$ **(ii)** $\log_{10} 12$ **(iii)** $\log_{10} 5$ **(iv)** $\log_5 12$

(v) $\log_{10} 360$ **(vi)** $\log_{10} \sqrt{2}$ **(vii)** $\log_{10} 6\frac{2}{3}$ **(viii)** $\log_{10} \frac{1}{4}$

Solution:

Method: Write each of the numbers in terms of 2, 3 and the base 10.

(i) $\log_{10} 6$

$\qquad 6 = 2 \times 3$

$\quad \therefore \ \log_{10} 6 = \log_{10} (2 \times 3)$

$\qquad\qquad = \log_{10} 2 + \log_{10} 3$ (L1)

$\qquad\qquad = p + q$

(ii) $\log_{10} 12$

$\qquad 12 = 2 \times 2 \times 3$

$\quad \therefore \ \log_{10} 12 = \log_{10} (2 \times 2 \times 3)$

$\qquad\qquad = \log_{10} 2 + \log_{10} 2 + \log_{10} 3$ (L 1)

$\qquad\qquad = p + p + q$

$\qquad\qquad = 2p + q$

(iii) $\log_{10} 5$

$\qquad 5 = \frac{10}{2}$

$\quad \therefore \ \log_{10} 5 = \log_{10} \frac{10}{2}$

$\qquad\qquad = \log_{10} 10 - \log_{10} 2$ (L2)

$\qquad\qquad = 1 - p$

(iv) $\log_5 12$

$\qquad = \dfrac{\log_{10} 12}{\log_{10} 5}$ (L4, change of base)

$\qquad = \dfrac{2p + q}{1 - p}$ [from **(ii)** and **(iii)**]

(v) $\log_{10} 360$

$360 = 2 \times 2 \times 3 \times 3 \times 10$

$\therefore \log_{10} 360$

$= \log_{10} (2 \times 2 \times 3 \times 3 \times 10)$

$= \log_{10} 2 + \log_{10} 2 + \log_{10} 3 + \log_{10} 3 + \log_{10} 10$ (L1)

$= p + p + q + q + 1$

$= 2p + 2q + 1$

(vi) $\log_{10} \sqrt{2}$

$\sqrt{2} = 2^{\frac{1}{2}}$

$\therefore \log_{10} \sqrt{2}$

$= \log_{10} 2^{\frac{1}{2}}$

$= \frac{1}{2} \log_{10} 2$ (L3)

$= \frac{1}{2} p$

(vii) $\log_{10} 6\frac{2}{3}$

$6\frac{2}{3} = \frac{20}{3} = \frac{10 \times 2}{3}$

$\therefore \log_{10} 6\frac{2}{3}$

$= \log_{10} \dfrac{10 \times 2}{3}$

$= \log_{10} 10 + \log_{10} 2 - \log_{10} 3$ (L1 and L2)

$= 1 + p - q$

(viii) $\log_{10} \frac{1}{4}$

$\dfrac{1}{4} = \dfrac{1}{2 \times 2}$

$\therefore \log_{10} \frac{1}{4}$

$= \log_{10} \dfrac{1}{2 \times 2}$

$= \log_{10} 1 - \log_{10} 2 - \log_{10} 2$ (L1 and L2)

$= 0 - p - p$ (L6)

$= -2p$

Example

If $p = \log 5\frac{1}{4}$, $q = \log 2\frac{1}{3}$, $r = \log 3\frac{1}{2}$, express $(p + q)$ in terms of r.

Solution:

$p + q$

$= \log 5\frac{1}{4} + \log 2\frac{1}{3}$

$= \log \dfrac{21}{4} + \log \dfrac{7}{3}$

$= \log \dfrac{21}{4} \times \dfrac{7}{3}$ (L1)

$= \log \dfrac{49}{4}$

$= \log \left(\dfrac{7}{2}\right)^2$

$= 2 \log \dfrac{7}{2}$ (L3)

$= 2 \log 3\frac{1}{2}$

$= 2r$

Example

(i)   If $\log_4 t = 2$, find t.

(ii)   If $\log_3 x = -1$, find x.

(iii)   If $\log_2 x = 3$ and $\log_2 y = 5$, evaluate $\log_2 y^x$.

Solution:

(i) $\log_4 t = 2$

       $\Rightarrow$ $t = 4^2$

       $\Rightarrow$ $t = 16$

(ii) $\log_3 x = -1$

       $\Rightarrow$ $x = 3^{-1}$

       $\Rightarrow$ $x = \frac{1}{3}$

(iii) $\log_2 x = 3$

       $\Rightarrow$ $x = 2^3$

       $\Rightarrow$ $x = 8$

           $\log_2 y^x$

           $= x \log_2 y$

           $= (8)\,(5) = 40$

Logarithm Equations

Use the properties of logs to:

> 1. Get a single log expression in the equation and change to index form
>
> or
>
> 2. Get a single log expression on both sides, cancel the logs and solve.

Example

Solve for x (i) $2 \log x = \log (3x + 4)$ (ii) $\log_2(1 + x) - \log_2 (1 - x) = 2$

Solution:

(i)

$$2 \log x = \log(3x + 4)$$
$$\Rightarrow \quad \log x^2 = \log(3x + 4)$$
$$\Rightarrow \quad x^2 = 3x + 4$$
$$\Rightarrow \quad x^2 - 3x - 4 = 0$$
$$\Rightarrow \quad (x - 4)(x + 1) = 0$$
$$\Rightarrow \quad x - 4 = 0 \quad \text{or} \quad x + 1 = 0$$
$$\Rightarrow \quad x = 4 \quad \text{or} \quad x = -1$$

$x = -1$ is rejected as substitution into the original equation yields $2 \log (-1)$, which is not defined.

Check $x = 4$ in original equation.

L.H.S $\quad x = 4$	R.H.S
$2 \log x$	$\log (3x + 4)$
$= 2 \log 4$	$= \log 16$
	$= \log 4^2$
	$= 2 \log 4$

$\therefore \quad x = 4$ is a solution.

(ii) $\log_2(1 + x) - \log_2 (1 - x) = 2$

$$\Rightarrow \quad \log_2\left(\frac{1 + x}{1 - x}\right) = 2$$
$$\Rightarrow \quad \frac{1 + x}{1 - x} = 2^2$$
$$\Rightarrow \quad \frac{1 + x}{1 - x} = 4$$
$$\Rightarrow \quad 1 + x = 4(1 - x)$$
$$\Rightarrow \quad 1 + x = 4 - 4x$$
$$\Rightarrow \quad x + 4x = 4 - 1$$
$$\Rightarrow \quad 5x = 3$$
$$\Rightarrow \quad x = \tfrac{3}{5}$$

Check $x = \tfrac{3}{5}$ in original equation.

L.H.S.	$x = \tfrac{3}{5}$ R.H.S.
$\log_2 (1 + x) - \log_2(1 - x)$	2
$= \log_2 (1 + \tfrac{3}{5}) - \log(1 - \tfrac{3}{5})$	
$= \log_2 \tfrac{8}{5} - \log_2 \tfrac{2}{5}$	
$= \log_2 (\tfrac{8}{5} \div \tfrac{2}{5})$	
$= \log_2 4$	
$= \log_2 2^2$	
$= 2 \log_2 2 = 2(1) = 2$	

$\therefore \quad x = \tfrac{3}{5}$ is a solution.

Example

Solve for x: $(\log_9 3)\left(\log_9 \dfrac{x}{2}\right) = \log_9 x$

Solution:

$$(\log_9 3)\left(\log_9 \dfrac{x}{2}\right) = \log_9 x$$

$\Rightarrow \qquad \frac{1}{2}\log_9 \dfrac{x}{2} = \log_9 x$

$\Rightarrow \qquad \log_9 \dfrac{x}{2} = 2\log_9 x$

$\Rightarrow \qquad \log_9 \dfrac{x}{2} = \log_9 x^2$

$\Rightarrow \qquad \dfrac{x}{2} = x^2 \qquad$ [both are to the base 9]

$\Rightarrow \qquad x = 2x^2$

$\Rightarrow \qquad 2x^2 - x = 0$

$\Rightarrow \qquad x(2x - 1) = 0$

$\Rightarrow \qquad x = 0 \quad$ or $\quad 2x - 1 = 0$

$\Rightarrow \qquad x = 0 \quad$ or $\quad x = \frac{1}{2}$

$x = 0$ is rejected as $\log_9 0$ or $\log_9 \frac{0}{2}$ is not defined.

Thus, the solution is $x = \frac{1}{2}$ (which can be verified).

$\log_9 3$

$= \log_9 9^{\frac{1}{2}}$

$= \frac{1}{2}\log_9 9$

$= \frac{1}{2}(1) = \frac{1}{2}$

Sometimes a change of base is required.

Example

Solve for x: $\log_4(3x + 1) = \log_2 (x - 1)$

Solution:

Change the left-hand side to base 2.

$$\log_4(3x + 1) = \log_2(x - 1)$$

$\Rightarrow \qquad \dfrac{\log_2 (3x + 1)}{\log_2 4} = \log_2 (x - 1)$

$\Rightarrow \qquad \dfrac{\log_2 (3x + 1)}{2} = \log_2 (x - 1) \qquad [\log_2 4 = 2]$

$\Rightarrow \qquad \log_2(3x + 1) = 2 \log_2(x - 1)$

$\Rightarrow \qquad \log_2(3x + 1) = \log_2(x - 1)^2$

$\Rightarrow \qquad (3x + 1) = (x - 1)^2 \qquad$ [both are to the base 2]

$\Rightarrow \qquad 3x + 1 = x^2 - 2x + 1$

$\Rightarrow \qquad x^2 - 5x = 0$

$\Rightarrow \qquad x(x - 5) = 0$

$\Rightarrow \qquad x = 0 \quad$ or $\quad x = 5$

$x = 0$ is rejected as it leads to $\log_2 (-1)$, which is undefined.

$x = 5$ gives $\log_4 16 = \log_2 4$

i.e. $\qquad\qquad 2 = 2$ (true)

Thus, $x = 5$ is a solution.

Undetermined Coefficients

When two expressions in x (or any other variable) are equal to one another for all values of x, we can equate the coefficients of the same powers of x in the two expressions.

Example

If $p(x + q)^2 + r = 2x^2 + 5x + 6$, for all x, find the value of p, of q and of r.

Solution:

Expand the left-hand side and equate coefficients.

$$p(x + q)^2 + r = 2x^2 + 5x + 6$$

$\Rightarrow \qquad p(x^2 + 2qx + q^2) + r = 2x^2 + 5x + 6$

$\Rightarrow \qquad px^2 + 2pqx + pq^2 + r = 2x^2 + 5x + 6$

$\Rightarrow \qquad p(x^2) + 2pq(x) + (pq^2 + r) = 2(x^2) + 5(x) + 6$

Equating coefficients of like terms:

$\Rightarrow \quad p = 2$ ①	$2pq = 5$ ②	$pq^2 + r = 6$ ③
	$2(2)q = 5$	$2(\frac{5}{4})^2 + r = 6$
	$4q = 5$	$2(\frac{25}{16}) + r = 6$
	$q = \frac{5}{4}$	$\frac{50}{16} + r = 6$
		$r = 6 - \frac{50}{16}$
		$r = \frac{23}{8}$

Example

If $(x + r)(2x^2 + sx + 4) = 2x^3 + x^2 - 11x + 12$, for all x, find the value of r and of s.

Solution:

$$(x + r)(2x^2 + sx + 4) = 2x^3 + x^2 - 11x + 12$$
$$2x^3 + sx^2 + 4x + 2rx^2 + rsx + 4r = 2x^3 + x^2 - 11x + 12$$
$$2x^3 + (s + 2r)x^2 + (4 + rs)x + 4r = 2x^3 + x^2 - 11x + 12$$

Equating coefficients of like terms:

$s + 2r = 1$ ①	$4 + rs = -11$ ②	$4r = 12$ ③
From ③ $\quad 4r = 12$	Put $r = 3$ into ① or ②	Test $r = 3$, $s = -5$ in ②
$\Rightarrow \quad r = 3$	$s + 2r = 1$ ①	$4 + rs = -11$ ②
	$s + 2(3) = 1$	$4 + (3)(-5) = -11$
	$s + 6 = 1$	$4 - 15 = -11$
	$s = -5$	$-11 = -11$ (true)

Thus, $r = 3$, $s = -5$.

Example

If $n^3 - 1 = a(n - 1)(n - 2)(n - 3) + b(n - 1)(n - 2) + c(n - 1) + d$, for all values of n, find the value of a, of b, of c and of d.

Solution:

Method 1: Expand the right-hand side and equate coefficients of like terms.

$$a(n - 1)(n - 2)(n - 3) + b(n - 1)(n - 2) + c(n - 1) + d$$
$$= a(n^3 - 6n^2 + 11n - 6) + b(n^2 - 3n + 2) + c(n - 1) + d$$
$$= an^3 - 6an^2 + 11an - 6a + bn^2 - 3bn + 2b + cn - c + d$$
$$= an^3 + (-6a + b)n^2 + (11a - 3b + c)n + (-6a + 2b - c + d)$$
$$n^3 - 1 = n^3 + 0n^2 + 0n - 1$$
$$\therefore \quad n^3 + 0n^2 + 0n - 1 = an^3 + (-6a + b)n^2 + (11a - 3b + c)n + (-6a + 2b - c + d)$$

60

Equating coefficients of like terms:

$a = 1$ ①	$-6a + b = 0$ ②	$11a - 3b + c = 0$ ③	$-6a + 2b - c + d = -1$ ④
	$-6(1) + b = 0$	$11(1) - 3(6) + c = 0$	$-6(1) + 2(6) - 7 + d = -1$
	$-6 + b = 0$	$11 - 18 + c = 0$	$-6 + 12 - 7 + d = -1$
	$b = 6$	$-7 + c = 0$	$-1 + d = -1$
		$c = 7$	$d = 0$

Method 2:   The left-hand side = right-hand side for all values of n.

Hence, by choosing suitable values of n, the values of a, b, c and d can be found.

$$n^3 - 1 = a(n - 1)(n - 2)(n - 3) + b(n - 1)(n - 2) + c(n - 1) + d$$

<u>Let $n = 1$:</u>

$\Rightarrow \qquad 1 - 1 = 0 + 0 + 0 + d$

$\therefore \qquad \quad d = 0$

<u>Let $n = 2$:</u>

$\Rightarrow \qquad 8 - 1 = 0 + 0 + c(2 - 1) + d$

$\Rightarrow \qquad \quad 7 = c + d$

$\Rightarrow \qquad \quad 7 = c + 0$

$\therefore \qquad \quad c = 7$

<u>Let $n = 3$:</u>

$\Rightarrow \qquad 27 - 1 = 0 + b(2)\,(1) + c(2) + d$

$\Rightarrow \qquad \quad 26 = 2b + 2c + d$

$\Rightarrow \qquad \quad 26 = 2b + 2(7) + 0$

$\Rightarrow \qquad \quad 26 = 2b + 14 + 0$

$\Rightarrow \qquad \quad 12 = 2b$

$\therefore \qquad \quad b = 6$

<u>Let $n = 0$:</u>

$\Rightarrow \qquad 0 - 1 = a(-1)\,(-2)(-3)$

$\qquad \qquad \qquad \quad + b(-1)(-2) + c(-1) + d$

$\Rightarrow \qquad \quad -1 = -6a + 2b - c + d$

$\Rightarrow \qquad \quad -1 = -6a + 2(6) - 7 + 0$

$\Rightarrow \qquad \quad -1 = -6a + 12 - 7$

$\Rightarrow \qquad \quad 6a = 6$

$\therefore \qquad \quad a = 1$

The values are the same as before.

Induction

Proof by induction involves two steps:

1. Prove that the proposition is true for the smallest value of n given in the question (usually $n = 0$ or $n = 1$).

2. Assuming the proposition is true for $n = k$, show that the proposition is true for $n = k + 1$.

Note: If it is true for $n = 1$, then step 2 ensures that it is true for $n = 2$. If it is true for $n = 2$, then step 2 ensures that it is true for $n = 3$, and so on.

We will use induction to prove propositions in 3 areas:

1. Divisibility **2. Inequalities** **3. Series**

1. Divisibility

Example

Prove that $4^n - 1$ is divisible by 3 for all $n \in N_0$.

Solution:

$P(n)$: $4^n - 1$ is divisible by 3 for all $n \in N_0$.

Step 1: $P(1)$: $4^1 - 1 = 4 - 1 = 3$, which is divisible by 3.

∴ $P(1)$ is true.

Step 2: Assume $P(k)$ is true, i.e. $4^k - 1$ is divisible by 3.

Test $P(k + 1)$: $4^{k+1} - 1$

$\qquad = 4.4^k - 1$

$\qquad = (3 + 1)4^k - 1$ [split 4 up into 3 + 1]

$\qquad = 3.4^k + 4^k - 1$

3.4^k is divisible by 3 and we assumed $4^k - 1$ is divisible by 3.

∴ $P(k + 1)$ is divisible by 3.

i.e. $P(k + 1)$ is true if $P(k)$ is true.

Hence, by the principle of mathematical induction $P(n)$ is true.

Example

Show by induction that 8 is a factor of $7^{2n+1} + 1$ for $n \in N_0$.

Solution:

$P(n)$: $7^{2n+1} + 1$ is divisible by 8 for all $n \in N_0$.

Step 1. $P(1)$: $7^3 + 1 = 344$, which is divisible by 8.

∴ $P(1)$ is true.

Step 2. Assume $P(k)$ is true, i.e., $7^{2k+1} + 1$ is divisible by 8.

Test $P(k + 1)$: $7^{2(k+1)+1} + 1$

$\qquad = 7^{2k+3} + 1$

$\qquad = 7^2.7^{2k+1} + 1$

$\qquad = 49.7^{2k+1} + 1$

$\qquad = (48 + 1).7^{2k+1} + 1$ [split 49 up into 48 + 1]

$\qquad = 48.7^{2k+1} + 7^{2k+1} + 1$

$\qquad = 48.7^{2k+1} + (7^{2k+1} + 1)$

$48 \cdot 7^{2k+1}$ is divisible by 8 and we assumed $(7^{2k+1} + 1)$ is divisible by 8.

$$\therefore \quad P(k + 1) \text{ is divisible by 8.}$$

$$\text{i.e.} \quad P(k + 1) \text{ is true if } P(k) \text{ is true.}$$

Hence, by the principle of mathematical induction $p(n)$ is true.

Example

Prove by induction that $7^n - 3^n$ is divisible by 4 for all $n \in N_0$.

Solution:

$$P(n): 7^n - 3^n \text{ is divisible by 4 for all } n \in N_0.$$

Step 1: $P(1): 7^1 - 3^1 = 7 - 3 = 4$, which is divisible by 4.

$$\therefore \quad P(1) \text{ is true.}$$

Step 2: Assume $P(k)$ is true, i.e. $7^k - 3^k$ is divisible by 4.

Test $P(k + 1): 7^{k+1} - 3^{k+1}$

$$= 7.7^k - 3.3^k$$

$$= (4 + 3)7^k - 3.3^k \qquad \text{[split 7 up into 4 + 3]}$$

$$= 4.7^k + 3.7^k - 3.3^k$$

$$= 4.7^k + 3(7^k - 3^k)$$

$4 \cdot 7^k$ is divisible by 4 and we assumed $(7^k - 3^k)$ is divisible by 4.

$$\therefore \quad P(k + 1) \text{ is divisible by 4.}$$

$$\text{i.e.} \quad P(k + 1) \text{ is true if } P(k) \text{ is true.}$$

Hence, by the principle of mathematical induction $P(n)$ is true.

Example

Prove by induction that $n^3 + 6n^2 + 8n$ is divisible by 3 for all $n \in N_0$.

Solution:

$$P(n): n^3 + 6n^2 + 8n \text{ is divisible by 3 for all } n \in N_0.$$

Step 1: $P(1): (1)^3 + 6(1)^2 + 8(1) = 1 + 6 + 8 = 15$, which is divisible by 3.

$$\therefore P(1) \text{ is true.}$$

Step 2: Assume $P(k)$ is true, i.e. $k^3 + 6k^2 + 8k$ is divisible by 3.

Test $P(k + 1): (k + 1)^3 + 6(k + 1)^2 + 8(k + 1)$

$$= (k^3 + 3k^2 + 3k + 1) + 6(k^2 + 2k + 1) + 8(k + 1)$$

$$= k^3 + 3k^2 + 3k + 1 + 6k^2 + 12k + 6 + 8k + 8$$

$$= (k^3 + 6k^2 + 8k) + (3k^2 + 15k + 15)$$

$$= (k^3 + 6k^2 + 8k) + 3(k^2 + 5k + 5)$$

$3(k^2 + 5k + 5)$ is divisible by 3 and we assumed $(k^3 + 6k^2 + 8k)$ is divisible by 3

$\therefore$ $P(k + 1)$ is divisible by 3.

i.e. $P(k + 1)$ is true if $P(k)$ is true.

Hence, by the principle of mathematical induction $P(n)$ is true.

2. Inequalities

Example

Prove by induction that $2n^2 > (n + 1)^2$, for $n \geq 3$, $n \in N$.

Solution:

$P(n)$: $2n^2 > (n + 1)^2$, for $n \geq 3$, $n \in N$.

Step 1: $P(3)$: $2(3)^2 > (3 + 1)^2$

$18 > 16$, which is true

$\therefore$ $P(3)$ is true.

Step 2: Assume $P(k)$ is true, i.e. $2k^2 > (k + 1)^2$

Test $P(k + 1)$: $2(k + 1)^2 > (k + 2)^2$

L.H.S: $2(k + 1)^2 = 2(k^2 + 2k + 1)$

$= 2k^2 + 4k + 2$

$> (k + 1)^2 + 4k + 2$ [using our assumption]

$= k^2 + 2k + 1 + 4k + 2$

$= (k^2 + 4k + 4) + 2k - 1$

$= (k + 2)^2 + 2k - 1$

$> (k + 2)^2$ [as $2k - 1 > 0$ for $k \geq 3$]

$\therefore$ $2(k + 1)^2 > (k + 2)^2$

i.e. $P(k + 1)$ is true if $P(k)$ is true.

Hence, by the principle of mathematical induction $P(n)$ is true.

Example

Prove, using the method of induction, that if $r > 0$, $\dfrac{1}{(1 + r)^n} \leq \dfrac{1}{(1 + nr)}$, for all $n \geq 1$.

Solution:

$P(n)$: If $r > 0$, $\dfrac{1}{(1 + r)^n} \leq \dfrac{1}{(1 + nr)}$, for all $n \geq 1$.

64

Step 1: $P(1)$: $\dfrac{1}{(1+r)} \le \dfrac{1}{(1+r)}$, which is true.

∴ $P(1)$ is true.

Step 2: Assume $P(k)$ is true, i.e. $\dfrac{1}{(1+r)^k} \le \dfrac{1}{(1+kr)}$.

Test $P(k+1)$: $\dfrac{1}{(1+r)^{k+1}} \le \dfrac{1}{1+(k+1)r}$

L.H.S.:

$$\dfrac{1}{(1+r)^{k+1}} \le \dfrac{1}{(1+r)(1+r)^k} \le \dfrac{1}{(1+r)(1+kr)} \qquad \text{[using our assumption]}$$

$$\le \dfrac{1}{1+kr+r+kr^2}$$

$$\le \dfrac{1}{1+(k+1)r+kr^2}$$

$$\le \dfrac{1}{1+(k+1)r} \qquad \text{[since } kr^2 > 0]$$

∴ $\dfrac{1}{(1+r)^{k+1}} \le \dfrac{1}{1+(k+1)r}$

∴ $P(k+1)$ is true if $P(k)$ is true.

Hence, by the principle of mathematical induction $P(n)$ is true.

Example

Prove by induction that $(a+b)^n \ge a^n + b^n$, for $a, b > 0$, $a, b \in \textbf{R}$.

Solution:

$P(n)$: $(a+b)^n \ge a^n + b^n$, for $a, b > 0$.

Step 1: $P(1)$: $(a+b)^1 \ge a^1 + b^1$

$a + b \ge a + b$, which is true.

∴ $P(1)$ is true.

Step 2: Assume $P(k)$ is true, i.e. $(a+b)^k \ge a^k + b^k$.

Test $P(k+1)$: $(a+b)^{k+1} \ge a^{k+1} + b^{k+1}$

L.H.S.: $(a+b)^{k+1} = (a+b)(a+b)^k \ge (a+b)(a^k + b^k)$ [using our assumption]

$\ge a^{k+1} + ab^k + ba^k + b^{k+1}$

$\ge a^{k+1} + b^{k+1}$ [as ab^k, $ba^k > 0$]

∴ $(a+b)^{k+1} \ge a^{k+1} + b^{k+1}$

∴ $P(k+1)$ is true if $P(k)$ is true.

Hence, by the principle of mathematical induction $P(n)$ is true.

Example

Prove by induction that $n! > 3^n$, for $n \geq 7$, $n \in N$.

Solution:

$$P(n): n! > 3^n, \text{ for } n \geq 7, n \in N.$$

Step 1: $P(7): 7! > 3^7$

$5\,040 > 2\,187$, which is true

$\therefore P(7)$ is true.

Step 2: Assume $P(k)$ is true, i.e. $k! > 3^k$

Test $P(k + 1): (k + 1)! > 3^{k+1}$

L.H.S.: $(k + 1)! = (k + 1)\, k! > (k + 1)3^k$ [using our assumption]

$> 3 \cdot 3^k$ [as $k \geq 7$]

$= 3^{k+1}$

$\therefore (k + 1)! > 3^{k+1}$

$\therefore P(k + 1)$ is true if $P(k)$ is true.

Hence, by the principle of mathematical induction $P(n)$ is true.

Example

Prove by induction that $(1 + x)^n \geq 1 + nx$, $x > -1$, $n \in N$.

Solution:

$$P(n): (1 + x)^n \geq 1 + nx, \, x > -1, \, n \in N.$$

Step 1: $P(0): (1 + x)^0 \geq 1 + (0)x$

$1 \geq 1$ which is true

$\therefore P(0)$ is true

Step 2: Assume $P(k)$ is true, i.e. $(1 + x)^k \geq 1 + kx$

Test $P(k + 1): (1 + x)^{k+1} \geq 1 + (k + 1)x$

L.H.S.: $(1 + x)^{k+1} = (1 + x)(1 + x)^k \geq (1 + x)(1 + kx)$ [using our assumption]

$= 1 + kx + x + kx^2$

$= 1 + (k + 1)x + kx^2$

$\geq 1 + (k + 1)x$ [as $kx^2 > 0$]

$\therefore (1 + x)^{k+1} \geq 1 + (k + 1)x$

$\therefore P(k + 1)$ is true if $P(k)$ is true.

Hence, by the principle of mathematical induction $P(n)$ is true.

3. Series

Example

Prove by mathematical induction that $1 + 2 + 3 + \cdots + n = \dfrac{n(n + 1)}{2}$, $n \in N_0$.

Solution:

$$P(n): S_n = 1 + 2 + 3 + \cdots + n = \frac{n(n + 1)}{2}, \quad n \in N_0$$

Step 1: $P(1): S_n = 1 = \dfrac{1(1 + 1)}{2} = 1$

$\therefore P(1)$ is true.

Step 2: Assume $P(k)$ is true, i.e. $S_k = 1 + 2 + 3 + \cdots + k = \dfrac{k(k + 1)}{2}$

Test $P(k + 1): S_{k+1} = 1 + 2 + 3 + \cdots + k + (k + 1) = \dfrac{(k + 1)(k + 2)}{2}$

L.H.S.: $(1 + 2 + 3 + \cdots + k) + (k + 1)$

$= \dfrac{k(k + 1)}{2} + (k + 1)$ [using our assumption]

$= (k + 1)\left(\dfrac{k}{2} + 1\right)$ [take out common factor $(k + 1)$]

$= (k + 1)\left(\dfrac{k + 2}{2}\right)$

$= \dfrac{(k + 1)(k + 2)}{2} =$ **R.H.S.**

$\therefore$ $P(k + 1)$ is true if $P(k)$ is true.

Hence, by the principle of mathematical induction $P(n)$ is true.

Example

Prove by mathematical induction that $1^3 + 2^3 + 3^3 + \cdots + n^3 = \dfrac{n^2}{4}(n + 1)^2$, $n \in N_0$.

Solution:

$$P(n): S_n = 1^3 + 2^3 + 3^3 + \cdots + n^3 = \frac{n^2}{4}(n + 1)^2, \quad n \in N_0.$$

Step 1: $P(1): S_1 = 1^3 = \dfrac{1^2}{4}(1 + 1)^2 = 1$, which is true.

$\therefore$ $P(1)$ is true.

Step 2: Assume $P(k)$ is true, i.e. $S_k = 1^3 + 2^3 + 3^3 + \cdots + k^3 = \dfrac{k^2}{4}(k + 1)^2$

Test $P(k + 1):$ $S_{k+1} = 1^3 + 2^3 + 3^3 + \cdots + k^3 + (k + 1)^3 = \dfrac{(k + 1)^2(k + 2)^2}{4}$

L.H.S.: $[1^3 + 2^3 + 3^3 + \cdots + k^3] + (k + 1)^3$

$= \dfrac{k^2(k + 1)^2}{4} + (k + 1)^3$ [using our assumption]

$= (k + 1)^2\left(\dfrac{k^2}{4} + k + 1\right)$ [take out common factor $(k + 1)^2$]

$= (k + 1)^2\left(\dfrac{k^2 + 4k + 4}{4}\right)$

$= \dfrac{(k + 1)^2(k + 2)^2}{4} = $ **R.H.S.**

$\therefore$ $P(k + 1)$ is true if $P(k)$ is true.

Hence, by the principle of mathematical induction $P(n)$ is true.

Example

Prove by mathematical induction that $\dfrac{1}{1.2} + \dfrac{1}{2.3} + \cdots + \dfrac{1}{n(n + 1)} = \dfrac{n}{n + 1}, n \in N_0$.

Solution:

$P(n): S_n = \dfrac{1}{1.2} + \dfrac{1}{2.3} + \cdots + \dfrac{1}{n(n + 1)} = \dfrac{n}{n + 1}, n \in N_0$.

Step 1: $P(1): S_1 = \dfrac{1}{1.2} = \dfrac{1}{1 + 1} = \dfrac{1}{2}$, which is true.

$\therefore$ is $P(1)$ true.

Step 2: Assume $P(k)$ is true, i.e. $S_k = \dfrac{1}{1.2} + \dfrac{1}{2.3} + \cdots + \dfrac{1}{k(k + 1)} = \dfrac{k}{k + 1}$

Test $P(k + 1):$ $S_{k+1} = \dfrac{1}{1.2} + \dfrac{1}{2.3} + \cdots + \dfrac{1}{k(k + 1)} + \dfrac{1}{(k + 1)(k + 2)} = \dfrac{k + 1}{k + 2}$

L.H.S.: $\left[\dfrac{1}{1.2} + \dfrac{1}{2.3} + \cdots + \dfrac{1}{k(k+1)}\right] + \dfrac{1}{(k+1)(k+2)}$

$= \dfrac{k}{(k+1)} + \dfrac{1}{(k+1)(k+2)}$ [using our assumption]

$= \dfrac{k(k+2)}{(k+1)(k+2)} + \dfrac{1}{(k+1)(k+2)}$ [multiply top and bottom of first fraction by $(k+2)$]

$= \dfrac{k^2 + 2k + 1}{(k+1)(k+2)} = \dfrac{(k+1)(k+1)}{(k+1)(k+2)} = \dfrac{k+1}{k+2} =$ **R.H.S.**

$\therefore$ $P(k+1)$ is true if $P(k)$ is true.

Hence, by the principle of mathematical induction $P(n)$ is true.

Example

Prove by induction that $a + ar + ar^2 + \cdots + ar^{n-1} = \dfrac{a(1 - r^n)}{1 - r}, r \neq 1$

Solution:

$$P(n): S_n = a + ar + ar^2 + \cdots + ar^{n-1} = \dfrac{a(1 - r^n)}{1 - r}, r \neq 1$$

Step 1: $P(1): S_1 = a = \dfrac{a(1 - r)}{1 - r} = a$, which is true.

$\therefore$ $P(1)$ is true.

Step 2:   Assume $P(k)$ is true, i.e. $S_k = a + ar + ar^2 + \cdots + ar^{k-1} = \dfrac{a(1 - r^k)}{1 - r}$

Test $P(k+1): S_{k+1} = a + ar + ar^2 + \cdots + ar^{k-1} + ar^k = \dfrac{a(1 - r^{k+1})}{1 - r}$

L.H.S.: $[a + ar + ar^2 + \cdots ar^{k-1}] + ar^k$

$= \dfrac{a(1 - r^k)}{1 - r} + ar^k$ [using our assumption]

$= \dfrac{a(1 - r^k)}{1 - r} + \dfrac{(1 - r)ar^k}{1 - r}$ $\left[\begin{array}{l}\text{multiply top and bottom of the} \\ \text{second fraction by } (1 - r)\end{array}\right]$

$= \dfrac{a - ar^k + ar^k - ar^{k+1}}{1 - r}$

$= \dfrac{a - ar^{k+1}}{1 - r} = \dfrac{a(1 - r^{k+1})}{1 - r} =$ **R.H.S.**

$\therefore$ $P(k+1)$ is true if $P(k)$ is true.

Hence, by the principle of mathematical induction $P(n)$ is true.

Chapter 2
Complex Numbers

Definitions

A **complex number** z is a number of the form $a + bi$, $a, b \in \mathbf{R}$ and $i = \sqrt{-1}$.
a is called the real part of z and b is called the imaginary part of z.

$i = \sqrt{-1}$, $i^2 = -1$, $i^3 = -i$ and $i^4 = 1$.

The modulus of $z = |z| = \sqrt{a^2 + b^2}$.

The argument of $z = \arg(z) = \theta = \tan^{-1}\dfrac{b}{a}$

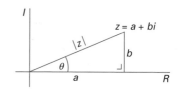

The conjugate of $z = \bar{z} = a - bi$ (only change sign of imaginary part)

(e.g. if $z = -2 - 5i$, then $\bar{z} = -2 + 5i$).

Equality: If two complex numbers are equal, then:

real parts = real parts   and   imaginary parts = imaginary parts

(e.g. if $a + bi = c + di$, then $a = c$ and $b = d$).

Powers of i

Every integer power of i is a member of the set $\{1, -1, i, -i\}$.

Example
Simplify each of the following: **(i)** i^{25} **(ii)** i^{102} **(iii)** i^{-21}

Solution:

[Key: look for i^4's, as each $i^4 = 1$].

(i) i^{25}

$= i^{24}i^1$

$= (i^4)^6 . i$

$= 1^6 . i$

$= i$

(ii) i^{102}

$= i^{100}i^2$

$= 1 . i^2$

$= i^2$

$= -1$

(iii) i^{-21}

$= \dfrac{1}{i^{21}}$ $= \dfrac{1}{i^{21}} \times \dfrac{i^3}{i^3}$

$= \dfrac{i^3}{i^{24}}$ $= \dfrac{i^3}{1}$

$= i^3 = -i$

Operations

Addition, **Subtraction** and **Multiplication** are the same as in ordinary algebra, except i^2, i^3 and i^4 are replaced by -1, $-i$ and 1, respectively.

Division: multiply top and bottom by the conjugate of the bottom.

Example

Let $z = -1 + \sqrt{3}i$, where $i^2 = -1$. Express z^2 in the form $x + yi$, $x, y \in R$.

Find the real value of k such that $z^2 + kz$ is (i) real (ii) a multiple of i.

Solution:

$$z^2 = (-1 + \sqrt{3}i)^2 = (-1 + \sqrt{3}i)(-1 + \sqrt{3}i) = 1 - \sqrt{3}i - \sqrt{3}i + 3i^2 = -2 - 2\sqrt{3}i$$

$$z^2 + kz = (-2 - 2\sqrt{3}\,i) + k(-1 + \sqrt{3}\,i)$$

$$= -2 - 2\sqrt{3}\,i - k + k\sqrt{3}\,i = (-2 - k) + (k\sqrt{3} - 2\sqrt{3}\,)i$$

(i) For $z^2 + kz$ to be real, the expression $(k\sqrt{3} - 2\sqrt{3}\,) = 0$

$\Rightarrow \quad k\sqrt{3} - 2\sqrt{3} = 0$

$\Rightarrow \quad\quad k - 2 = 0$

$\quad\quad\quad k = 2$

(ii) For $z^2 + kz$ to be a multiple of i, the expression $(-2 - k) = 0$.

$\Rightarrow \quad -2 - k = 0$

$\Rightarrow \quad\quad -k = 2$

$\Rightarrow \quad\quad k = -2$

Example

Express $i^{30} - 2i^{11}$ in the form $a + bi$, $a, b \in R$, $i = \sqrt{-1}$.

Solution:

$i^{30} = i^{28}.i^2 = (1)(-1) = -1$

$i^{11} = i^8.i^3 = (1)(-i) = -i$

Thus, $i^{30} - 2i^{11} = -1 - 2(-i) = -1 + 2i$.

Example

(i) Find the real part of $\dfrac{1}{(1 - 2i)^2}$.

(ii) If $\dfrac{2 - \sqrt{2}i}{2 + \sqrt{2}i} = p + qi$, find the values of p and q and, hence, evaluate $p^2 + q^2$.

Solution:

(i) $(1 - 2i)^2 = (1 - 2i)(1 - 2i) = 1 - 2i - 2i - 4 = -3 - 4i$

Thus, $\dfrac{1}{(1 - 2i)^2} = \dfrac{1}{-3 - 4i} = \dfrac{1}{-3 - 4i} \cdot \dfrac{-3 + 4i}{-3 + 4i}$

$$= \dfrac{-3 + 4i}{25} = -\dfrac{3}{25} + \dfrac{4}{25}i$$

Thus, the real part of $\dfrac{1}{(1 - 2i)^2}$ is $-\dfrac{3}{25}$.

(ii) $\dfrac{2 - \sqrt{2}i}{2 + \sqrt{2}i} = \dfrac{2 - \sqrt{2}i}{2 + \sqrt{2}i} \cdot \dfrac{2 - \sqrt{2}i}{2 - \sqrt{2}i}$

$$= \dfrac{4 - 2\sqrt{2}i - 2\sqrt{2}i - 2}{4 + 2} = \dfrac{2 - 4\sqrt{2}i}{6} = \dfrac{1}{3} - \dfrac{2\sqrt{2}}{3}i = p + qi$$

Thus, $p = \tfrac{1}{3}$, $q = -\tfrac{2\sqrt{2}}{3}$

$$p^2 + q^2 = (\tfrac{1}{3})^2 + (-\tfrac{2\sqrt{2}}{3})^2 = \tfrac{1}{9} + \tfrac{8}{9} = \tfrac{9}{9} = 1$$

Example

Given $\dfrac{2}{z} = \dfrac{1}{u} + \dfrac{1}{v}$, where $u = 2 - i$, $v = 1 + 2i$,

express z in the form $a + bi$ and, hence, evaluate $|z|$.

Solution:

$$\dfrac{1}{u} + \dfrac{1}{v} = \dfrac{1}{2 - i} + \dfrac{1}{1 + 2i} = \dfrac{1 + 2i + 2 - i}{(2 - i)(1 + 2i)} = \dfrac{3 + i}{4 + 3i}$$

Thus, $\dfrac{2}{z} = \dfrac{3 + i}{4 + 3i}$

$\Rightarrow \quad (3 + i)z = 8 + 6i$

$$z = \dfrac{8 + 6i}{3 + i} = \dfrac{8 + 6i}{3 + i} \cdot \dfrac{3 - i}{3 - i} = \dfrac{30 + 10i}{10} = 3 + i$$

Thus, $|z| = |3 + i| = \sqrt{3^2 + 1^2} = \sqrt{9 + 1} = \sqrt{10}$

Example

The complex number $u = 4 + 3i$, where $i^2 = -1$.

(i) Find the complex number $v = p + qi$, p, $q \in R$, where $uv = 10 - 5i$.

(ii) Verify that $|u + v + 3 - 5i| = 4\sqrt{5}$.

Solution:

(i) **Method 1** (using division)

$$uv = 10 - 5i$$

$$(4 + 3i)\,v = 10 - 5i$$

$$v = \frac{10 - 5i}{4 + 3i}$$

$$v = \frac{10 - 5i}{4 + 3i} \cdot \frac{4 - 3i}{4 - 3i}$$

$$v = \frac{40 - 30i - 20i - 15}{25}$$

$$v = \frac{25 - 50i}{25}$$

$$v = 1 - 2i$$

(i) **Method 2** (using equality)

$$uv = 10 - 5i$$

$$(4 + 3i)(p + qi) = 10 - 5i$$

$$4p + 4qi + 3pi + 3qi^2 = 10 - 5i$$

$$\underset{R}{4p} + \underset{I}{4qi} + \underset{I}{3pi} - \underset{R}{3q} = \underset{R}{10} - \underset{I}{5i}$$

$$4p - 3q = 10 \quad \text{and} \quad 3p + 4q = -5$$

Solving these simultaneous equations gives $p = 1$ and $q = -2$.

Thus, $v = p + qi = 1 - 2i$.

(ii) $u + v + 3 - 5i = 4 + 3i + 1 - 2i + 3 - 5i = 8 - 4i$

Thus, $|u + v + 3 - 5i| = |8 - 4i| = \sqrt{8^2 + 4^2} = \sqrt{64 + 16} = \sqrt{80} = \sqrt{16}\sqrt{5} = 4\sqrt{5}$.

Example

Evaluate $\left(\dfrac{-1 + \sqrt{3}i}{\sqrt{3} + i} \right)^{98}$.

Solution:

$$\frac{-1 + \sqrt{3}i}{\sqrt{3} + i} = \frac{(-1 + \sqrt{3}i)}{(\sqrt{3} + i)} \cdot \frac{(\sqrt{3} - i)}{(\sqrt{3} - i)} \quad \left[\begin{array}{l} \text{[multiply top and bottom} \\ \text{by } \sqrt{3} - i,\ \text{conjugate of } \sqrt{3} + i] \end{array} \right]$$

$$= \frac{-\sqrt{3} + i + 3i + \sqrt{3}}{3 - i^2} = \frac{4i}{4} = i$$

Thus, $\left(\dfrac{-1 + \sqrt{3}i}{\sqrt{3} + i} \right)^{98} = i^{98} = i^{96} \cdot i^2 = (1)(-1) = -1$

Example

Evaluate $\left|\dfrac{z-1}{1-\bar{z}}\right|$, $z \in C$.

Solution:

Let $z = a + bi$, then $\bar{z} = a - bi$

Note: $\left|\dfrac{z_1}{z_2}\right| = \dfrac{|z_1|}{|z_2|}$

$$\left|\frac{z-1}{1-\bar{z}}\right| = \frac{|z-1|}{|1-\bar{z}|}$$

$$= \frac{|a+bi-1|}{|1-(a-bi)|} = \frac{|(a-1)+bi|}{|(1-a)+bi|} = \frac{\sqrt{(a-1)^2+b^2}}{\sqrt{(1-a)^2+b^2}}$$

$$= \frac{\sqrt{a^2-2a+1+b^2}}{\sqrt{1-2a+a^2+b^2}} = \frac{\sqrt{a^2-2a+1+b^2}}{\sqrt{a^2-2a+1+b^2}} = 1$$

Example

$z_1 = 4 - 2i$, $z_2 = -2 - 6i$. If $z_2 - pz_1 = qi$, $p, q \in R$, find p and q.

Solution:

$$z_2 - pz_1 = qi$$

The right-hand side has no real part, hence a 0, representing the real part, should be placed on the right-hand side.

Now the equation is:

$$z_2 - pz_1 = 0 + qi \quad \text{[put 0 in for real part]}$$

$$\Rightarrow \quad (-2-6i) - p(4-2i) = 0 + qi \quad \text{[substitute for } z_1 \text{ and } z_2\text{]}$$

$$-2 - 6i - 4p + 2pi = 0 + qi \quad \text{[remove the brackets]}$$

$$R \quad I \quad R \quad I \quad R \quad I \quad \text{[identify real and imaginary parts]}$$

Real parts = Real parts   **Imaginary parts = Imaginary parts**

$$\Rightarrow \quad -2 - 4p = 0 \quad \text{①} \qquad\qquad -6 + 2p = q \quad \text{②}$$

Solve between the equations ① and ②:

$$-2 - 4p = 0 \quad \text{①} \qquad\qquad \text{Substitute } p = -\tfrac{1}{2} \text{ into equation ②}$$

$$\Rightarrow \qquad -4p = 2 \qquad\qquad\qquad -6 + 2p = q$$

$$\Rightarrow \qquad 4p = -2 \qquad\qquad \Rightarrow \quad -6 + 2(-\tfrac{1}{2}) = q$$

$$\Rightarrow \qquad p = \tfrac{-2}{4} = -\tfrac{1}{2} \qquad\qquad \Rightarrow \qquad -6 - 1 = q$$

$$\Rightarrow \qquad\qquad -7 = q$$

Solution: $p = -\tfrac{1}{2}$, $q = -7$

Example

Express $\dfrac{1 + i \tan \theta}{1 - i \tan \theta}$ in the form $\cos k\theta + i \sin k\theta$, $k \in \mathbf{R}$.

Solution:

$$\dfrac{1 + i \tan \theta}{1 - i \tan \theta} = \dfrac{1 + i\left(\dfrac{\sin \theta}{\cos \theta}\right)}{1 - i\left(\dfrac{\sin \theta}{\cos \theta}\right)} = \dfrac{\cos\theta + i \sin \theta}{\cos \theta - i \sin \theta} \qquad \begin{bmatrix} \text{multiply each} \\ \text{part by } \cos \theta \end{bmatrix}$$

$$\dfrac{\cos \theta + i \sin \theta}{\cos \theta - i \sin \theta} = \dfrac{\cos \theta + i \sin \theta}{\cos \theta - i \sin \theta} \cdot \dfrac{\cos \theta + i \sin \theta}{\cos \theta + i \sin \theta} \qquad \begin{bmatrix} \text{multiply top and bottom by} \\ \text{the conjugate of the botttom} \end{bmatrix}$$

$$= \dfrac{\cos^2\theta + i \cos \theta \sin \theta + i \sin \theta \cos \theta - \sin^2 \theta}{\cos^2\theta + \sin^2\theta}$$

$$= (\cos^2\theta - \sin^2 \theta) + i(2 \sin \theta \cos \theta) \qquad [\text{as } \sin^2\theta + \cos^2 \theta = 1]$$

$$= \cos 2\theta + i \sin 2\theta$$

Example

Find two complex numbers, z_1 and z_2, such that $2z\bar{z} + 3(z - \bar{z}) = 2(7 - 6i)$.
Evaluate $|z_1.z_2|$.

Solution:

Let $z = a + bi$, $\Rightarrow$ $\bar{z} = a - bi$.

Given: $2z\bar{z} + 3(z - \bar{z}) = 2(7 - 6i)$

$\Rightarrow$ $2(a + bi)(a - bi) + 3(a + bi - a + bi) = 14 - 12i$

$\Rightarrow$ $2(a^2 + b^2) \quad + \quad 3(2bi) \quad = 14 - 12i$

$\Rightarrow$ $2a^2 + 2b^2 \quad + \quad 6bi \quad = 14 - 12i$

$\Rightarrow$ $2a^2 + 2b^2 = 14$ ① and $6b = -12$ ②

From ② $6b = -12 \Rightarrow b = -2$ (put this into ①)

$2a^2 + 2b^2 = 14$ ①	$z = a + bi$
$\Rightarrow \quad a^2 + b^2 = 7$	Thus, $\quad z_1 = \sqrt{3} - 2i$
$\Rightarrow \quad a^2 + (-2)^2 = 7$	and $\quad z_2 = -\sqrt{3} - 2i$
$\Rightarrow \quad a^2 + 4 = 7$	$|z_1.z_2| = |z_1|.|z_2|$
$\Rightarrow \quad a^2 = 3$	$= \left|\sqrt{3} - 2i\right|.\left|-\sqrt{3} - 2i\right|$
$\Rightarrow \quad a = \pm\sqrt{3}$	$= \sqrt{7}.\sqrt{7} = 7$

Example

Evaluate $\sqrt{5 + 12i}$.

Solution:

$$\text{Let } a + bi = \sqrt{5 + 12i}, \ a, b \in \mathbf{R}.$$

$\Rightarrow \quad (a + bi)^2 = (\sqrt{5 + 12i})^2 \qquad$ [square both sides]

$a^2 + 2abi - b^2 = 5 + 12i \qquad$ [remove brackets]

$\quad R \quad\ \ I \quad R \quad\ R \quad I \qquad$ [identify real and imaginary parts]

Real parts = Real parts $\qquad\qquad$ Imag. parts = Imag. parts

$\qquad a^2 - b^2 = 5 \quad ① \qquad\qquad\qquad 2ab = 12 \quad ②$

Solve between equations ① and ②:

② $\quad 2ab = 12$	① $\qquad a^2 - b^2 = 5$
$ab = 6$	$a^2 - \left(\dfrac{6}{a}\right)^2 = 5 \left[\text{replace } b \text{ with } \dfrac{6}{a}\right]$
$b = \left(\dfrac{6}{a}\right)$	$a^2 - \dfrac{36}{a^2} = 5$
put this into equation ①	$a^4 - 36 = 5a^2$
	$a^4 - 5a^2 - 36 = 0$
	$(a^2 - 9)(a^2 + 4) = 0$
	$a^2 - 9 = 0 \qquad$ or $\qquad a^2 + 4 = 0$
	$a^2 = 9 \qquad$ or $\qquad a^2 = -4$
	$a = \pm 3 \qquad$ or $\qquad a = \pm 2i$

As $a, b \in \mathbf{R}$, the result $a = \pm 2i$ is rejected.

$$b = \frac{6}{a}$$

$a = 3$	$a = -3$
$b = \dfrac{6}{3}$	$b = \dfrac{6}{-3}$
$= 2$	$= -2$
$a = 3, b = 2$	$a = -3, b = -2$

Thus, $\sqrt{5 + 12i} = 3 + 2i$

or $\qquad \sqrt{5 + 12i} = -3 - 2i$.

Note: Another way of asking the same question is:

If $z^2 = 5 + 12i$, find all the values of z, or

if $(p + qi)^2 = 5 + 12i$, find the values of p and q, $p, q \in \mathbf{R}$.

Example

If $z^2 = 2 - 2\sqrt{3}i$, express z in the form $a + bi$, $a, b \in \mathbf{R}$ and $i = \sqrt{1}$.

Solution:

$$\text{Let } z = a + bi, \; a, b \in \mathbf{R}$$

$$z^2 = 2 - 2\sqrt{3}i \quad \text{[given]}$$

$$\Rightarrow \quad (a + bi)^2 = 2 - 2\sqrt{3}\,i$$

$$\Rightarrow \quad a^2 + 2abi - b^2 = 2 - 2\sqrt{3}i$$

$$\qquad \; R \quad \; I \quad \; R \quad R \qquad \; I$$

$$\Rightarrow a^2 - b^2 = 2 \;\; \text{①} \quad \text{and} \quad 2ab = -2\sqrt{3} \;\; \text{②} \quad \text{[equating real and imag. parts]}$$

We now solve between equations ① and ②:

② $\quad 2ab = -2\sqrt{3}$	① $\qquad\qquad\qquad a^2 - b^2 = 2$
$ab = -\sqrt{3}$	$a^2 - \left(\dfrac{-\sqrt{3}}{a}\right)^2 = 2$
$b = \left(-\dfrac{\sqrt{3}}{a}\right)$	$a^2 - \dfrac{3}{a^2} = 2$
put this into equation ①	$a^4 - 3 = 2a^2$
	$a^4 - 2a^2 - 3 = 0$
	$(a^2 - 3)(a^2 + 1) = 0$
	$a^2 - 3 = 0 \qquad \text{or} \qquad a^2 + 1 = 0$
	$a^2 = 3 \qquad\quad \text{or} \qquad\quad a^2 = -1$
	$a = \pm\sqrt{3} \qquad \text{or} \qquad a = \pm i$

As $a, b \in \mathbf{R}$, the result $a = \pm i$ is rejected.

$$b = \frac{-\sqrt{3}}{a} \qquad\qquad \text{Thus, } z = \sqrt{3} - i \; \text{ or } \; z = -\sqrt{3} + i.$$

$a = \sqrt{3}$	$a = -\sqrt{3}$
$b = \dfrac{-\sqrt{3}}{\sqrt{3}}$	$b = \dfrac{-\sqrt{3}}{-\sqrt{3}}$
$= -1$	$= 1$
$a = \sqrt{3}, b = -1$	$a = -\sqrt{3}, b = 1$

Complex Polynomial Equations

Conjugate Roots Theorem

> If all the coefficients of a polynomial equation are **real**, then all complex roots occur as conjugate pairs.

Example

If $-2 + 3i$ is a root of the equation $z^2 + pz + q = 0$, $p, q \in R$, write down the other root and, hence, find the value of p and the value of q.

Solution:

All the coefficients are real.

$\therefore$ if $-2 + 3i$ is a root, then $-2 - 3i$ is also a root.

$$z^2 - (\text{sum of the roots})\, z + (\text{product of the roots}) = 0$$

$$\Rightarrow \quad z^2 - (-2 + 3i - 2 - 3i)\, z + (-2 + 3i)(-2 - 3i) = 0$$

$$\Rightarrow \quad z^2 + 4z + 13 = 0$$

Compare to $z^2 + pz + q = 0$

$$\therefore \quad p = 4, q = 13$$

Example

Show that $(1 - 3i)$ is a root of the equation $2z^3 - 3z^2 + 18z + 10 = 0$ and find the other roots.

Solution:

Put in $(1 - 3i)$ for z.

$$2z^3 - 3z^2 + 18z + 10$$

$$2(1 - 3i)^3 - 3(1 - 3i)^2 + 18(1 - 3i) + 10$$

$$= 2(-26 + 18i) - 3(-8 - 6i) + 18(1 - 3i) + 10$$

$$= -52 + 36i + 24 + 18i + 18 - 54i + 10$$

$$= 0$$

$(1 - 3i)^2$

$$= (1 - 3i)(1 - 3i)$$

$$= -8 - 6i$$

$(1 - 3i)^3$

$$= (1 - 3i)^2(1 - 3i)$$

$$= (-8 - 6i)(1 - 3i)$$

$$= -26 + 18i$$

$\therefore$ $1 - 3i$ is a root and $1 + 3i$ is also a root (as coefficients are real).

We construct the quadratic factor using:

$z^2 - $ (sum of the roots)$z + $ (product of the roots)

$z^2 - (1 - 3i + 1 + 3i)z + (1 - 3i)(1 + 3i)$

giving $z^2 - 2z + 10$.

Dividing $2z^3 - 3z^2 + 18z + 10$ by $z^2 - 2z + 10$ gives $2z + 1$

$\therefore$ the third factor is $2z + 1$.

Let $2z + 1 = 0$

$\Rightarrow \quad 2z = -1$

$\Rightarrow \quad z = -\frac{1}{2}$

Thus, the roots are $1 - 3i,\ 1 + 3i,\ -\frac{1}{2}$.

Division

$$
\begin{array}{r}
2z + 1 \\
z^2 - 2z + 10 \overline{)\, 2z^3 - 3z^2 + 18z + 10} \\
\underline{2z^3 - 4z^2 + 20z} \\
z^2 - 2z + 10 \\
\underline{z^2 - 2z + 10} \\
0
\end{array}
$$

Note: We did not have to use long division to get the third factor.

$$2z^3 - 3z^2 + 18z + 10 = (z^2 - 2z + 10)(2z + k)$$

Comparing constants of both sides, we get $10k = 10$, $\therefore k = 1$.
Thus, the third factor is $2z + 1$.

Example

Solve $z^2 + (i - 2)z + 3 - i = 0$. Say why the roots do not occur in conjugate pairs.

Solution:

$$z^2 + (i - 2)z + 3 - i = 0$$

$$\Rightarrow \quad z^2 + (i - 2)z + (3 - i) = 0 \qquad \text{[write in the form } az^2 + bz + c = 0]$$

$$z = \frac{-b \pm \sqrt{b^2 - 4ac}}{2a}$$

$$a = 1$$
$$b = (i - 2)$$
$$c = (3 - i)$$

$$= \frac{-(i - 2) \pm \sqrt{(i - 2)^2 - 4.1.(3 - i)}}{2(1)}$$

$$= \frac{-i + 2 \pm \sqrt{-1 - 4i + 4 - 12 + 4i}}{2} = \frac{-i + 2 \pm \sqrt{-9}}{2} = \frac{-i + 2 \pm 3i}{2}$$

$$z_1 = \frac{-i + 2 + 3i}{2} = \frac{2 + 2i}{2} = 1 + i$$

$$z_2 = \frac{-i + 2 - 3i}{2} = \frac{2 - 4i}{2} = 1 - 2i$$

Thus, the roots are $1 + i,\ 1 - 2i$.

They are not conjugates because not all of the coefficients are real.

Example

Evaluate $\sqrt{-2i}$, giving your answers in the form $\pm(a + bi)$.

Hence, solve $z^2 - 3(1 + i)z + 5i = 0$.

Solution:

$$\sqrt{-2i} = \sqrt{0 - 2i}$$

Let $$a + bi = \sqrt{0 - 2i}$$

$\Rightarrow$ $$(a + bi)^2 = (\sqrt{0 - 2i})^2 \quad \text{[square both sides]}$$

$\Rightarrow$ $a^2 + 2abi - b^2 = 0 - 2i$

$\therefore$ $a^2 - b^2 = 0$ and $2ab = -2$

Solving simultaneously (see earlier example) gives $a = 1, b = -1$ or $a = -1, b = 1$.

$\sqrt{-2i} = a + bi = 1 - i$ or $-1 + i$

Thus, $\sqrt{-2i} = \pm(1 - i)$

$z^2 - 3(1 + i)z + 5i = 0$

$\Rightarrow$ $z^2 + (-3 - 3i)z + 5i = 0$ $\qquad\qquad$ [in the form $az^2 + bz + c = 0$]

$$z = \frac{-b \pm \sqrt{b^2 - 4ac}}{2a}$$

$$\boxed{\begin{array}{l} a = 1 \\[4pt] b = (-3 - 3i) \\[4pt] c = 5i \end{array}}$$

$$= \frac{-(-3 - 3i) \pm \sqrt{(-3 - 3i)^2 - 4.1.(5i)}}{2(1)}$$

$$= \frac{3 + 3i \pm \sqrt{9 + 18i - 9 - 20i}}{2}$$

$$= \frac{3 + 3i \pm \sqrt{-2i}}{2}$$

$$= \frac{3 + 3i \pm (1 - i)}{2} \qquad\qquad \text{[put in } (1 - i) \text{ for } \sqrt{-2i}\text{]}$$

$$z_1 = \frac{3 + 3i + (1 - i)}{2} = \frac{3 + 3i + 1 - i}{2} = \frac{4 + 2i}{2} = 2 + i$$

$$z_2 = \frac{3 + 3i - (1 - i)}{2} = \frac{3 + 3i - 1 + i}{2} = \frac{2 + 4i}{2} = 1 + 2i$$

Thus, the roots are $2 + i, 1 + 2i$.

Note: It makes no difference whether we substitute $1 - i$ or $-1 + i$ for $\sqrt{-2i}$.

Example

$f(z) = z^2 + (p + 2i)z + (1 + qi)$, $p, q \in \mathbf{R}$

(i)   If $f(-1 + i) = 0$, find the value of p and the value of q.

(ii) Find the other root.

Solution:

$$f(z) = z^2 + (p + 2i)z + (1 + qi)$$

Given $f(-1 + i) = 0$.

$\therefore$ $(-1 + i)^2 + (p + 2i)(-1 + i) + (1 - qi) = 0$ [put in $(-1 + i)$ for z]

$\Rightarrow$ $1 - 2i - 1 - p + pi - 2i - 2 + 1 + qi = 0$

$\Rightarrow$ $(-p - 1) + (p + q - 4)i = 0$

$\Rightarrow$ $-p - 1 = 0$ and $p + q - 4 = 0$

Solving these simultaneous equations gives $p = -1$, $q = 5$.

Thus, $z^2 + (p + 2i)z + (1 + qi) = 0$

becomes $z^2 + (-1 + 2i)z + (1 + 5i) = 0$ [put in $p = -1$, $q = 5$]

Let $a + bi$ be the other root.

Thus, the roots are $a + bi$ and $-1 + i$.

The sum of the roots is $-(-1 + 2i) = 1 - 2i$.

$\therefore$ $a + bi - 1 + i = 1 - 2i$

$\Rightarrow$ $a + bi = 1 - 2i + 1 - i$

$\Rightarrow$ $a + bi = 2 - 3i$

Thus, the other root is $2 - 3i$.

De Moivre's Theorem

$$[r(\cos \theta + i \sin \theta)]^n = r^n (\cos n\theta + i \sin n\theta)$$

Applications of De Moivre's Theorem

1.   Powers of complex numbers, e.g. $(1 + i)^{10}$.
2.   Proving trigonometrical identities.
3.   Finding roots (always use **general** polar form).

Before looking at De Moivre's Theorem let us first write some numbers, given in Cartesian form, in polar form.

Example

Write each of the following in polar form:

(i) $1 + i$ 　　　　(ii) $-1 - \sqrt{3}i$ 　　　　(iii) $-\frac{\sqrt{3}}{2} + \frac{1}{2}i$ 　　　　(iv) $-3i$

Solution:

(i) $1 + i$

$$r = |1 + i| = \sqrt{1^2 + 1^2} = \sqrt{2}$$

$$\tan \theta = \frac{1}{1} = 1 \implies \theta = \frac{\pi}{4}$$

$$\therefore \ 1 + i = \sqrt{2}\left(\cos\frac{\pi}{4} + i\sin\frac{\pi}{4}\right)$$

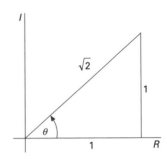

(ii) $-1 - \sqrt{3}i$

$$r = |-1 - \sqrt{3}i| = \sqrt{1^2 + (\sqrt{3})^2} = \sqrt{4} = 2$$

$$\tan \alpha = \frac{\sqrt{3}}{1} = \sqrt{3} \ \therefore \ \alpha = \frac{\pi}{3}$$

$$\implies \theta = \pi + \frac{\pi}{3} = \frac{4\pi}{3}$$

$$\therefore \ -1 - \sqrt{3}i = 2\left(\cos\frac{4\pi}{3} + i\sin\frac{4\pi}{3}\right)$$

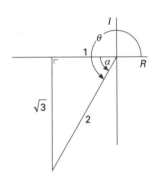

(iii) $-\frac{\sqrt{3}}{2} + \frac{1}{2}i$

$$r = \left|-\frac{\sqrt{3}}{2} + \frac{1}{2}i\right| = \sqrt{\left(\frac{\sqrt{3}}{2}\right)^2 + \left(\frac{1}{2}\right)^2} = \sqrt{\frac{3}{4} + \frac{1}{4}} = \sqrt{1} = 1$$

$$\tan \alpha = \frac{\frac{1}{2}}{\frac{\sqrt{3}}{2}} = \frac{1}{\sqrt{3}} \implies \alpha = \frac{\pi}{6}$$

$$\theta = \pi - \frac{\pi}{6} = \frac{5\pi}{6}$$

$$\therefore \ -\frac{\sqrt{3}}{2} + \frac{1}{2}i = \cos\frac{5\pi}{6} + i\sin\frac{5\pi}{6}$$

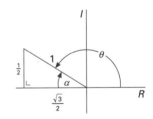

(iv) $-3i = 0 - 3i$

$$r = |0 - 3i| = \sqrt{0^2 + 3^2} = \sqrt{9} = 3$$

$$\theta = \frac{3\pi}{2}$$

$$\therefore \ -3i = 3\left(\cos\frac{3\pi}{2} + i\sin\frac{3\pi}{2}\right)$$

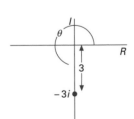

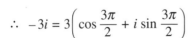

Sometimes we are given a number in polar form $r(\cos\theta + i\sin\theta)$, and asked to write it in Cartesian form, $x + yi$. Again, it is good practice to draw a diagram.

Example

Express in the form $x + yi$:

(i) $3\left(\cos\dfrac{3\pi}{4} + i\sin\dfrac{3\pi}{4}\right)$

(ii) $\cos\left(-\dfrac{5\pi}{6}\right) + i\sin\left(-\dfrac{5\pi}{6}\right)$

Solution:

(i) $\dfrac{3\pi}{4}$ is in the 2nd quadrant

$$\cos\dfrac{3\pi}{4} = -\cos\dfrac{\pi}{4} = -\dfrac{1}{\sqrt{2}}$$

$$\sin\dfrac{3\pi}{4} = \sin\dfrac{\pi}{4} = \dfrac{1}{\sqrt{2}}$$

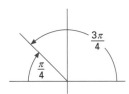

$$\therefore\ 3\left(\cos\dfrac{3\pi}{4} + i\sin\dfrac{3\pi}{4}\right) = 3\left(-\dfrac{1}{\sqrt{2}} + \dfrac{1}{\sqrt{2}}i\right) = -\dfrac{3}{\sqrt{2}} + \dfrac{3}{\sqrt{2}}i$$

(ii) $-\dfrac{5\pi}{6}$ is in the 3rd quadrant

$$\cos\left(-\dfrac{5\pi}{6}\right) = -\cos\dfrac{\pi}{6} = -\dfrac{\sqrt{3}}{2}$$

$$\sin\left(-\dfrac{5\pi}{6}\right) = -\sin\dfrac{\pi}{6} = -\dfrac{1}{2}$$

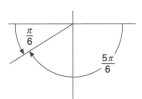

$$\therefore\ \cos\left(-\dfrac{5\pi}{6}\right) + i\sin\left(-\dfrac{5\pi}{6}\right) = -\dfrac{\sqrt{3}}{2} - \dfrac{1}{2}i$$

---

1. Powers of Complex Numbers

Write the complex number in polar form, apply De Moivre's Theorem and simplify the result.

Example

Express $(-1 + i)^{10}$ in the form $x + yi$.

Solution:

$$r = |-1 + i| = \sqrt{(-1)^2 + 1^2} = \sqrt{1 + 1} = \sqrt{2}$$

$$\tan\alpha = \dfrac{1}{1} = 1 \ \Rightarrow\ \alpha = \dfrac{\pi}{4}$$

$$\theta = \pi - \dfrac{\pi}{4} = \dfrac{3\pi}{4}$$

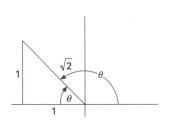

$$\therefore\quad (-1 + i) = \sqrt{2}\left(\cos\dfrac{3\pi}{4} + i\sin\dfrac{3\pi}{4}\right)$$

$$\therefore \quad (-1+i)^{10} = \sqrt{2}^{10}\left[\cos 10\left(\frac{3\pi}{4}\right) + i \sin 10\left(\frac{3\pi}{4}\right)\right]$$

$$= 32\left(\cos\frac{30\pi}{4} + i \sin\frac{30\pi}{4}\right)$$

$$= 32\left(\cos\frac{3\pi}{2} + i \sin\frac{3\pi}{2}\right)$$

$$= 32(0 - i) = 0 - 32i$$

$$\frac{30\pi}{4}$$

$$= 7\tfrac{1}{2}\pi$$

$$= 6\pi + 1\tfrac{1}{2}\pi$$

$$= \frac{3\pi}{2}$$

Example

Evaluate $\left(\dfrac{1-\sqrt{3}i}{4}\right)^{12}$.

Solution:

$$\frac{1-\sqrt{3}i}{4} = \frac{1}{4} - \frac{\sqrt{3}}{4}i$$

$$r = \left|\frac{1}{4} - \frac{\sqrt{3}}{4}i\right| = \sqrt{\left(\frac{1}{4}\right)^2 + \left(\frac{\sqrt{3}}{4}\right)^2} = \sqrt{\frac{1}{16} + \frac{3}{16}} = \sqrt{\frac{1}{4}} = \frac{1}{2}$$

$$\tan\alpha = \frac{\dfrac{\sqrt{3}}{4}}{\dfrac{1}{4}} = \frac{\sqrt{3}}{1} = \sqrt{3} \implies \alpha = \frac{\pi}{3}$$

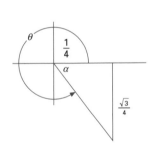

$$\theta = 2\pi - \frac{\pi}{3} = \frac{5\pi}{3}$$

$$\therefore \quad \frac{1-\sqrt{3}i}{4} = \frac{1}{2}\left[\cos\frac{5\pi}{3} + i\sin\frac{5\pi}{3}\right]$$

$$\therefore \quad \left(\frac{1-\sqrt{3}i}{4}\right)^{12} = \left[\frac{1}{2}\left(\cos\frac{5\pi}{3} + i\sin\frac{5\pi}{3}\right)\right]^{12}$$

$$= \left(\frac{1}{2}\right)^{12}\left[\cos 12\left(\frac{5\pi}{3}\right) + i\sin 12\left(\frac{5\pi}{3}\right)\right]$$

$$= \frac{1}{2^{12}}(\cos 20\pi + i\sin 20\pi)$$

$$= \frac{1}{4\,096}(\cos 0 + i\sin 0)$$

$$= \frac{1}{4\,096}(1 + 0i) = \frac{1}{4\,096}$$

2. Trigonometrical Identities

Example

Using De Moivre's Theorem, prove that:

(i) $\cos 4\theta = 8 \cos^4 \theta - 8 \cos^2 \theta + 1$

(ii) $\sin 4\theta = 4 \cos^3 \theta \sin \theta - 4 \cos \theta \sin^3 \theta.$

Express $\tan 4\theta$ in terms of $\tan \theta$.

Solution:

By De Moivre's Theorem: $\cos 4\theta + i \sin 4\theta = (\cos \theta + i \sin \theta)^4$

$$= \cos^4\theta + 4 \cos^3 \theta \, (i \sin \theta) + 6 \cos^2 \theta \, (i \sin \theta)^2 + 4 \cos \theta \, (i \sin \theta)^3 + (i \sin \theta)^4$$

$$= \cos^4 \theta + i \, 4 \cos^3 \theta \sin \theta - 6 \cos^2 \theta \sin^2 \theta - i \, 4 \cos \theta \sin^3 \theta + \sin^4 \theta$$

$$= \cos^4 \theta - 6 \cos^2 \theta \sin^2 \theta + \sin^4 \theta + i(4 \cos^3 \theta \sin \theta - 4 \cos \theta \sin^3 \theta)$$

(i) Equating real parts

$$\cos 4\theta = \cos^4\theta - 6 \cos^2 \theta \sin^2 \theta + \sin^4\theta \quad \text{①}$$

$$= \cos^4\theta - 6 \cos^2 \theta \, (1 - \cos^2 \theta) + (1 - \cos^2 \theta)^2$$

$$= \cos^4 \theta - 6 \cos^2 \theta + 6 \cos^4 \theta + 1 - 2 \cos^2 \theta + \cos^4 \theta$$

$$\therefore \cos 4\theta = 8 \cos^4 \theta - 8 \cos^2 \theta + 1$$

(ii) Equating imaginary parts:

$$\sin 4\theta = 4 \cos^3 \theta \sin \theta - 4 \cos \theta \sin^3 \theta \quad \text{②}$$

$$\tan 4\theta = \frac{\sin 4\theta}{\cos 4\theta} = \frac{4 \cos^3 \theta \sin \theta - 4 \cos \theta \sin^3 \theta}{\cos^4\theta - 6 \cos^2 \theta \sin^2\theta + \sin^4\theta} \qquad \text{[using ① and ②]}$$

$$= \frac{4 \tan \theta - 4 \tan^3 \theta}{1 - 6 \tan^2 \theta + \tan^4\theta} \qquad \left[\begin{array}{l} \text{dividing top and bottom} \\ \text{by } \cos^4 \theta \end{array}\right]$$

3. Finding Roots (Always use general polar form)

Rectangular form $\rightarrow$ Polar form $\rightarrow$ General polar form $\rightarrow$ Apply De Moivre's Theorem
$\rightarrow n = 0, \ 1, 2,$ etc.

Example

If 1, w_1 and w_2 are the roots of the equation $z^3 - 1 = 0$, show that:

(i) $w_1^2 = w_2$ (ii) $w_1^3 = 1$ (iii) $1 + w_1 + w_2 = 0$.

Solution:

$$z^3 - 1 = 0$$
$$z^3 = 1$$
$$z^3 = 1 + 0i$$
$$z = (1 + 0i)^{\frac{1}{3}}$$
$$r = |\,1 + 0i\,| = \sqrt{1^2 + 0} = \sqrt{1} = 1$$
$$\theta = 0$$

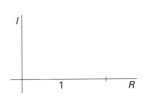

Polar form: $(1 + 0i) = \cos 0 + i \sin 0$

General polar form: $(1 + 0i) = \cos(2n\pi + 0) + i \sin(2n\pi + 0)$
$$(1 + 0i) = \cos 2n\pi + i \sin 2n\pi$$
$$\therefore \ (1 + 0i)^{\frac{1}{3}} = (\cos 2n\pi + i \sin 2n\pi)^{\frac{1}{3}}$$
$$= \cos \frac{2n\pi}{3} + i \sin \frac{2n\pi}{3} \quad \text{[applying De Moivre's Theorem]}$$

Let $n = 0$: $\cos 0 + i \sin 0 = 1 + 0i = 1$

Let $n = 1$: $\cos \dfrac{2\pi}{3} + i \sin \dfrac{2\pi}{3} = -\dfrac{1}{2} + \dfrac{\sqrt{3}}{2} i = w_1$

Let $n = 2$: $\cos \dfrac{4\pi}{3} + i \sin \dfrac{4\pi}{3} = -\dfrac{1}{2} - \dfrac{\sqrt{3}}{2} i = w_2$

(Note: Putting $n = 3, 4, 5, \ldots$ regenerates the same roots.)

(i) $w_1^2 = \left(-\dfrac{1}{2} + \dfrac{\sqrt{3}}{2} i \right)^2 = \left(-\dfrac{1}{2} \right)^2 + 2\left(-\dfrac{1}{2} \right)\left(\dfrac{\sqrt{3}}{2} i \right) + \left(\dfrac{\sqrt{3}}{2} i \right)^2$

$\qquad = \dfrac{1}{4} - \dfrac{\sqrt{3}}{2} i - \dfrac{3}{4}$

$\qquad = -\dfrac{1}{2} - \dfrac{\sqrt{3}}{2} i = w_2$

(ii) $\quad w_1^3 = w_1^2 . w_1 = \left(-\dfrac{1}{2} - \dfrac{\sqrt{3}}{2} i \right)\left(-\dfrac{1}{2} + \dfrac{\sqrt{3}}{2} i \right)$

$\qquad\qquad = \dfrac{1}{4} - \dfrac{\sqrt{3}}{4} i + \dfrac{\sqrt{3}}{4} i + \dfrac{3}{4} = 1$

(iii) $1 + w_1 + w_2 = 1 + \left(-\dfrac{1}{2} + \dfrac{\sqrt{3}}{2} i \right) + \left(-\dfrac{1}{2} - \dfrac{\sqrt{3}}{2} i \right)$

$\qquad\qquad\qquad = 1 - \dfrac{1}{2} + \dfrac{\sqrt{3}}{2} i - \dfrac{1}{2} - \dfrac{\sqrt{3}}{2} i = 0$

Chapter **3**
Matrices

Order of a Matrix

The **order** of a matrix gives the number of rows and columns it has. A matrix with m rows and n columns has order $(m \times n)$.

Here are some matrices, for example:

$$A = \begin{pmatrix} 2 \\ -3 \end{pmatrix} \qquad B = \begin{pmatrix} 1 & -1 \\ 2 & 5 \end{pmatrix} \qquad C = (-5 \quad 8)$$

order   order   order
(2×1) (2×2) (1×2)

A **square** matrix has the same number of rows and columns; its order is of the form $(m \times m)$.
The **transpose** of a matrix M, written M^T, is obtained by interchanging the rows and columns.
For example:

If $M = \begin{pmatrix} -1 & 5 \\ 3 & -2 \end{pmatrix}$, then $M^T = \begin{pmatrix} -1 & 3 \\ 5 & -2 \end{pmatrix}$.

Equal Matrices

If two matrices are equal, then their corresponding elements must be equal. For example:

If $\begin{pmatrix} a & c \\ b & d \end{pmatrix} = \begin{pmatrix} -1 & 4 \\ 3 & -5 \end{pmatrix}$ then $\begin{array}{ll} a = -1 & c = 4 \\ b = 3 & d = -5. \end{array}$

Addition, Subtraction and Multiplication by a Scalar

Matrices can only be added, or subtracted, if they are of the same order. Simply add, or subtract, corresponding elements. This gives a matrix of the same order. To multiply a matrix by a scalar (a number), multiply each element of the matrix by the number.

Note: Matrix addition is commutative and associative.

Example

If $A = \begin{pmatrix} 3 & 1 \\ -2 & 4 \end{pmatrix}$, $B = \begin{pmatrix} 4 & -1 \\ 3 & 0 \end{pmatrix}$ and $C = \begin{pmatrix} 9 & -13 \\ 2 & -1 \end{pmatrix}$

(i) find $3A - 4B^T$ (ii) find a 2×2 matrix X, such that $2A - 3X = C$.

Solution:

$$B = \begin{pmatrix} 4 & -1 \\ 3 & 0 \end{pmatrix} \Rightarrow B^T = \begin{pmatrix} 4 & 3 \\ -1 & 0 \end{pmatrix}$$

(i) $\quad 3A - 4B^T = 3\begin{pmatrix} 3 & 1 \\ -2 & 4 \end{pmatrix} - 4\begin{pmatrix} 4 & 3 \\ -1 & 0 \end{pmatrix}$

$$= \begin{pmatrix} 9 & 3 \\ -6 & 12 \end{pmatrix} - \begin{pmatrix} 16 & 12 \\ -4 & 0 \end{pmatrix}$$

$$= \begin{pmatrix} 9-16 & 3-12 \\ -6+4 & 12-0 \end{pmatrix} = \begin{pmatrix} -7 & -9 \\ -2 & 12 \end{pmatrix}$$

(ii) Let $X = \begin{pmatrix} p & r \\ q & s \end{pmatrix}$.

$$2A - 3X = C$$

$$\Rightarrow 2\begin{pmatrix} 3 & 1 \\ -2 & 4 \end{pmatrix} - 3\begin{pmatrix} p & r \\ q & s \end{pmatrix} = \begin{pmatrix} 9 & -13 \\ 2 & -1 \end{pmatrix}$$

$$\Rightarrow \begin{pmatrix} 6 & 2 \\ -4 & 8 \end{pmatrix} - \begin{pmatrix} 3p & 3r \\ 3q & 3s \end{pmatrix} = \begin{pmatrix} 9 & -13 \\ 2 & -1 \end{pmatrix}$$

$$\Rightarrow \begin{pmatrix} 6-3p & 2-3r \\ -4-3q & 8-3s \end{pmatrix} = \begin{pmatrix} 9 & -13 \\ 2 & -1 \end{pmatrix}$$

$\Rightarrow \quad 6 - 3p = 9$	$-4 - 3q = 2$	$2 - 3r = -13$	$8 - 3s = -1$
$\Rightarrow \quad -3p = 3$	$-3q = 6$	$-3r = -15$	$-3s = -9$
$\Rightarrow \quad p = -1$	$q = -2$	$r = 5$	$s = 3$

Thus, $X = \begin{pmatrix} p & r \\ q & s \end{pmatrix} = \begin{pmatrix} -1 & 5 \\ -2 & 3 \end{pmatrix}$.

Example

Simplify $\cos\theta \begin{pmatrix} \cos\theta & \sin\theta \\ -\sin\theta & \cos\theta \end{pmatrix} + \sin\theta \begin{pmatrix} \sin\theta & -\cos\theta \\ \cos\theta & \sin\theta \end{pmatrix}$.

Solution:

$$\cos\theta \begin{pmatrix} \cos\theta & \sin\theta \\ -\sin\theta & \cos\theta \end{pmatrix} + \sin\theta \begin{pmatrix} \sin\theta & -\cos\theta \\ \cos\theta & \sin\theta \end{pmatrix}$$

$$= \begin{pmatrix} \cos^2\theta & \cos\theta\sin\theta \\ -\cos\theta\sin\theta & \cos^2\theta \end{pmatrix} + \begin{pmatrix} \sin^2\theta & -\sin\theta\cos\theta \\ \sin\theta\cos\theta & \sin^2\theta \end{pmatrix}$$

$$= \begin{pmatrix} \cos^2\theta + \sin^2\theta & 0 \\ 0 & \cos^2\theta + \sin^2\theta \end{pmatrix} = \begin{pmatrix} 1 & 0 \\ 0 & 1 \end{pmatrix}$$

Example

$A = \begin{pmatrix} 4 & 3 \\ -1 & 7 \end{pmatrix}$, $B = \begin{pmatrix} 3 & 4 \\ 1 & 2 \end{pmatrix}$ and $C = \begin{pmatrix} -1 & 1 \\ 2 & -5 \end{pmatrix}$.

Solve for l and m, $lB + mC = A$, $l, m \in \mathbf{R}$.

Solution:

$$lB + mC = A$$

$$\Rightarrow \quad l\begin{pmatrix} 3 & 4 \\ 1 & 2 \end{pmatrix} + m\begin{pmatrix} -1 & 1 \\ 2 & -5 \end{pmatrix} = \begin{pmatrix} 4 & 3 \\ -1 & 7 \end{pmatrix}$$

$$\Rightarrow \quad \begin{pmatrix} 3l & 4l \\ l & 2l \end{pmatrix} + \begin{pmatrix} -m & m \\ 2m & -5m \end{pmatrix} = \begin{pmatrix} 4 & 3 \\ -1 & 7 \end{pmatrix}$$

$$\Rightarrow \quad \begin{pmatrix} 3l - m & 4l + m \\ l + 2m & 2l - 5m \end{pmatrix} = \begin{pmatrix} 4 & 3 \\ -1 & 7 \end{pmatrix}$$

$$\Rightarrow \quad 3l - m = 4 \quad \text{and} \quad 4l + m = 3$$

Solving these equations gives $l = 1$ and $m = -1$.

Note: The other two equations, $l + 2m = -1$ and $2l - 5m = 7$, are satisfied by these values.

Multiplication of Matrices

> Multiply each row of the first matrix by each column of the second matrix.

Memory aid: 'Row by Column'

Two matrices can be multiplied only if the number of columns in the first matrix equals the number of rows in the second.

If M is a $p \times q$ matrix and N is a $q \times r$ matrix, then the product MN will be a matrix of order $p \times r$.

$$\begin{array}{ccc} M.N & = & MN \\ \underbrace{(p \times q).(q \times r)} & & (p \times r) \end{array}$$

The 2×2 identity matrix $I = \begin{pmatrix} 1 & 0 \\ 0 & 1 \end{pmatrix}$.

If M is any matrix, then $IM = M = MI$.

Note: $M^2 = M.M$ and $M^3 = M.M.M$, etc.

$$I = I^2 = I^3 = I^4 = I^N$$

The **determinant** of a 2×2 matrix $A = \begin{pmatrix} a & c \\ b & d \end{pmatrix}$ is the number $ad - bc = \det (A)$.

If $\det (A) = 0$ (i.e. $ad - bc = 0$, A is called a singular matrix.

The **inverse** of the matrix A, written A^{-1}, is the matrix such that:

$$AA^{-1} = I = A^{-1}A$$

$$\text{If } A = \begin{pmatrix} a & c \\ b & d \end{pmatrix}, \text{ then } A^{-1} = \frac{1}{ad - bc}\begin{pmatrix} d & -c \\ -b & a \end{pmatrix}.$$

1. Exchange the elements in the leading diagonal.

$$\begin{pmatrix} d & c \\ b & a \end{pmatrix}$$

2. Change the signs of the elements on the other diagonal.

$$\begin{pmatrix} d & -c \\ -b & a \end{pmatrix}$$

3. Multiply by $\dfrac{1}{ad - bc}$.

$$\frac{1}{ad - bc}\begin{pmatrix} d & -c \\ -b & a \end{pmatrix}$$

Example

Let $M = \begin{pmatrix} 1 & -2 \\ 3 & 1 \end{pmatrix}$ and $A = \begin{pmatrix} 7 & 10 \\ 21 & 23 \end{pmatrix}$.

(i) Simplify $M^{-1}A$. (ii) If $MB = 2M + A$, express B in matrix form.

Solution:

(i) $M^{-1} = \dfrac{1}{(1)(1) - (3)(-2)}\begin{pmatrix} 1 & 2 \\ -3 & 1 \end{pmatrix} = \dfrac{1}{7}\begin{pmatrix} 1 & 2 \\ -3 & 1 \end{pmatrix}$

$M^{-1}A = \dfrac{1}{7}\begin{pmatrix} 1 & 2 \\ -3 & 1 \end{pmatrix}\begin{pmatrix} 7 & 10 \\ 21 & 23 \end{pmatrix} = \dfrac{1}{7}\begin{pmatrix} 49 & 56 \\ 0 & -7 \end{pmatrix} = \begin{pmatrix} 7 & 8 \\ 0 & -1 \end{pmatrix}$

(ii) Method 1:

$$MB = 2M + A$$

$$\Rightarrow \quad M^{-1}MB = 2M^{-1}M + M^{-1}A \quad \text{[premultiply each matrix by } M^{-1}]$$

$$\Rightarrow \quad B = 2I + M^{-1}A$$

$$= \begin{pmatrix} 2 & 0 \\ 0 & 2 \end{pmatrix} + \begin{pmatrix} 7 & 8 \\ 0 & -1 \end{pmatrix} = \begin{pmatrix} 9 & 8 \\ 0 & 1 \end{pmatrix}$$

Method 2:

Let $B = \begin{pmatrix} p & r \\ q & s \end{pmatrix}$

$$MB = 2M + A$$

$$\begin{pmatrix} 1 & -2 \\ 3 & 1 \end{pmatrix}\begin{pmatrix} p & r \\ q & s \end{pmatrix} = \begin{pmatrix} 2 & -4 \\ 6 & 2 \end{pmatrix} + \begin{pmatrix} 7 & 10 \\ 21 & 23 \end{pmatrix}$$

$$\begin{pmatrix} p - 2q & r - 2s \\ 3p + q & 3r + s \end{pmatrix} = \begin{pmatrix} 9 & 6 \\ 27 & 25 \end{pmatrix}$$

$$\left.\begin{array}{c} p - 2q = 9 \\ 3p + q = 27 \end{array}\right\} \Rightarrow \begin{array}{cc} p = 9 & r - 2s = 6 \\ q = 0 & 3r + s = 25 \end{array}\left.\begin{array}{c} \\ \end{array}\right\} \Rightarrow \begin{array}{c} r = 8 \\ s = 1 \end{array}$$

$$\therefore \quad B = \begin{pmatrix} 9 & 8 \\ 0 & 1 \end{pmatrix}$$

Example

If $M = \begin{pmatrix} 3 & 5 \\ 2 & 3 \end{pmatrix}$ and $N = \begin{pmatrix} -1 & 3 \\ -1 & 2 \end{pmatrix}$, verify that $(MN)^{-1} = N^{-1}M^{-1}$.

Solution:

$$MN = \begin{pmatrix} 3 & 5 \\ 2 & 3 \end{pmatrix}\begin{pmatrix} -1 & 3 \\ -1 & 2 \end{pmatrix} = \begin{pmatrix} -8 & 19 \\ -5 & 12 \end{pmatrix}$$

$$(MN)^{-1} = \frac{1}{(-8)(12) - (-5)(19)}\begin{pmatrix} 12 & -19 \\ 5 & -8 \end{pmatrix} = -1\begin{pmatrix} 12 & -19 \\ 5 & -8 \end{pmatrix} = \begin{pmatrix} -12 & 19 \\ -5 & 8 \end{pmatrix}$$

$$M^{-1} = \frac{1}{(3)(3) - (2)(5)}\begin{pmatrix} 3 & -5 \\ -2 & 3 \end{pmatrix} = -1\begin{pmatrix} 3 & -5 \\ -2 & 3 \end{pmatrix} = \begin{pmatrix} -3 & 5 \\ 2 & -3 \end{pmatrix}$$

$$N^{-1} = \frac{1}{(-1)(2) - (-1)(3)}\begin{pmatrix} 2 & -3 \\ 1 & -1 \end{pmatrix} = 1\begin{pmatrix} 2 & -3 \\ 1 & -1 \end{pmatrix} = \begin{pmatrix} 2 & -3 \\ 1 & -1 \end{pmatrix}$$

$$N^{-1}M^{-1} = \begin{pmatrix} 2 & -3 \\ 1 & -1 \end{pmatrix}\begin{pmatrix} -3 & 5 \\ 2 & -3 \end{pmatrix} = \begin{pmatrix} -12 & 19 \\ -5 & 8 \end{pmatrix}$$

Thus, $(MN)^{-1} = N^{-1}M^{-1}$.

Example

$$M = \begin{pmatrix} \lambda - 2 & 1 \\ 2 & \lambda - 3 \end{pmatrix}, \quad \lambda \in R.$$

If the determinant of M is zero (i.e. M is singular), find the values of λ.

Solution:

$$\det(M) = 0 \quad \text{[given]}$$
$$\Rightarrow \quad (\lambda - 2)(\lambda - 3) - (2)(1) = 0 \quad \text{[i.e. } ad - bc = 0\text{]}$$
$$\Rightarrow \quad \lambda^2 - 5\lambda + 6 - 2 = 0$$
$$\Rightarrow \quad \lambda^2 - 5\lambda + 4 = 0$$
$$\Rightarrow \quad (\lambda - 4)(\lambda - 1) = 0$$
$$\lambda = 4 \quad \text{or} \quad \lambda = 1$$

Example

If $A = \begin{pmatrix} \cos\theta & \sin\theta \\ \sin\theta & -\cos\theta \end{pmatrix}$, show that $A^{-1} = A$ and hence evaluate $A^2 - I$.

Solution:

$$A = \begin{pmatrix} \cos\theta & \sin\theta \\ \sin\theta & -\cos\theta \end{pmatrix}$$

$$A^{-1} = \frac{1}{-\cos^2\theta - \sin^2\theta} \begin{pmatrix} -\cos\theta & -\sin\theta \\ -\sin\theta & \cos\theta \end{pmatrix}$$

$$= \frac{1}{-(\cos^2\theta + \sin^2\theta)} \begin{pmatrix} -\cos\theta & -\sin\theta \\ -\sin\theta & \cos\theta \end{pmatrix}$$

$$= -1 \begin{pmatrix} -\cos\theta & -\sin\theta \\ -\sin\theta & \cos\theta \end{pmatrix} = \begin{pmatrix} \cos\theta & \sin\theta \\ \sin\theta & -\cos\theta \end{pmatrix} = A$$

$$\therefore \quad A = A^{-1}$$
$$\Rightarrow \quad A.A = A.A^{-1} \quad \text{[premultiply both sides by } A\text{]}$$
$$\therefore \quad A^2 = I$$

Thus, $A^2 - I = I - I = 0$.

Example

(i) Find the coefficient of xy in the quadratic form:

$$(x \quad yi)\begin{pmatrix} 1 & 1-i \\ 1+i & -1 \end{pmatrix}\begin{pmatrix} x \\ -yi \end{pmatrix}$$

(ii) Evaluate:

$$(1 \quad i)\begin{pmatrix} 3 & 2-i \\ 2+i & 3 \end{pmatrix}\begin{pmatrix} 1 \\ -i \end{pmatrix}$$

Solution:

(Remember: $i^2 = -1$, $i^3 = -i$, $i^4 = 1$)

(i)
$$(x \quad yi)\begin{pmatrix} 1 & 1-i \\ 1+i & -1 \end{pmatrix}\begin{pmatrix} x \\ -yi \end{pmatrix}$$

$$= (x \quad yi)\begin{pmatrix} x - yi - y \\ x + xi + yi \end{pmatrix}$$

$$= x^2 - xyi - xy + xyi - xy - y^2$$

$$= x^2 - 2xy - y^2$$

$\therefore$ coefficient of $xy = -2$

(ii)
$$(1 \quad i)\begin{pmatrix} 3 & 2-i \\ 2+i & 3 \end{pmatrix}\begin{pmatrix} 1 \\ -i \end{pmatrix}$$

$$= (1 \quad i)\begin{pmatrix} 3 - 2i - 1 \\ 2 + i - 3i \end{pmatrix}$$

$$= (1 \quad i)\begin{pmatrix} 2 - 2i \\ 2 - 2i \end{pmatrix}$$

$$= 2 - 2i + 2i + 2$$

$$= 4$$

Example

If $M = \begin{pmatrix} a & c \\ b & d \end{pmatrix} = \begin{pmatrix} 4 & 1 \\ 16 & -2 \end{pmatrix}$, solve $\lambda^2 - (a+d)\lambda + ad - bc = 0$.

Hence, find k_1 and k_2 such that:

$$M\begin{pmatrix} 1 \\ k_1 \end{pmatrix} = \lambda_1 \begin{pmatrix} 1 \\ k_1 \end{pmatrix} \quad \text{and} \quad M\begin{pmatrix} 1 \\ k_2 \end{pmatrix} = \lambda_2 \begin{pmatrix} 1 \\ k_2 \end{pmatrix}$$

where λ_1, λ_2 are the roots of the quadratic equation above.

Solution:

$\begin{pmatrix} a & c \\ b & d \end{pmatrix} = \begin{pmatrix} 4 & 1 \\ 16 & -2 \end{pmatrix}$, thus, $a = 4$, $b = 16$, $c = 1$ and $d = -2$.

$$\lambda^2 - (a+d)\lambda + ad - bc = 0$$
$$\Rightarrow \quad \lambda^2 - (4-2)\lambda + (4)(-2) - (16)(1) = 0$$
$$\Rightarrow \quad \lambda^2 - 2\lambda - 24 = 0$$
$$\Rightarrow \quad (\lambda - 6)(\lambda + 4) = 0$$
$$\Rightarrow \quad \lambda = 6 \quad \text{or} \quad \lambda = -4$$

Thus, $\lambda_1 = 6$ and $\lambda_2 = -4$ (order does not matter).

$$M\begin{pmatrix} 1 \\ k_1 \end{pmatrix} = \lambda_1 \begin{pmatrix} 1 \\ k_1 \end{pmatrix} \qquad\qquad M\begin{pmatrix} 1 \\ k_2 \end{pmatrix} = \lambda_2 \begin{pmatrix} 1 \\ k_2 \end{pmatrix}$$

$$\Rightarrow \quad \begin{pmatrix} 4 & 1 \\ 16 & -2 \end{pmatrix}\begin{pmatrix} 1 \\ k_1 \end{pmatrix} = 6\begin{pmatrix} 1 \\ k_1 \end{pmatrix} \qquad \Rightarrow \quad \begin{pmatrix} 4 & 1 \\ 16 & -2 \end{pmatrix}\begin{pmatrix} 1 \\ k_2 \end{pmatrix} = -4\begin{pmatrix} 1 \\ k_2 \end{pmatrix}$$

$$\Rightarrow \quad \begin{pmatrix} 4 + k_1 \\ 16 - 2k_1 \end{pmatrix} = \begin{pmatrix} 6 \\ 6k_1 \end{pmatrix} \qquad \Rightarrow \quad \begin{pmatrix} 4 + k_2 \\ 16 - 2k_2 \end{pmatrix} = \begin{pmatrix} -4 \\ -4k_2 \end{pmatrix}$$

$$\Rightarrow \quad 4 + k_1 = 6 \ \text{ or } \ 16 - 2k_1 = 6k_1 \qquad \Rightarrow \quad 4 + k_2 = -4 \ \text{ or } \ 16 - 2k_2 = -4k_2$$

$$\Rightarrow \qquad\qquad k_1 = 2 \qquad\qquad\qquad \Rightarrow \qquad\qquad k_2 = -8$$

Thus, $k_1 = 2$ and $k_2 = -8$.

Example

If $M = \begin{pmatrix} 7 & 4 \\ 4 & 1 \end{pmatrix}$, find the slope of the line represented by $M\begin{pmatrix} x \\ y \end{pmatrix} = 9\begin{pmatrix} x \\ y \end{pmatrix}$.

Solution:

$$M\begin{pmatrix} x \\ y \end{pmatrix} = 9\begin{pmatrix} x \\ y \end{pmatrix}$$

$$\Rightarrow \qquad \begin{pmatrix} 7 & 4 \\ 4 & 1 \end{pmatrix}\begin{pmatrix} x \\ y \end{pmatrix} = 9\begin{pmatrix} x \\ y \end{pmatrix}$$

$$\Rightarrow \qquad \begin{pmatrix} 7x + 4y \\ 4x + y \end{pmatrix} = \begin{pmatrix} 9x \\ 9y \end{pmatrix}$$

$\Rightarrow \quad 7x + 4y = 9x$ ①	$\Rightarrow \quad 4x + y = 9y$ ②
$\Rightarrow \quad -2x + 4y = 0$	$\Rightarrow \quad 4x - 8y = 0$
$\Rightarrow \quad x - 2y = 0$	$\Rightarrow \quad x - 2y = 0$

(we get the same line $x - 2y = 0$ in each case)

The slope of the line $x - 2y = 0$ is $\frac{1}{2}$.

Thus, the slope of the line represented by $M\begin{pmatrix} x \\ y \end{pmatrix} = 9\begin{pmatrix} x \\ y \end{pmatrix}$ is $\frac{1}{2}$.

Example

Given $\lambda M + \mu I = M^2$ and $M = \begin{pmatrix} 5 & -2 \\ 0 & 4 \end{pmatrix}$,

find the value of λ and the value of μ, λ, $\mu \in \mathbf{R}$.

Solution:

$$M^2 = M.M = \begin{pmatrix} 5 & -2 \\ 0 & 4 \end{pmatrix}\begin{pmatrix} 5 & -2 \\ 0 & 4 \end{pmatrix} = \begin{pmatrix} 25 & -18 \\ 0 & 16 \end{pmatrix}$$

$$\lambda M + \mu I = M^2$$

$$\Rightarrow \qquad \lambda\begin{pmatrix} 5 & -2 \\ 0 & 4 \end{pmatrix} + \mu\begin{pmatrix} 1 & 0 \\ 0 & 1 \end{pmatrix} = \begin{pmatrix} 25 & -18 \\ 0 & 16 \end{pmatrix}$$

$$\Rightarrow \qquad \begin{pmatrix} 5\lambda & -2\lambda \\ 0 & 4\lambda \end{pmatrix} + \begin{pmatrix} \mu & 0 \\ 0 & \mu \end{pmatrix} = \begin{pmatrix} 25 & -18 \\ 0 & 16 \end{pmatrix}$$

$\Rightarrow \qquad 5\lambda + \mu = 25$ ① $\qquad\qquad -2\lambda = -18$ ① $\qquad\qquad 4\lambda + \mu = 16$ ③

Solving these equations gives $\lambda = 9$, $\mu = -20$.

Using Matrices to Solve Simultaneous Equations

Example

Solve the simultaneous equations $\begin{array}{l} x - 2y = 3 \\ 3x + y = -1 \end{array}$ by matrix methods.

Solution:

First we must express the equations in matrix form:

$$\begin{pmatrix} 1 & -2 \\ 3 & 1 \end{pmatrix}\begin{pmatrix} x \\ y \end{pmatrix} = \begin{pmatrix} 3 \\ -1 \end{pmatrix}$$

$$\Rightarrow \quad \begin{pmatrix} 1 & -2 \\ 3 & 1 \end{pmatrix}^{-1}\begin{pmatrix} 1 & -2 \\ 3 & 1 \end{pmatrix}\begin{pmatrix} x \\ y \end{pmatrix} = \begin{pmatrix} 1 & -2 \\ 3 & 1 \end{pmatrix}^{-1}\begin{pmatrix} 3 \\ -1 \end{pmatrix} \quad \left[\begin{array}{l}\text{premultiply both sides by} \\ \text{the inverse of } \begin{pmatrix} 1 & -2 \\ 3 & 1 \end{pmatrix}\end{array}\right]$$

$$\Rightarrow \qquad \begin{pmatrix} 1 & 0 \\ 0 & 1 \end{pmatrix}\begin{pmatrix} x \\ y \end{pmatrix} = \frac{1}{(1)(1) - (-2)(3)}\begin{pmatrix} 1 & 2 \\ -3 & 1 \end{pmatrix}\begin{pmatrix} 3 \\ -1 \end{pmatrix}$$

$$\Rightarrow \qquad \begin{pmatrix} x \\ y \end{pmatrix} = \frac{1}{7}\begin{pmatrix} 1 \\ -10 \end{pmatrix}$$

$$\Rightarrow \qquad \begin{pmatrix} x \\ y \end{pmatrix} = \begin{pmatrix} \frac{1}{7} \\ -\frac{10}{7} \end{pmatrix}$$

Thus, $x = \frac{1}{7}$, $y = -\frac{10}{7}$.

Example

Express the simultaneous equations $3(x - 2) - 7y = 0$ and $\frac{x}{3} - \frac{y}{2} = -\frac{1}{6}$ in matrix form and use matrix methods to solve them.

Solution:

Write each equation in the form $ax + by = k$ (where a, b and k are whole numbers)

$$3(x - 2) - 7y = 0 \qquad\qquad \frac{x}{3} - \frac{y}{2} = -\frac{1}{6}$$

$$\Rightarrow \quad 3x - 6 - 7y = 0 \qquad\qquad \Rightarrow \quad 2x - 3y = -1 \quad \text{[multiply each part by 6]}$$

$$\Rightarrow \quad 3x - 7y = 6$$

Now the question is: solve $\begin{matrix} 3x - 7y = 6 \\ 2x - 3y = -1 \end{matrix}$ using matrix methods.

In matrix form: $\begin{pmatrix} 3 & -7 \\ 2 & -3 \end{pmatrix}\begin{pmatrix} x \\ y \end{pmatrix} = \begin{pmatrix} 6 \\ -1 \end{pmatrix}$

$$\Rightarrow \begin{pmatrix} 3 & -7 \\ 2 & -3 \end{pmatrix}^{-1}\begin{pmatrix} 3 & -7 \\ 2 & -3 \end{pmatrix}\begin{pmatrix} x \\ y \end{pmatrix} = \begin{pmatrix} 3 & -7 \\ 2 & -3 \end{pmatrix}^{-1}\begin{pmatrix} 6 \\ -1 \end{pmatrix} \qquad \left[\begin{matrix} \text{premultiply both sides by} \\ \text{the inverse of } \begin{pmatrix} 3 & -7 \\ 2 & -3 \end{pmatrix} \end{matrix}\right]$$

$$\Rightarrow \begin{pmatrix} 1 & 0 \\ 0 & 1 \end{pmatrix}\begin{pmatrix} x \\ y \end{pmatrix} = \frac{1}{(3)(-3) - (2)(-7)}\begin{pmatrix} -3 & 7 \\ -2 & 3 \end{pmatrix}\begin{pmatrix} 6 \\ -1 \end{pmatrix}$$

$$\Rightarrow \begin{pmatrix} x \\ y \end{pmatrix} = \frac{1}{5}\begin{pmatrix} -25 \\ -15 \end{pmatrix}$$

$$\Rightarrow \begin{pmatrix} x \\ y \end{pmatrix} = \begin{pmatrix} -5 \\ -3 \end{pmatrix}$$

Thus, $x = -5$, $y = -3$.

Diagonal Matrices

A **diagonal matrix** is a matrix of the form $\begin{pmatrix} a & 0 \\ 0 & b \end{pmatrix}$.

Diagonal matrices have the following property:

$$\begin{pmatrix} a & 0 \\ 0 & b \end{pmatrix}^n = \begin{pmatrix} a^n & 0 \\ 0 & b^n \end{pmatrix}$$

Example

If $M = \begin{pmatrix} 2 & 0 \\ 0 & 5 \end{pmatrix}$, find M^2, M^3 and write down an expression for M^{50}.

Solution:

$$M^2 = \begin{pmatrix} 2 & 0 \\ 0 & 5 \end{pmatrix}\begin{pmatrix} 2 & 0 \\ 0 & 5 \end{pmatrix} = \begin{pmatrix} 4 & 0 \\ 0 & 25 \end{pmatrix} = \begin{pmatrix} 2^2 & 0 \\ 0 & 5^2 \end{pmatrix}$$

$$M^3 = M^2 M = \begin{pmatrix} 4 & 0 \\ 0 & 25 \end{pmatrix}\begin{pmatrix} 2 & 0 \\ 0 & 5 \end{pmatrix} = \begin{pmatrix} 8 & 0 \\ 0 & 125 \end{pmatrix} = \begin{pmatrix} 2^3 & 0 \\ 0 & 5^3 \end{pmatrix}$$

$$M^{50} = \begin{pmatrix} 2 & 0 \\ 0 & 5 \end{pmatrix}^{50} = \begin{pmatrix} 2^{50} & 0 \\ 0 & 5^{50} \end{pmatrix}$$

Example

Evaluate $\begin{pmatrix} 2 & -3 \\ 1 & -2 \end{pmatrix}^{10}$.

Solution

$$\begin{pmatrix} 2 & -3 \\ 1 & -2 \end{pmatrix}^2 = \begin{pmatrix} 2 & -3 \\ 1 & -2 \end{pmatrix}\begin{pmatrix} 2 & -3 \\ 1 & -2 \end{pmatrix} = \begin{pmatrix} 1 & 0 \\ 0 & 1 \end{pmatrix}$$

$$\begin{pmatrix} 2 & -3 \\ 1 & -2 \end{pmatrix}^{10} = \left[\begin{pmatrix} 2 & -3 \\ 1 & -2 \end{pmatrix}^2\right]^5 = \begin{pmatrix} 1 & 0 \\ 0 & 1 \end{pmatrix}^5 = \begin{pmatrix} 1^5 & 0 \\ 0 & 1^5 \end{pmatrix} = \begin{pmatrix} 1 & 0 \\ 0 & 1 \end{pmatrix}$$

Example

If $N = \begin{pmatrix} 4 & 3 \\ 3 & -4 \end{pmatrix}$ and $P = \begin{pmatrix} 3 & -1 \\ 1 & 3 \end{pmatrix}$:

(i) Find P^{-1}.

(ii) Show that $P^{-1}NP$ is a diagonal matrix.

(iii) Show that $(P^{-1}NP)^6 = P^{-1}N^6P$.

(iv) Hence, find N^6.

Solution:

(i) $P^{-1} = \dfrac{1}{(3)(3) - (1)(-1)} \begin{pmatrix} 3 & 1 \\ -1 & 3 \end{pmatrix} = \dfrac{1}{10} \begin{pmatrix} 3 & 1 \\ -1 & 3 \end{pmatrix}$

(ii) $P^{-1}NP = \dfrac{1}{10} \begin{pmatrix} 3 & 1 \\ -1 & 3 \end{pmatrix} \begin{pmatrix} 4 & 3 \\ 3 & -4 \end{pmatrix} \begin{pmatrix} 3 & -1 \\ 1 & 3 \end{pmatrix}$

$= \dfrac{1}{10} \begin{pmatrix} 3 & 1 \\ -1 & 3 \end{pmatrix} \begin{pmatrix} 15 & 5 \\ 5 & -15 \end{pmatrix} = \dfrac{1}{10} \begin{pmatrix} 50 & 0 \\ 0 & -50 \end{pmatrix}$

$\Rightarrow P^{-1}NP = \begin{pmatrix} 5 & 0 \\ 0 & -5 \end{pmatrix}$ [a diagonal matrix]

(iii) $(P^{-1}NP)^6 = P^{-1}NP.P^{-1}NP.P^{-1}NP.P^{-1}NP.P^{-1}NP.P^{-1}NP$

$= P^{-1}NININININININP$ [as $PP^{-1} = I$]

$= P^{-1}N^6P$ [as $NI = N$]

(iv) $P^{-1}N^6P = (P^{-1}NP)^6$

$\Rightarrow P^{-1}N^6P = \begin{pmatrix} 5 & 0 \\ 0 & -5 \end{pmatrix}^6$

$\Rightarrow P^{-1}N^6P = \begin{pmatrix} 5^6 & 0 \\ 0 & -5^6 \end{pmatrix} = \begin{pmatrix} 5^6 & 0 \\ 0 & 5^6 \end{pmatrix}$ $[-5^6 = 5^6]$

$\Rightarrow P^{-1}N^6P = 5^6 \begin{pmatrix} 1 & 0 \\ 0 & 1 \end{pmatrix} = 5^6 I$

We now premultiply both sides by P and postmultiply both sides by P^{-1}.

$\Rightarrow PP^{-1}N^6PP^{-1} = P5^6IP^{-1} = 5^6PIP^{-1}$

$\Rightarrow IN^6I = 5^6PP^{-1}$

$\Rightarrow N^6 = 5^6 I = 5^6 \begin{pmatrix} 1 & 0 \\ 0 & 1 \end{pmatrix} = \begin{pmatrix} 5^6 & 0 \\ 0 & 5^6 \end{pmatrix}$

Example

If $A = \begin{pmatrix} 2 & 0 \\ 0 & 3 \end{pmatrix}$, prove by induction that $A^n = \begin{pmatrix} 2^n & 0 \\ 0 & 3^n \end{pmatrix}$, for $n \geq 2$, $n \in N$.

Solution:

$$P(n): \begin{pmatrix} 2 & 0 \\ 0 & 3 \end{pmatrix}^n = \begin{pmatrix} 2^n & 0 \\ 0 & 3^n \end{pmatrix}, \text{ for } n \geq 2, n \in N$$

Step 1:

$$P(2): \begin{pmatrix} 2 & 0 \\ 0 & 3 \end{pmatrix}^2 = \begin{pmatrix} 2 & 0 \\ 0 & 3 \end{pmatrix}\begin{pmatrix} 2 & 0 \\ 0 & 3 \end{pmatrix} = \begin{pmatrix} 4 & 0 \\ 0 & 9 \end{pmatrix} = \begin{pmatrix} 2^2 & 0 \\ 0 & 3^3 \end{pmatrix}, \text{ which is true,}$$

$\therefore$ $P(2)$ is true.

Step 2: Assume $P(k)$ is true, i.e. $\begin{pmatrix} 2 & 0 \\ 0 & 3 \end{pmatrix}^k = \begin{pmatrix} 2^k & 0 \\ 0 & 3^k \end{pmatrix}$

Test $P(k + 1)$: $\begin{pmatrix} 2 & 0 \\ 0 & 3 \end{pmatrix}^{k+1} = \begin{pmatrix} 2^{k+1} & 0 \\ 0 & 3^{k+1} \end{pmatrix}$

L.H.S.: $\begin{pmatrix} 2 & 0 \\ 0 & 3 \end{pmatrix}^{k+1} = \begin{pmatrix} 2 & 0 \\ 0 & 3 \end{pmatrix}^k\begin{pmatrix} 2 & 0 \\ 0 & 3 \end{pmatrix}$

$$= \begin{pmatrix} 2^k & 0 \\ 0 & 3^k \end{pmatrix}\begin{pmatrix} 2 & 0 \\ 0 & 3 \end{pmatrix} \quad \text{[using our assumption]}$$

$$= \begin{pmatrix} 2^{k+1} & 0 \\ 0 & 3^{k+1} \end{pmatrix} = \text{R.H.S.}$$

$\therefore$ $P(k + 1)$ is true, assuming $P(k)$ is true.

Hence, by the principle of mathematical induction $P(n)$ is true.

Chapter **4**
Sequences and Series

Basics

A sequence is a list of numbers, usually derived from a rule, e.g. 2, 5, 8, 11, 14, ...
A series is a sequence 'added up', e.g. $2 + 5 + 8 + 11 + 14 + \cdots$
u_n is the nth term. In the above series, $u_n = 3n - 1$.

S_n is the sum of the first n terms and is written $\sum\limits_{r=1}^{n} u_r$.

The sum to infinity $S_\infty = \lim\limits_{n \to \infty} S_n$ and can be written $\sum\limits_{n=1}^{\infty} u_n$.

Arithmetic Sequences and Series

$$a, a + d, a + 2d, a + 3d, ...$$

$$a = \text{first term} = u_1, \qquad d = \text{common difference}$$

1. $u_n = a + (n - 1)d$

2. $u_n - u_{n-1} = \text{constant} = d$

3. $S_n = \frac{n}{2}[2a + (n - 1)d]$

4. If three terms, u_n, u_{n+1}, u_{n+2}, are in arithmetic sequence, then:

$$u_{n+2} - u_{n+1} = u_{n+1} - u_n$$

Geometric Sequences and Series

$$a, ar, ar^2, ar^3, \ldots$$

$$a = \text{first term} = u_1 \qquad r = \text{common ratio}$$

1. $u_n = ar^{n-1}$

2. $\dfrac{u_n}{u_{n-1}} = \text{constant} = r$

3. (a) $S_n = \dfrac{a(r^n - 1)}{r - 1}$ $(r > 1 \text{ or } r < -1)$

    (b) $S_n = \dfrac{a(1 - r^n)}{1 - r}$ $(-1 < r < 1)$

4. $S_\infty = \dfrac{a}{1-r}$ $(-1 < r < 1)$

If $|r| \geq 1$, S_∞ does not exist.

5. If three terms, u_n, u_{n+1}, u_{n+2}, are in geometric sequence, then:

$$\frac{u_{n+2}}{u_{n+1}} = \frac{u_{n+1}}{u_n}$$

For all series: $u_n = S_n - S_{n-1}$

Example

The first three terms of an arithmetic sequence are 6, –9, and x.
The first three terms of a geometric sequence are –9, x and y.
Find the value of x and the value of y.

Solution:

Arithmetic sequence

$$6, -9, x$$

$$u_3 - u_2 = u_2 - u_1 \quad ①$$

$$\Rightarrow \quad x - (-9) = -9 - 6$$

$$x + 9 = -15$$

$$x = -24$$

put $x = -24$ into ②

Geometric sequence

$$-9, x, y$$

$$\frac{u_3}{u_2} = \frac{u_2}{u_1} \quad ②$$

$$\Rightarrow \quad \frac{y}{x} = \frac{x}{-9}$$

$$-9y = x^2$$

$$-9y = (-24)^2$$

$$-9y = 576$$

$$y = -64$$

Example

The sum to infinity of a geometric series is 36 and the second term of the series is 8.
Find two possible series.

Solution:

Let the series be $a + ar + ar^2 + \cdots$

Given the sum to infinity is 36:

$$\therefore \quad \frac{a}{1-r} = 36$$

$$\Rightarrow \quad a = 36(1-r) \quad ①$$

Given the second term is 8:

$$\therefore \quad ar = 8 \quad ②$$

We now solve between ① and ②

$$ar = 8 \dots ②$$

$$36(1 - r)\,r = 8 \qquad \text{[replace } a \text{ with } 36(1 - r)\text{]}$$

$\Rightarrow \qquad (36 - 36r)r = 8$

$\Rightarrow \qquad 36r - 36r^2 = 8$

$\Rightarrow \qquad -36r^2 + 36r - 8 = 0 \qquad$ [everything to the left]

$\Rightarrow \qquad 36r^2 - 36r + 8 = 0 \qquad$ [change all signs]

$\Rightarrow \qquad 9r^2 - 9r + 2 = 0 \qquad$ [divide across by 4]

$\Rightarrow \qquad (3r - 2)(3r - 1) = 0 \qquad$ [factorise]

$\Rightarrow \qquad 3r - 2 = 0 \quad \text{or} \quad 3r - 1 = 0 \qquad$ [let each factor $= 0$]

$\Rightarrow \qquad 3r = 2 \quad \text{or} \quad 3r = 1$

$\Rightarrow \qquad r = \frac{2}{3} \ \text{or} \ r = \frac{1}{3}$

$$ar = 8 \dots ②$$

$$\Rightarrow r = \frac{8}{r}$$

$r = \frac{2}{3}$	$r = \frac{1}{3}$
$a = \dfrac{8}{\frac{2}{3}}$	$a = \dfrac{8}{\frac{1}{3}}$
$a = 12$	$a = 24$

∴ We have two series which obey the two given conditions:

(i) $a = 12$, $r = \frac{2}{3}$, the series is $12 + 8 + 5\frac{1}{3} + \cdots$

(ii) $a = 24$, $r = \frac{1}{3}$, the series is $24 + 8 + 2\frac{2}{3} + \cdots$

Example

Prove that:
(i) the sequence $u_n = 2 - 4n$ is arithmetic.
(ii) the sequence $u_n = 5 . 2^n$ is geometric.
(iii) for any series $u_n = S_n - S_{n-1}$.

Solution:

(i) $u_n = 2 - 4n$

$u_{n-1} = 2 - 4(n - 1) = 6 - 4n$

$u_n - u_{n-1}$

$= (2 - 4n) - (6 - 4n)$

$= 2 - 4n - 6 + 4n$

$= -4$ [a constant]

Thus, the sequence is arithmetic.

(ii) $u_n = 5 . 2^n$

$u_{n-1} = 5 . 2^{n-1}$

$\dfrac{u_n}{u_{n-1}} = \dfrac{5 . 2^n}{5 . 2^{n-1}}$

$= \dfrac{2^n}{2^{n-1}}$

$= 2^{n-n+1} = 2$ [a constant]

Thus, the sequence is geometric.

(iii) $S_n = u_1 + u_2 + u_3 + \cdots + u_{n-2} + u_{n-1} + u_n$

$S_{n-1} = u_1 + u_2 + u_3 + \cdots + u_{n-2} + u_{n-1}$

$\overline{S_n - S_{n-1} = u_n}$ [subtracting]

Thus, $u_n = S_n - S_{n-1}$.

Example

In an arithmetic sequence, the sum of three consecutive terms is 24 and the product of these terms is 312. Find two possible sets of values for these terms.

Solution:

Let the three terms be $a - d, a, a + d$.

(Note: using $a, a + d$ and $a + 2d$ leads to more complicated algebra.)

Given: $a - d + a + a + d = 24$ ①

$\Rightarrow \qquad 3a = 24$

$\Rightarrow \qquad a = 8$

(put $a = 8$ into ②)

Given: $(a - d)(a)(a + d) = 312$ ②

$(8 - d)(8)(8 + d) = 312$

$8(8 - d)(8 + d) = 312$

$8(64 - d^2) = 312$

$64 - d^2 = 39$

$d^2 = 25$

$d = \pm 5$

The three terms are $a - d, a, a + d$.

If $d = 5$, terms are $8 - 5, 8, 8 + 5$, i.e. 3, 8, 13.

If $d = -5$, terms are $8 + 5, 8, 8 - 5$, i.e. 13, 8, 3.

Example

In an arithmetic sequence, $u_5 = 1$ and $S_4 + S_{10} = 29$. Find a and d.
If $S_n = -120$, find n.

Solution:

In an arithmetic sequence, $u_n = a + (n-1)d$ and $S_n = \frac{n}{2}[2a + (n-1)d]$.

Given: $\qquad\qquad\qquad\qquad\qquad u_5 = 1$

$\Rightarrow \qquad\qquad\qquad\qquad a + 4d = 1 \qquad$ ①

Given: $\qquad\qquad\qquad\qquad S_4 + S_{10} = 29$

$\Rightarrow \qquad \frac{4}{2}[2a + 3d] + \frac{10}{2}[2a + 9d] = 29$

$\Rightarrow \qquad\qquad 4a + 6d + 10a + 45d = 29$

$\Rightarrow \qquad\qquad\qquad 14a + 51d = 29 \qquad$ ②

Solving between ① and ② gives $a = 13$ and $d = -3$.

Given: $\qquad\qquad S_n = -120$

$\Rightarrow \qquad \frac{n}{2}[2a + (n-1)d] = -120 \qquad$ [we know a and b; find n]

$\Rightarrow \quad \frac{n}{2}[26 + (n-1)(-3)] = -120 \qquad$ [put in $a = 13$, $d = -3$]

$\Rightarrow \qquad \frac{n}{2}[26 - 3n + 3] = -120$

$\Rightarrow \qquad\quad \frac{n}{2}(29 - 3n) = -120$

$\Rightarrow \qquad\quad 29n - 3n^2 = -240$

$\Rightarrow \qquad 3n^2 - 29n - 240 = 0$

$\Rightarrow \qquad (3n + 16)(n - 15) = 0$

$\Rightarrow \qquad\qquad n = -\dfrac{16}{3} \quad$ or $\quad n = 15$

Reject $\qquad\qquad\qquad n = -\dfrac{16}{3}$.

Thus, $\qquad\qquad\qquad n = 15$.

Note: If n is a fraction, or a negative number, ignore it, because for sequences and series n must be a positive whole number.

Example

Three consecutive terms of an arithmetic series are x, y, x^2, where $x < 0$.

Three consecutive terms of a geometric series are x, x^2, y.

Find the value of x and the value of y.

Solution:

Arithmetic series:

$$u_{n+2} - u_{n+1} = u_{n+1} - u_n$$

$\Rightarrow$ $\qquad x^2 - y = y - x$

$\Rightarrow$ $\qquad x^2 + x = 2y \quad \text{①}$

Geometric series:

$$\frac{u_{n+2}}{u_{u+1}} = \frac{u_{n+1}}{u_n}$$

$$\frac{y}{x^2} = \frac{x^2}{x}$$

$$y = \frac{x^4}{x}$$

$$y = x^3 \quad \text{②}$$

We now solve between equations ① and ②

$$x^2 + x = 2y \quad \text{①}$$

$\downarrow$

$$x^2 + x = 2x^3 \quad [y = x^3]$$

$$2x^3 - x^2 - x = 0$$

$$x(2x^2 - x - 1) = 0$$

$$x(2x + 1)(x - 1) = 0$$

$\Rightarrow \quad x = 0, \ x = -\tfrac{1}{2} \quad \text{or} \quad x = 1$

Thus, $x = -\tfrac{1}{2}$ [as given $x < 0$]

$$y = x^3 \quad \text{②}$$

$$y = (-\tfrac{1}{2})^3 = -\tfrac{1}{8}$$

$\therefore \qquad x = -\tfrac{1}{2}, y = -\tfrac{1}{8}$

Example

The sum of the first n terms of the series $u_1 + u_2 + u_3 + \cdots + u_n$ is given by $n(n-1)$.

(i)   Express u_n in terms of n.

(ii) If u_n, u_{n+1}, u_{n+2} and u_{n+3} are four terms of the series, calculate the value of

$$(u_{n+3}^2 - u_{n+1}^2) - (u_{n+2}^2 - u_n^2).$$

Solution:

(i) $u_n = S_n - S_{n-1}$

$\qquad = n(n-1) - (n-1)(n-2) \qquad$ [Given: $S_n = n(n-1)$]

$\qquad = n^2 - n - n^2 + 3n - 2$

$\qquad = 2n - 2$

105

(ii) $u_n = 2n - 2$

$u_{n+1} = 2(n + 1) - 2 = 2n + 2 - 2 = 2n$

$u_{n+2} = 2(n + 2) - 2 = 2n + 4 - 2 = 2n + 2$

$u_{n+3} = 2(n + 3) - 2 = 2n + 6 - 2 = 2n + 4$

$(u_{n+3}^2 - u_{n+1}^2) - (u_{n+2}^2 - u_n^2)$

$= u_{n+3}^2 - u_{n+1}^2 - u_{n+2}^2 + u_n^2$

$= (2n + 4)^2 - (2n)^2 - (2n + 2)^2 + (2n - 2)^2$

$= 4n^2 + 16n + 16 - 4n^2 - 4n^2 - 8n - 4 + 4n^2 - 8n + 4$

$= 16$

Example

In a geometric series, $S_2 = 3$ and $S_4 = 15$. Find two expressions for u_n.

Solution:

Given: $S_2 = 3$

$\Rightarrow$ $a + ar = 3$ ①

Given: $S_4 = 15$

$\Rightarrow$ $a + ar + ar^2 + ar^3 = 15$ ②

Now subtract ① from ②

$a + ar + ar^2 + ar^3 = 15$ ②

$a + ar \qquad\qquad = 3$ ①

$ar^2 + ar^3 = 12$ ③

Now divide ③ by ①

$$\frac{①}{②} = \frac{ar^2 + ar^3}{a + ar} = \frac{12}{3}$$

$$\Rightarrow \qquad \frac{ar^2(1 + r)}{a(1 + r)} = 4$$

$$r^2 = 4$$

$$r = \pm 2$$

$a + ar = 3$

$r = 2: \quad a + 2a = 3$

$3a = 3$

$a = 1$

$u_n = ar^{n-1} = 1 . 2^{n-1} = 2^{n-1}$

$a + ar = 3$

$r = -2: \quad a - 2a = 3$

$-a = 3$

$a = -3$

$u_n = ar^{n-1} = -3(-2)^{n-1}$

Example

Given that $\dfrac{1}{b+c}, \dfrac{1}{c+a}, \dfrac{1}{a+b}$ are three consecutive terms of an arithmetic sequence,

show that a^2, b^2 and c^2 are also three consecutive terms of an arithmetic sequence.

Solution:

$\dfrac{1}{b+c}, \dfrac{1}{c+a}, \dfrac{1}{a+b}$ are in arithmetic sequence.

$$u_{n+2} - u_{n+1} = u_{n+1} - u_n$$

Thus, $\dfrac{1}{a+b} - \dfrac{1}{c+a} = \dfrac{1}{c+a} - \dfrac{1}{b+c}$

$$\dfrac{(c+a)(b+c)-(a+b)(b+c)=(a+b)(b+c)-(a+b)(c+a)}{(a+b)(c+a)(b+c)}$$

$$\left[\begin{array}{l}\text{common denominator}\\(a+b)(c+a)(b+c)\end{array}\right]$$

$$cb + c^2 + ab + ac - ab - ac - b^2 - bc = ab + ac + b^2 + bc - ac - a^2 - bc - ab$$

$$c^2 - b^2 = b^2 - a^2$$

Thus, a^2, b^2, c^2 are in arithmetic sequence as $u_{n+2} - u_{n+1} = u_{n+1} - u_n$.

Note: An alternating series is one made from two different series. Consider the next example.

Example

One sequence of alternating terms of the series $1 + 2 + 3 + 4 + 5 + 8 + \cdots$
forms an arithmetic sequence, while the other forms a geometric sequence.
Find S_{20} of each series and hence S_{40} of the series.

Solution:

Arithmetic series	*Geometric series*

Arithmetic series

$1 + 3 + 5 + \cdots$

$a = 1, \quad d = 2$

$S_n = \frac{n}{2}[2a + (n-1)d]$

$S_{20} = \frac{20}{2}[2(1) + (19)(2)]$

$\qquad = 10[2 + 38]$

$\qquad = 10(40)$

$\qquad = 400$

Geometric series

$2 + 4 + 8 + \cdots$

$a = 2, \quad r = 2$

$S_n = \dfrac{a(r^n - 1)}{r - 1}$

$S_{20} = \dfrac{2(2^{20} - 1)}{2 - 1}$

$\qquad = 2(1\,048\,576 - 1)$

$\qquad = 2\,097\,150$

Thus, $S_{40} = (S_{20}$ of the arithmetic series$) + (S_{20}$ of the geometric series$)$

$\qquad = 400 + 2\,097\,150 = 2\,097\,550.$

Example

Prove that for $0 < \theta < \frac{\pi}{2}$ the geometric series

$\sin 2\theta - \sin 2\theta \cos 2\theta + \sin 2\theta \cos^2 2\theta - \sin 2\theta \cos^3 2\theta + \cdots$

has a sum to infinity, and that this sum to infinity is $\tan \theta$.

Solution:

$$\sin 2\theta - \sin 2\theta \cos 2\theta + \sin 2\theta \cos^2 2\theta - \sin 2\theta \cos^3 2\theta + \cdots$$

$$r = \frac{u_2}{u_1}$$

$$= \frac{-\sin 2\theta \cos 2\theta}{\sin 2\theta}$$

$$= -\cos 2\theta$$

If $0 < \theta < \frac{\pi}{2}$

$$|-\cos 2\theta| < 1$$

i.e. $\qquad |r| < 1$

Thus, the sum to infinity exists.

$$S_\infty = \frac{a}{1 - r}$$

$$= \frac{\sin 2\theta}{1 + \cos 2\theta}$$

$$= \frac{2 \sin \theta \cos \theta}{1 + \cos^2 \theta - \sin^2 \theta}$$

$$= \frac{2 \sin \theta \cos \theta}{1 - \sin^2 \theta + \cos^2 \theta}$$

$$= \frac{2 \sin \theta \cos \theta}{2 \cos^2 \theta}$$

$$= \frac{\sin \theta}{\cos \theta} = \tan \theta$$

Example

$$\sum_{n=0}^{\infty} \left(\frac{3}{2x + 1} \right)^n = 1 + \frac{3}{2x + 1} + \left(\frac{3}{2x + 1} \right)^2 + \left(\frac{3}{2x + 1} \right)^3 + \cdots$$

is a geometric series.

(i)   Find, in terms of x, the sum to infinity of the series.

(ii)   If the sum to infinity of the series is $\frac{2}{3}$, find the value of x.

(iii) Determine the set of values of x for which the sum to infinity exists.

Solution:

This is a geometric series with $a = 1$ and $r = \dfrac{3}{2x + 1}$.

(i) $S_\infty = \dfrac{a}{1 - r}$

$= \dfrac{1}{1 - \dfrac{3}{2x + 1}}$

$= \dfrac{2x + 1}{2x + 1 - 3}$

$= \dfrac{2x + 1}{2x - 2}$

(ii) Given: $S_\infty = \dfrac{2}{3}$

$\Rightarrow \quad \dfrac{2x + 1}{2x - 2} = \dfrac{2}{3}$

$\Rightarrow \quad 6x + 3 = 4x - 4$

$\Rightarrow \quad 2x = -7$

$\Rightarrow \quad x = -\dfrac{7}{2}$

(iii) S_∞ exists if $|r| < 1$

i.e. $\left| \dfrac{3}{2x + 1} \right| < 1$

$\dfrac{3^2}{(2x + 1)^2} < 1$ [square both sides]

$9 < (2x + 1)^2$ [multiply both sides by $(2x + 1)^2$]

$9 < 4x^2 + 4x + 1$

$4x^2 + 4x + 1 > 9$ [swop sides]

$4x^2 + 4x - 8 > 0$

$x^2 + x - 2 > 0$

Let $x^2 + x - 2 = 0$ [replace > with =]

$(x + 2)(x - 1) = 0$

$x = -2$ or $x = 1$

Test 0 (inside the roots) in the original inequality.

$\left| \dfrac{3}{2(0) + 1} \right| < 1$

$3 < 1$ false, $\therefore$ solution does not lie between the roots.

$\therefore$ S_∞ exists for $x < -2 \cup x > 1$.

Example

Find the greatest value of x in the interval $0 < x < \frac{\pi}{2}$ for which

$$(1 + \sin^2 x + \sin^4 x + \sin^6 x + \cdots + \sin^{2(n-1)}x + \cdots) \le 4$$

Solution:

$$1 + \sin^2 x + \sin^4 x + \sin^6 x + \cdots$$

This is an infinite geometric series with $a = 1$ and $r = \sin^2 x$.

In the given interval, $|\sin^2 x| < 1$, thus a sum to infinity exists.

$$S_\infty = \frac{a}{1 - r} = \frac{1}{1 - \sin^2 x} = \frac{1}{\cos^2 x}$$

Given: $S_\infty \le 4$, thus the max. value $= 4$

$\therefore \quad \dfrac{1}{\cos^2 x} = 4$

$\Rightarrow \quad 4\cos^2 x = 1$

$\Rightarrow \quad \cos^2 x = \dfrac{1}{4}$

$\Rightarrow \quad \cos x = \pm\dfrac{1}{2}$

$\cos x = \dfrac{1}{2}$

$\Rightarrow \quad x = \dfrac{\pi}{3}$

$\cos x = -\dfrac{1}{2}$

$\Rightarrow \quad x = -\dfrac{2\pi}{3}$ [ignore]

$\left[\text{as outside } 0 < x < \dfrac{\pi}{2}\right]$

Thus, the max. value is $x = \dfrac{\pi}{3}$.

Example

The fifth, seventh and twelfth terms of an arithmetic sequence are consecutive terms for a geometric sequence. Find the common ratio r of the geometric sequence.

Solution:

Arithmetic sequence: $\qquad u_5 = a + 4d \qquad\qquad u_7 = a + 6d \qquad\qquad u_{12} = a + 11d$

$\qquad\qquad\qquad\qquad\qquad\quad \downarrow \qquad\qquad\qquad\qquad\quad \downarrow \qquad\qquad\qquad\qquad\quad \downarrow$

Geometric sequence: $\qquad u_1 \qquad\qquad\qquad\qquad\quad u_2 \qquad\qquad\qquad\qquad\quad u_3$

$\qquad$ Common ratio $= r = \dfrac{u_3}{u_2} = \dfrac{u_2}{u_1}$

$\Rightarrow \qquad\qquad \dfrac{a + 11d}{a + 6d} = \dfrac{a + 6d}{a + 4d}$

$\Rightarrow \qquad (a + 11d)(a + 4d) = (a + 6d)(a + 6d)$

$\Rightarrow \qquad a^2 + 15ad + 44d^2 = a^2 + 12ad + 36d^2$

$\Rightarrow \qquad\quad 15ad + 44d^2 = 12ad + 36d^2$

$\Rightarrow \qquad\quad 15a + 44d = 12a + 36d \qquad [d \neq 0]$

$\Rightarrow \qquad\qquad\qquad 3a = -8d$

$\Rightarrow \qquad\qquad\qquad a = -\tfrac{8}{3}d$

$\qquad r = \dfrac{a + 11d}{a + 6d} = \dfrac{-\tfrac{8}{3}d + 11d}{-\tfrac{8}{3}d + 6d} = \dfrac{-8d + 33d}{-8d + 18d} = \dfrac{25d}{10d} = \dfrac{25}{10} = \dfrac{5}{2}$

Example

(i) The sum to infinity of the geometric series $a + a^2 + a^3 + \cdots$ is $5a$ $(a \neq 0)$. Find the common ratio r.

(ii) If a, b and c are three consecutive terms of a geometric sequence, show that $\log a$, $\log b$ and $\log c$ are three consecutive terms of an arithmetic sequence $(a, b$ and $c > 0)$.

Solution:

(i) $a + a^2 + a^3 + \cdots$

This is a geometric series with $a = a$ and $r = a$.

Given: $\qquad S_\infty = 5a$

$\Rightarrow \qquad \dfrac{a}{1 - r} = 5a$

$\Rightarrow \qquad \dfrac{a}{1 - a} = 5a$

$\Rightarrow \qquad a = 5a - 5a^2$

$\Rightarrow \qquad 5a^2 - 4a = 0$

$\Rightarrow \qquad a(5a - 4) = 0$

$\Rightarrow \quad a = 0 \quad$ or $\quad a = \dfrac{4}{5}$

but $a \neq 0$, $\therefore\ a = \dfrac{4}{5}$

Thus, $r = \dfrac{4}{5}$.

(ii) a, b and c are in a geometric sequence.

Thus, $\qquad \dfrac{c}{b} = \dfrac{b}{a}$

$\Rightarrow \qquad \log \dfrac{c}{b} = \log \dfrac{b}{a} \qquad$ [take logs]

$\Rightarrow \qquad \log c - \log b = \log b - \log a$

Thus, $\log a$, $\log b$ and $\log c$ are three consecutive terms in an arithmetic sequence.

[i.e. $u_{n+2} - u_{n+1} = u_{n+1} - u_n$]

Example

Ten markers are placed on the ground in a straight line, at intervals of 6 metres. During a training session, a player, 6 m from the first marker, has to run to the first marker and back to the start, then run to the second marker and back to the start, and so on in succession until she runs to the tenth marker and back.

Calculate the total distance run by the player.

Solution:

Diagram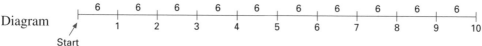

The player runs to the first marker and back. This is a distance of 12 m.

To the second marker and back the distance is 24 m and so on.

Thus, the total distance run is given by:

$12 + 24 + 36 + 48 + 60 + 72 + 84 + 96 + 108 + 120 = 660$ m

Alternatively, this is obviously an arithmetic series where $a = 12$ and $d = 12$, $n = 10$ and we require S_{10}.

$$S_n = \tfrac{n}{2}[2a + (n - 1)d]$$

$$S_{10} = \tfrac{10}{2}[2(12) + (10 - 1)12] \quad [a = 12, d = 12, n = 10]$$

$$= 5[24 + 108]$$

$$= 5[132]$$

$$= 660 \text{ m [same answer as above]}.$$

Example

If an object is dropped, the distance s metres through which it falls freely in t seconds is given by $s = 16t^2$.

(i) Show that the distances through which it falls during each second form an arithmetic sequence.

(ii) How far will the object fall in each of the 1st second, 2nd second and 3rd second?

(iii) How far will it travel in the first 20 seconds?

113

Solution:

(i) We are given S_n in disguise.

$S_n = 16n^2$ (where S_n is the total distance travelled in the number of seconds so far)

To prove that the distances travelled each second form an arithmetic sequence, we must prove that $u_n - u_{n-1} = $ constant.

$u_n = S_n - S_{n-1}$

$= (16n^2) - (16n^2 - 32n + 16)$

$= 16n^2 - 16n^2 + 32n - 16$

$= 32n - 16$

$S_{n-1} = 16(n-1)^2$

$= 16(n^2 - 2n + 1)$

$= 16n^2 - 32n + 16$

$u_n - u_{n-1}$

$= (32n - 16) - (32n - 48)$

$= 32n - 16 - 32n + 48$

$= 32$ [a constant]

$u_{n-1} = 32(n-1) - 16$

$= 32n - 32 - 16$

$= 32n - 48$

$\therefore$ the distances which the object falls in each second form an arithmetic sequence.

(ii) $u_n = 32n - 16$

Distance fallen in 1st second $= T_1 = 32(1) - 16 = 32 - 16 = 16$ m

Distance fallen in 2nd second $= T_2 = 32(2) - 16 = 64 - 16 = 48$ m

Distance fallen in 3rd second $= T_3 = 32(3) - 16 = 96 - 16 = 80$ m

(**Note:** Distances travelled each second form an arithmetic sequence, where $a = 16$ and $d = 32$.)

(iii) $\qquad S_n = 16n^2$

$\Rightarrow \qquad S_{20} = 16(20)^2 = 16(400) = 6\,400$ m

or $\qquad S_n = \frac{n}{2}[2a + (n-1)d]$

$\Rightarrow \qquad S_{20} = \frac{20}{2}[2(16) + 19(32)] \quad [a = 16, d = 32, n = 20]$

$= 10(32 + 608)$

$= 10(640)$

$= 6\,400$ m

Example

A ball is dropped from a height of 81 cm. If the ball bounces $\frac{2}{3}$ of its previous height on each bounce, what is the total vertical distance the ball has travelled when it strikes the ground for the 6th time?

Solution:

Diagram:

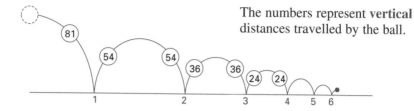

The numbers represent **vertical distances travelled by the ball.**

In addition to the original drop of 81 cm, there are 5 complete bounces which form a geometric series, i.e. Distance = 81 + (108 + 72 + 48 + ···).

The series in the brackets is a geometric series with $a = 108$ and $r = \frac{2}{3}$ (as each height is $\frac{2}{3}$ of the previous height).

We want to find the sum of the first five terms, S_5.

$$S_n = \frac{a(1 - r^n)}{1 - r}$$

$$S_5 = \frac{108\left[1 - \left(\frac{2}{3}\right)^5\right]}{1 - \frac{2}{3}} = \frac{108\left(1 - \frac{32}{243}\right)}{\frac{1}{3}} = \frac{108\left(\frac{211}{243}\right)}{\frac{1}{3}}$$

$$= 108\left(\frac{211}{243}\right)\left(\frac{3}{1}\right) = 281\frac{1}{3}$$

Thus, the total vertical distance travelled = $81 + 281\frac{1}{3} = 362\frac{1}{3}$ cm.

Recurring Decimals as Infinite Geometric Series

Example

Express (i) $0\cdot\dot{4}$ (ii) $1\cdot\dot{2}\dot{5}$ (iii) $2\cdot3\dot{7}\dot{0}$ in the form $\dfrac{p}{q}$, $p, q \in N_0$.

Solution:

(i) $\quad 0\cdot\dot{4} = 0\cdot444 \cdots$

$$= 0\cdot4 + 0\cdot04 + 0\cdot004 + \cdots$$

$$= \frac{4}{10} + \frac{4}{100} + \frac{4}{1000} + \cdots$$

This is an infinite geometric series with $a = \dfrac{4}{10}$ and $r = \dfrac{1}{10}$.

$$S_\infty = \frac{a}{1-r} = \frac{\frac{4}{10}}{1 - \frac{1}{10}} = \frac{4}{10-1} = \frac{4}{9}$$

Thus, $0\cdot\dot{4} = \frac{4}{9}$.

(ii) $\quad 1\cdot\dot{2}\dot{5} = 1\cdot252525 \ldots$

$$= 1 + (0\cdot25 + 0\cdot0025 + 0\cdot000025)$$

$$= 1 + \left(\frac{25}{100} + \frac{25}{10\,000} + \frac{25}{1\,000\,000} + \cdots \right)$$

The series in the brackets is an infinite geometric series with $a = \dfrac{25}{100}$ and $r = \dfrac{1}{100}$.

$$S_\infty = \frac{a}{1-r} = \frac{\frac{25}{100}}{1 - \frac{1}{100}} = \frac{25}{100-1} = \frac{25}{99}$$

Thus, $1\cdot\dot{2}\dot{5} = 1 + \frac{25}{99} = \frac{124}{99}$.

(iii) $\quad 2\cdot3\dot{7}\dot{0} = 2\cdot370370370\ldots$

$$= 2 + 0\cdot370 + 0\cdot000370 + 0\cdot000000370 + \cdots$$

$$= 2 + \left(\frac{370}{1\,000} + \frac{370}{1\,000\,000} + \frac{370}{1\,000\,000\,000} + \cdots \right)$$

$$= 2 + \left(\frac{37}{100} + \frac{37}{100\,000} + \frac{37}{100\,000\,000} + \cdots \right)$$

The series in the brackets is an infinite geometric series with $a = \dfrac{37}{100}$ and $r = \dfrac{1}{1\,000}$.

$$S_\infty = \frac{a}{1-r} = \frac{\dfrac{37}{100}}{1 - \dfrac{1}{1\,000}} = \frac{370}{1\,000 - 1} = \frac{370}{999} = \frac{10}{27}$$

Thus, $2 \cdot 3\dot{7}\dot{0} = 2 + \frac{10}{27} = \frac{64}{27}$.

The next example shows how a question on the sum of a finite geometric sequence can be formed.

Example

Show that the nth term of the sequence 5, 55, 555, 5555, ...
can be written as the sum of n terms of a geometric series and have the value of $\frac{5}{9}(10^n - 1)$.

Hence, find the sum of the first n terms of the sequence.

Solution:

$u_1 = 5$
$u_2 = 55 = 5 + 50 = 5 + 5.10$
$u_3 = 555 = 5 + 50 + 500 = 5 + 5.10 + 5.10^2$
$u_4 = 5555 = 5 + 50 + 500 + 5\,000 = 5 + 5.10 + 5.10^2 + 5.10^3$
$u_n = 5 + 5.10 + 5.10^2 + 5.10^3 + 5.10^4 + \cdots + 5.10^{n-1}$

This is a finite geometric series with $a = 5$ and $r = 10$.

Thus, $u_n = S_n$ of the geometric series

$$= \frac{a(r^n - 1)}{r - 1} = \frac{5(10^n - 1)}{10 - 1} = \frac{5}{9}(10^n - 1)$$

(i.e. $u_1 = \frac{5}{9}(10^1 - 1)$, $u_2 = \frac{5}{9}(10^2 - 1)$, $u_3 = \frac{5}{9}(10^3 - 1)$, etc.)

$S_n = u_1 + u_2 + u_3 + \cdots + u_n$

$\quad = \frac{5}{9}(10^1 - 1) + \frac{5}{9}(10^2 - 1) + \frac{5}{9}(10^3 - 1) + \cdots + \frac{5}{9}(10^n - 1)$

$\quad = \frac{5}{9}(10 - 1 + 10^2 - 1 + 10^3 - 1 + \cdots + 10^n - 1)$

$\quad = \frac{5}{9}\ [(10 + 10^2 + 10^3 + \cdots + 10^n) - (1 + 1 + 1 + 1 + \cdots + 1)]$

$\quad = \frac{5}{9}\left[\dfrac{10(10^n - 1)}{10 - 1} - n\right] \quad [a = 10, r = 10, n \text{ times}]$

$\quad = \frac{5}{9}\left[\dfrac{10}{9}(10^n - 1) - n\right]$

$\quad = \dfrac{50}{81}(10^n - 1) - \dfrac{5}{9}n$

Example

(i) Show that $\sum\limits_{r=1}^{n} \ln 2^r$ is an arithmetic series.

(ii) Find an expression for $\sum\limits_{r=1}^{n} \ln 2^r$. Hence, or otherwise, evaluate $\sum\limits_{r=1}^{10} \ln 2^r$.

(iii) Find the value of n for which $\sum\limits_{r=1}^{2n} \ln 2^r = \ln 2^{78}$.

Solution:

(i) $\sum\limits_{r=1}^{n} \ln 2^r = \sum\limits_{r=1}^{n} r \ln 2 = \ln 2 + 2 \ln 2 + 3 \ln 2 + \cdots + n \ln 2$

Thus, $u_n = n \ln 2 \qquad u_{n-1} = (n-1)\ln 2 = n \ln 2 - \ln 2$

$u_n - u_{n-1} = (n \ln 2) - (n \ln 2 - \ln 2)$

$\qquad\qquad = n \ln 2 - n \ln 2 + \ln 2$

$\qquad\qquad = \ln 2$ (a constant, i.e. common difference $= d = \ln 2$)

Thus, the series is arithmetic.

(ii) $\sum\limits_{r=1}^{n} \ln 2^r$ is an arithmetic series with $a = \ln 2$ and $d = \ln 2$.

$S_n = \frac{n}{2}[2a + (n-1)d]$

$\quad = \frac{n}{2}[2 \ln 2 + (n-1)\ln 2]$

$\quad = \frac{n}{2}[2 \ln 2 + n \ln 2 - \ln 2]$

$\quad = \frac{n}{2}[n \ln 2 + \ln 2]$

$\quad = \frac{n}{2}[(n+1)\ln 2]$

$\quad = \frac{1}{2}n(n+1)\ln 2$

$\sum\limits_{r=1}^{10} \ln 2^r$

$= S_{10}$

$= \frac{1}{2}(10)(10+1)\ln 2$

$= 5(11) \ln 2$

$= 55 \ln 2$

(iii) $\sum\limits_{r=1}^{2n} \ln 2^r$

$= S_{2n}$

$= \frac{1}{2}(2n)(2n+1)\ln 2$

$= n(2n+1)\ln 2$

Thus, $\sum\limits_{r=1}^{2n} \ln 2^r = \ln 2^{78}$

$\Rightarrow \qquad n(2n+1)\ln 2 = 78 \ln 2$

$\Rightarrow \qquad\qquad n(2n+1) = 78$

$\Rightarrow \qquad\qquad 2n^2 + n - 78 = 0$

$\Rightarrow \qquad (2n+13)(n-6) = 0$

$\Rightarrow \qquad n = -\dfrac{13}{2} \quad$ or $\quad n = 6$

Thus, $n = 6$. $\left[\text{ignore } n = -\dfrac{13}{2}\right]$

Limits

A sequence has a limit if $\lim\limits_{n\to\infty} u_n$ exists.

If $\lim\limits_{n\to\infty} u_n$ does not exist, then the sequence does not have a limit.

Two fundamental limits:

1. $\lim\limits_{n\to\infty} \dfrac{1}{n^p} = 0,$ if $p > 0$

2. $\lim\limits_{n\to\infty} r^n = 0,$ if $-1 < r < 1$

To find $\lim\limits_{n\to\infty} u_n$, do the following:

1. Divide top and bottom by the dominant term.
   (The dominant term is the largest term as $n \to \infty$.)
2. Use fundamental limits 1 and 2 above.

Example

Find   (i) $\lim\limits_{n\to\infty} \dfrac{3n - 4}{7n + 2}$

(ii) $\lim\limits_{n\to\infty} \dfrac{5n^2 + 3n - 2}{4n^2 - 2n + 7}$

(iii) $\lim\limits_{n\to\infty} \dfrac{2n^3 - 4n^2}{n^2 + 2n}$

(iv) $\lim\limits_{n\to\infty} \dfrac{\sqrt{2n^2 + 3}}{n}$

(v) $\lim\limits_{n\to\infty} \dfrac{3^n + 4^n}{5 \cdot 4^n}$

Solution:

(i) $\dfrac{3n - 4}{7n + 2}$ [dominant term is n]

[divide each part by n]

$$\lim\limits_{n\to\infty} \frac{3n - 4}{7n - 2} = \lim\limits_{n\to\infty} \frac{3 - \dfrac{4}{n}}{7 - \dfrac{2}{n}} = \frac{3 - 0}{7 - 0} = \frac{3}{7}$$

119

(ii) $\dfrac{5n^2 + 3n - 2}{4n^2 - 2n + 7}$ [dominant term is n^2]

[divide each part by n^2]

$$\lim_{n\to\infty} \frac{5n^2 + 3n - 2}{4n^2 - 2n + 7} = \lim_{n\to\infty} \frac{5 + \dfrac{3}{n} - \dfrac{2}{n^2}}{4 - \dfrac{2}{n} + \dfrac{7}{n^2}} = \frac{5 + 0 - 0}{4 - 0 - 0} = \frac{5}{4}$$

(iii) $\dfrac{2n^3 - 4n^2}{n^2 + 2n}$ [dominant term is n^3]

[divide each part by n^3]

$$\lim_{n\to\infty} \frac{2n^3 - 4n^2}{n^2 + 2n} = \lim_{n-\infty} \frac{2 - \dfrac{4}{n}}{\dfrac{1}{n} + \dfrac{2}{n^2}} = \frac{2 - 0}{0 + 0} = \frac{2}{0} \text{ [undefined]}$$

i.e. it has no limit.

(iv) $\displaystyle\lim_{n\to\infty} \frac{\sqrt{2n^2 + 3}}{n} = \lim_{n\to\infty} \sqrt{\frac{2n^2 + 3}{n^2}} = \sqrt{\lim_{n\to\infty} \frac{2n^2 + 3}{n^2}}$

$= \sqrt{\lim \dfrac{2 + \dfrac{3}{n^2}}{1}}$ $\begin{bmatrix} \text{take } \sqrt{\ } \text{ outside;} \\ \text{makes no difference as } n \to \infty \end{bmatrix}$

$= \sqrt{\dfrac{2 + 0}{1}}$

$= \sqrt{2}$ [dominant term is n^2]

[divide each part by n^2]

(v) $\displaystyle\lim_{n\to\infty} \frac{3^n + 4^n}{5.4^n}$ [dominant term is 4^n]

[divide each part by 4^n]

$= \displaystyle\lim_{n\to\infty} \frac{\dfrac{3^n}{4^n} + 1}{5} = \lim_{n\to\infty} \frac{\left(\dfrac{3}{4}\right)^n + 1}{5} = \frac{0 + 1}{5} = \frac{1}{5}$

Note: $\displaystyle\lim_{n\to\infty} \left(\tfrac{3}{4}\right)^n = 0$ as $-1 < \tfrac{3}{4} < 1$

Series of Powers of Natural Numbers

1. $\displaystyle\sum_{r=1}^{n} k = k + k + k + \cdots + k = nk$

2. $\displaystyle\sum_{r=1}^{n} r = 1 + 2 + 3 + \cdots + n = \frac{n}{2}(n + 1)$

3. $\displaystyle\sum_{r=1}^{n} r^2 = 1^2 + 2^2 + 3^2 + \cdots + n^2 = \frac{n}{6}(n + 1)(2n + 1)$

We use these to find an expression for S_n if $u_n = an^2 + bn + c$.

Note: (i) Each of these formulae can be proved using induction.

(ii) $\sum [f(n) + g(n)] = \sum f(n) + \sum g(n)$

Example

The nth term of a series is given by $u_n = n(n + 1)$. Evaluate $\displaystyle\sum_{n=1}^{30} u_n$.

Solution:

$$\sum_{n=1}^{30} u_n = \sum_{n=1}^{30} n(n + 1) = \sum_{n=1}^{30} (n^2 + n) = \sum_{n=1}^{30} n^2 + \sum_{n=1}^{30} n$$

But $\sum n^2 = \frac{n}{6}(n + 1)(2n + 1)$ and $\sum n = \frac{n}{2}(n + 1)$.

Thus, $\displaystyle\sum_{n=1}^{30} n^2 + \sum_{n=1}^{30} n = \frac{30}{6}(30 + 1)(60 + 1) + \frac{30}{2}(30 + 1)$

$$= 5(31)(61) + 15(31)$$

$$= 9\,455 + 465 = 9\,920$$

Example

The nth term of a series is given by $u_n = (1 - n)^2$.

Find an expression, in terms of n, for $\displaystyle\sum_{r=1}^{n}(1 - r)^2$ and, hence, evaluate $\displaystyle\sum_{n=1}^{20}(1 - n)^2$.

Solution:

$$u_n = (1 - n)^2 = 1 - 2n + n^2$$

$$S_n = \sum_{r=1}^{n} u_r = \sum_{r=1}^{n}(1 - 2r + r^2)$$

$$= \sum_{r=1}^{n} 1 - 2\sum_{r=1}^{n} r + \sum_{r=1}^{n} r^2$$

$$= n - 2\frac{n}{2}(n + 1) + \frac{n}{6}(n + 1)(2n + 1)$$

$$= n - n(n + 1) + \frac{n}{6}(n + 1)(2n + 1)$$

$$= n\left[1 - (n + 1) + \frac{(n + 1)(2n + 1)}{6}\right]$$

$$= n\left[\frac{6 - 6(n + 1) + (n + 1)(2n + 1)}{6}\right]$$

$$= \frac{n}{6}(6 - 6n - 6 + 2n^2 + 3n + 1)$$

$$= \frac{n}{6}(2n^2 - 3n + 1)$$

Thus, $\displaystyle S_{20} = \sum_{n=1}^{20}(1 - n)^2 = \frac{20}{6}[2(20)^2 - 3(20) + 1]$

$$= \frac{10}{3}(800 - 60 + 1)$$

$$= \frac{10}{3}(741)$$

$$= 2\,470$$

Example

Show that the sum of the numbers in the rth bracket of the series

$(1) + (1 + 2) + (1 + 2 + 3) + (1 + 2 + 3 + 4) + \cdots$ is $\frac{r}{2}(r + 1)$.

Hence, show that the sum of the n brackets is $\frac{n}{6}(n + 1)(n + 2)$.

Solution:

rth bracket: $(1 + 2 + 3 + \cdots + r)$

This is an arithmetic series with $a = 1$, $d = 1$ and $n = r$.

$$S_n = \frac{n}{2}[2a + (n - 1)d] = \frac{r}{2}[2 + (r - 1)(1)] = \frac{r}{2}(r + 1)$$

Thus, the nth term of the series of brackets is given by $u_n = \frac{n}{2}(n + 1)$.

$$S_n = \sum_{r=1}^{n} u_r = \sum_{r=1}^{n} \frac{r}{2}(r + 1)$$

$$= \frac{1}{2}\sum_{r=1}^{n}(r^2 + r)$$

$$= \frac{1}{2}\left[\sum_{r=1}^{n} r^2 + \sum_{r=1}^{n} r\right]$$

$$= \frac{1}{2}\left[\frac{n}{6}(n + 1)(2n + 1) + \frac{n}{2}(n + 1)\right]$$

$$= \frac{1}{12}[n(n + 1)(2n + 1) + 3n(n + 1)]$$

$$= \frac{1}{12}n(n + 1)(2n + 1 + 3)$$

$$= \frac{1}{12}n(n + 1)(2n + 4)$$

$$= \frac{1}{12}n(n + 1)2(n + 2)$$

$$= \frac{n}{6}(n + 1)(n + 2)$$

Example

If $S_n = \dfrac{1}{n} \sqrt{1 + 2 + 3 + 4 + \cdots + n}$, find $\lim\limits_{n \to \infty} S_n$.

Solution:

$$S_n = \frac{1}{n} \sqrt{1 + 2 + 3 + 4 + \cdots + n}$$

$$= \frac{1}{n} \sqrt{\frac{n}{2}(n + 1)} \qquad\qquad \left[1 + 2 + 3 + 4 + \cdots + n = \frac{n}{2}(n + 1) \right]$$

$$= \sqrt{\frac{n(n + 1)}{2n^2}}$$

$$= \sqrt{\frac{n^2 + n}{2n^2}}$$

$$\lim_{n \to \infty} S_n = \lim_{n \to \infty} \sqrt{\frac{n^2 + n}{2n^2}} \qquad \text{[dominant term is } n^2 \text{]}$$

$$= \sqrt{\lim_{n \to \infty} \frac{n^2 + n}{2n^2}} \qquad \text{[take } \sqrt{} \text{ outside, makes no difference as } n \to \infty\text{]}$$

$$= \sqrt{\lim \frac{1 + \dfrac{1}{n}}{2}} \qquad \text{[divide each part by } n^2\text{]}$$

$$= \sqrt{\frac{1 + 0}{2}} = \sqrt{\frac{1}{2}} = \frac{\sqrt{1}}{\sqrt{2}} = \frac{1}{\sqrt{2}} \quad \text{or} \quad \frac{\sqrt{2}}{2}$$

Series of the Form $\displaystyle\sum_{n=1}^{\infty} \frac{1}{n(n + 1)}$

Partial fractions enable us to find a concise expression for S_n by telescoping the series and then using the **'method of differences'**, as the following examples show. It also shows how to find the sum to infinity for this type of series.

Example

Find A and B if $\dfrac{2}{n(n + 2)} = \dfrac{A}{n} + \dfrac{B}{n + 2}$.

Find **(i)** S_n **(ii)** $\lim\limits_{n \to \infty} S_n$.

Solution:

$$\frac{2}{n(n+2)} = \frac{A}{n} + \frac{B}{n+2}$$

$$\Rightarrow \qquad 2 = A(n+2) + B(n)$$

(as this is true for all values of n, we choose two suitable values).

Let $n = -2$: $2 = A(0) + B(-2)$ $\Rightarrow$ $-2B = 2$ $\Rightarrow$ $B = -1$

Let $n = 0$: $2 = A(2) + B(0)$ $\Rightarrow$ $2A = 2$ $\Rightarrow$ $A = 1$

Thus, $\dfrac{2}{n(n+2)} = \dfrac{1}{n} - \dfrac{1}{n+2}$

(i)   Find S_n

$$u_1 = \frac{1}{1} - \frac{1}{3}$$

$$u_2 = \frac{1}{2} - \frac{1}{4}$$

$$u_3 = \frac{1}{3} - \frac{1}{5}$$

$$u_4 = \frac{1}{4} - \frac{1}{6}$$

$$\vdots \qquad \vdots \qquad \vdots$$

$$\vdots \qquad \vdots \qquad \vdots$$

$$u_{n-3} = \frac{1}{n-3} - \frac{1}{n+1}$$

$$u_{n-2} = \frac{1}{n-2} - \frac{1}{n}$$

$$u_{n-1} = \frac{1}{n-1} - \frac{1}{n+1}$$

$$u_n = \frac{1}{n} - \frac{1}{n+2}$$

(add) $S_n = 1 + \dfrac{1}{2} - \dfrac{1}{n+1} - \dfrac{1}{n+2}$

$$S_n = \frac{3}{2} - \frac{1}{n+1} - \frac{1}{n+2}$$

(ii)   Find $\lim\limits_{n\to\infty} S_n$

$$S_n = \frac{3}{2} - \frac{1}{n+1} - \frac{1}{n+2}$$

$$\lim_{n\to\infty} S_n = \lim_{n\to\infty}\left(\frac{3}{2} - \frac{1}{n+1} - \frac{1}{n+2}\right)$$

[dominant term is n in each of the last two fractions]

$$= \lim_{n\to\infty}\left(\frac{3}{2} - \frac{\frac{1}{n}}{1+\frac{1}{n}} - \frac{\frac{1}{n}}{1+\frac{2}{n}}\right)$$

$$= \frac{3}{2} - \frac{0}{1+0} - \frac{0}{1+0}$$

$$= \frac{3}{2} - 0 - 0$$

$$= \frac{3}{2}$$

Thus, $\lim\limits_{n\to\infty} S_n = \dfrac{3}{2}$.

Sometimes u_n is not given, as in the next example.

Example

Find u_n of the series $\dfrac{1}{3.5} + \dfrac{1}{4.6} + \dfrac{1}{5.7} + \dfrac{1}{6.8} + \cdots$

Evaluate $\displaystyle\sum_{n=1}^{\infty} u_n$.

Solution:

Find u_n.

Consider the set of first digits.

3, 4, 5, 6, ...

is an arithmetic series

with $a = 3, d = 1$

$$u_n = a + (n - 1)d$$
$$= 3 + (n - 1)(1)$$
$$= n + 2$$

Consider the set of second digits.

5, 6, 7, 8, ...

is an arithmetic series

with $a = 5, d = 1$

$$u_n = a + (n - 1)d$$
$$= 5 + (n - 1)(1)$$
$$= n + 4$$

Thus, $\qquad u_n = \dfrac{1}{(n + 2)(n + 4)}$

Let $\dfrac{1}{(n + 2)(n + 4)} = \dfrac{A}{n + 2} + \dfrac{B}{n + 4}$

$\Rightarrow \qquad\qquad 1 = A(n + 4) + B(n + 2)$

Let $n = -4$: $\quad 1 = A(0) + B(-2) \qquad \Rightarrow \qquad -2B = 1 \qquad \Rightarrow \qquad B = -\dfrac{1}{2}$

Let $n = -2$: $\quad 1 = A(2) + B(0) \qquad \Rightarrow \qquad 2A = 1 \qquad \Rightarrow \qquad A = \dfrac{1}{2}$

Thus, $\quad \dfrac{1}{(n + 2)(n + 4)} = \dfrac{\frac{1}{2}}{n + 2} - \dfrac{\frac{1}{2}}{n + 4}$

$$= \dfrac{1}{2(n + 2)} - \dfrac{1}{2(n + 4)}.$$

Now find S_n.

$$u_1 = \frac{1}{2.3} - \frac{1}{2.5}$$

$$u_2 = \frac{1}{2.4} - \frac{1}{2.6}$$

$$u_3 = \frac{1}{2.5} - \frac{1}{2.7}$$

$$u_4 = \frac{1}{2.6} - \frac{1}{2.8}$$

$$\vdots \qquad \vdots \qquad \vdots$$

$$\vdots \qquad \vdots \qquad \vdots$$

$$u_{n-3} = \frac{1}{2(n-1)} - \frac{1}{2(n+1)}$$

$$u_{n-2} = \frac{1}{2n} - \frac{1}{2(n+2)}$$

$$u_{n-1} = \frac{1}{2(n+1)} - \frac{1}{2(n+3)}$$

$$u_n = \frac{1}{2(n+2)} - \frac{1}{2(n+4)}$$

(add) $S_n = \dfrac{1}{2.3} + \dfrac{1}{2.4} - \dfrac{1}{2(n+3)} - \dfrac{1}{2(n+4)}$

$$= \frac{7}{24} - \frac{1}{2(n+3)} - \frac{1}{2(n+4)}$$

Evaluate $\displaystyle\sum_{n=1}^{\infty} u_n$ (i.e. S_∞)

i.e. $\displaystyle\lim_{n\to\infty} S_n$ or simply S_∞

$$S_n = \frac{7}{24} - \frac{1}{2(n+3)} - \frac{1}{2(n+4)}$$

$$\lim_{n\to\infty} S_n = \lim_{n\to\infty} \left(\frac{7}{24} - \frac{1}{2(n+3)} - \frac{1}{2(n+4)} \right)$$

[dominant term is n]

$$= \lim_{n \to \infty} \frac{7}{24} - \frac{\frac{1}{n}}{2\left(1 + \frac{3}{n}\right)} - \frac{\frac{1}{n}}{2\left(1 + \frac{4}{n}\right)}$$

$$= \frac{7}{24} - \frac{0}{2} - \frac{0}{2}$$

$$= \frac{7}{24}$$

Thus, $\sum\limits_{n=1}^{\infty} u_n = \frac{7}{24}$.

Series of the form $\sum\limits_{n=0}^{\infty} nx^n$

A series can be formed by multiplying, term by term, the terms of an arithmetic series and a geometric series, called '**Arithmetic–geometric**' series.

Arithmetic series: $a_0 + a_1 + a_2 + a_3 + \cdots + a_n$

Geometric series: $1 + x + x^2 + x^3 + \cdots + x^n$

New series: $a_0 + a_1x + a_2x^2 + a_3x^3 + \cdots + a_nx^n$

Example

Find S_n of the series: $4 + 5x + 6x^2 + 7x^3 + \cdots + (n + 3)x^{n-1}$.

If $|x| < 1$, find $\lim\limits_{n \to \infty} S_n$. Hence, or otherwise, evaluate $\sum\limits_{r=1}^{\infty} (r + 3)\left(\frac{1}{3}\right)^{r-1}$.

Solution:

$$S_n = 4 + 5x + 6x^2 + 7x^3 + \cdots + (n + 3)x^{n-1}$$

$$xS_n = \quad\quad 4x + 5x^2 + 6x^3 + \cdots + (n + 2)x^{n-1} + (n + 3)x^n$$

$$(1 - x)S_n = 4 + (x + x^2 + x^3 + \cdots + x^{n-1}) - (n + 3)x^n$$

[multiply by x, the common ratio of the geometric series]

The series in the brackets is a geometric series with $a = x$, $r = x$ and $(n - 1)$ terms.

Thus, S_n for this series $= \dfrac{a(1 - r^{n-1})}{1 - r} = \dfrac{x(1 - x^{n-1})}{1 - x}$.

$$(1 - x)S_n = 4 + \frac{x(1 - x^{n-1})}{1 - x} - (n + 3)x^n$$

$$S_n = \frac{4}{(1 - x)} + \frac{x(1 - x^{n-1})}{(1 - x)^2} - \frac{(n + 3)x^n}{1 - x}$$

If $|x| < 1$, then as $n \to \infty$, $x^n \to 0$, $x^{n-1} \to 0$.

Thus, $\lim_{n \to \infty} S_n = \frac{4}{1 - x} + \frac{x(1 - 0)}{(1 - x)^2} - \frac{(n + 3)(0)}{1 - x}$

$$= \frac{4}{1 - x} + \frac{x}{(1 - x)^2} = \frac{4(1 - x) + x}{(1 - x)^2} = \frac{4 - 3x}{(1 - x)^2} = S_\infty$$

$$\sum_{r=1}^{\infty} (r + 3)\left(\frac{1}{3}\right)^{r-1} = 4 + 5\left(\frac{1}{3}\right) + 6\left(\frac{1}{3}\right)^2 + 7\left(\frac{1}{3}\right)^2 + \cdots = S_\infty$$

This is exactly the same as the original series with $x = \frac{1}{3}$.

Thus, $\sum_{r=1}^{\infty} (r + 3)\left(\frac{1}{3}\right) = \dfrac{4 - 3\left(\dfrac{1}{3}\right)}{\left(1 - \dfrac{1}{3}\right)^2}$ $\left[\text{put in } x = \dfrac{1}{3} \text{ into } \dfrac{4 - 3x}{(1 - x)^2}\right]$

$$= \frac{4 - 1}{\dfrac{4}{9}} = \frac{36 - 9}{4} = \frac{27}{4}.$$

Sometimes u_n is not given, as in the next example.

Example

Find (i) u_n (ii) S_n and (iii) S_{20} of the series:

$$2 + 3.2 + 4.2^2 + 5.2^3 + \cdots$$

Solution:

(i) $2 + 3.2 + 4.2^2 + 5.2^3 + \cdots$

This series is a combination of an arithmetic series and a geometric series.

Thus, we need to find u_n separately for each of these series and combine the results.

Arithmetic series: $2 + 3 + 4 + 5 + \cdots$, $u_n = a + (n - 1)d = 2 + (n - 1)(1) = n + 1$

Geometric series: $2^0 + 2^1 + 2^2 + 2^3 + \cdots$, $u_n = ar^{n-1} = 1.2^{n-1} = 2^{n-1}$

Thus, for the new series, $u_n = (n + 1)2^{n-1}$

(ii) $S_n = 2 + 3.2 + 4.2^2 + 5.2^3 + \cdots + n2^{n-2} + (n + 1)2^{n-1}$

$2S_n = \qquad 2.2 + 3.2^2 + 4.2^3 + \qquad \cdots \quad + \qquad n2^{n-1} + (n + 1)2^n$

$-S_n = 2 + (2 + 2^2 + 2^3 + \qquad \cdots \quad + \qquad 2^{n-1}) - (n + 1)2^n$

[multiply by 2, the common ratio of the geometric series]

$$\left[\begin{array}{l} \text{The series in the brackets is a geometric series with } a = 2, \ r = 2 \text{ and } (n-1) \text{ terms.} \\[6pt] \text{Thus, } S_n \text{ for this series } = \dfrac{a(r^{n-1} - 1)}{r - 1} = \dfrac{2(2^{n-1} - 1)}{2 - 1} = 2^n - 2. \end{array}\right]$$

Thus, $-S_n = 2 + (2 + 2^2 + 2^3 + \cdots + 2^{n-1}) - (n + 1)2^n$

$-S_n = 2 + (2^n - 2) - n2^n - 2^n$

$-S_n = 2 + 2^n - 2 - n2^n - 2^n$

$-S_n = -n2^n$

$S_n = n2^n$

(iii) $\quad S_n = n2^n$

$\therefore \quad S_{20} = 20(2)^{20} = 20(1\ 048\ 576) = 20\ 971\ 520.$

Example

If $f(x) = \sum\limits_{n=1}^{\infty} nx^{n-1}$, for $-1 < x < 1$, show that:

$$x f(x) = \sum_{r=2}^{\infty} rx^{r-1} - \sum_{r=2}^{\infty} x^{r-1}$$

Hence, find the value of $f(x)$.

Solution:

$$f(x) = \sum_{n=1}^{\infty} nx^{n-1} = 1 + 2x + 3x^2 + \cdots \quad \text{for } -1 < x < 1$$

$$xf(x) = x + 2x^2 + 3x^3 + \cdots.$$

$$\sum_{r=2}^{\infty} rx^{r-1} = 2x + 3x^2 + 4x^3 + \cdots$$

$$\sum_{r=2}^{\infty} x^{r-1} = x + x^2 + x^3 + \cdots$$

$\Rightarrow \quad \sum rx^{r-1} - \sum x^{r-1} = (2x + 3x^2 + 4x^3 + \cdots) - (x + x^2 + x^3 + \cdots)$

$$= x + 2x^2 + 3x^3 + \cdots$$

$$= xf(x)$$

$$f(x) = 1 + 2x - 3x^2 + 4x^3 + \cdots + \quad nx^{n-1} + (n + 1)x^n + \cdots$$

$$xf(x) = \quad x + 2x^2 + 3x^3 + \cdots + (n - 1)x^{n-1} + \quad nx^n + \cdots$$

$$\overline{\rule{11cm}{0.4pt}}$$

$$(1 - x)f(x) = 1 + \quad x + \quad x^2 + x^3 + \cdots + \quad x^{n-1} + \quad x^n + \cdots$$

This is an infinite geometric series with $a = 1$ and $r = x$, where $-1 < x < 1$.

Thus, $S_\infty = \dfrac{a}{1-r} = \dfrac{1}{1-x}$

Thus, $(1-x)f(x) = 1 + x + x^2 + x^3 + \cdots$

$\Rightarrow \quad (1-x)f(x) = \dfrac{1}{1-x}$

$\Rightarrow \qquad f(x) = \dfrac{1}{(1-x)^2}$

Factorials, $n!$

Notation: $\quad n! = n(n-1)(n-2)(n-3) \ldots (3)(2)(1)$

i.e. the product of all the integers from n to 1, inclusive.

Note: $\quad 10! = 10.9! = 10.9.8!$ (and so on)

$\qquad n! = n(n-1)! = n(n-1)(n-2)!$ (and so on)

$\qquad 0! = 1$

When simplifying factorials, it is good practice to start with the larger factorial and work down to the smaller one.

Example

Simplify $\dfrac{3!\, n!}{(n-2)!\, 2n}$.

Solution:

$$\dfrac{3!\, n!}{(n-2)!2n} = \dfrac{3.2.1.n(n-1)(n-2)!}{(n-2)!2n} \quad [n! = n(n-1)(n-2)!]$$

$$= 3(n-1) = 3n - 3$$

Example

Factorise $(n+1)! + n^2(n-1)!$

Solution:

$\quad (n+1)! + n^2(n-1)!$

$= (n+1)(n)(n-1)! + n^2(n-1)! \qquad [(n+1)! = (n+1)n(n-1)!]$

$= n(n-1)!(n+1+n) \qquad\qquad$ [take out common factors n and $(n-1)!$]

$= n!(2n+1) \qquad\qquad\qquad\quad [n! = n(n-1)!]$

$= (2n+1)n!$

Example

Solve: (i) $\dfrac{(n-2)!}{n!} = \dfrac{1}{56}$ (ii) $\dfrac{(2n)!}{(2n-1)!} = \dfrac{5!}{3!}$

Solution

(i) $\qquad\qquad \dfrac{(n-2)!}{n!} = \dfrac{1}{56}$

$\Rightarrow \quad \dfrac{(n-2)!}{n(n-1)(n-2)!} = \dfrac{1}{56}$

$\Rightarrow \qquad\qquad \dfrac{1}{n(n-1)} = \dfrac{1}{56}$

$\qquad\qquad\qquad n(n-1) = 56$

$\qquad\qquad\qquad n^2 - n - 56 = 0$

$\qquad\qquad\qquad (n-8)(n+7) = 0$

$\Rightarrow \qquad\qquad n = 8 \quad \text{or} \quad n = -7$

$n = -7$ is rejected as $n!$ is defined for natural numbers only.

Thus, $n = 8$.

(ii) $\qquad\qquad \dfrac{(2n)!}{(2n-1)!} = \dfrac{5!}{3!}$

$\Rightarrow \quad \dfrac{(2n)(2n-1)!}{(2n-1)!} = \dfrac{5.4.3!}{3!}$

$\Rightarrow \qquad\qquad 2n = 20$

$\Rightarrow \qquad\qquad n = 10$

The $\binom{n}{r}$ notation

$$\binom{n}{r} = \dfrac{n!}{r!(n-r)!} = \dfrac{n(n-1)(n-2)\ldots(n-r+1)}{r!}$$

Notes: 1. $\binom{n}{r} = \binom{n}{n-r}$ e.g. $\binom{10}{2} = \binom{10}{8}$

2. $\binom{n}{0} = \binom{n}{n} = 1$ 3. $\binom{n}{1} = n$

Memory aid: $\binom{n}{r} = \dfrac{n!}{r!(n-r)!} = \dfrac{\text{top!}}{\text{bottom!}(\text{top}-\text{bottom})!}$

Example

(i) Solve $\binom{n+2}{2} = 36, n \in N$ (ii) Write down all the couples (x, y) for which

$$\binom{4}{x} = \binom{4}{y}$$

Solution:

(i) $\binom{n+2}{2} = 36$

$\Rightarrow \quad \dfrac{(n+2)(n+1)}{2.1} = 36$

$\Rightarrow \quad n^2 + 3n + 2 = 72$

$\Rightarrow \quad n^2 + 3n - 70 = 0$

$\Rightarrow \quad (n+10)(n-7) = 0$

$\Rightarrow \quad n = -10 \text{ or } n = 7$

reject -10, as $-10 \notin N$.

Thus, $n = 7$.

(ii) $\binom{4}{x} = \binom{4}{y}$

$\Rightarrow \qquad x + y = 4$

Both x and y must be positive whole numbers. Thus, the couples are:

$(0 \ \ 4), (1, \ 3), (2, \ 2), (3, \ 1), (4, \ 0)$

Example

Prove that (i) $\binom{n}{r} = \binom{n}{n-r}$ (ii) $r\binom{n}{r} = n\binom{n-1}{r-1}$

Solution:

Memory aid: $\binom{top}{bottom} = \dfrac{top!}{bottom!\,(top - bottom)!}$

(i) L.H.S. $= \binom{n}{r} = \dfrac{n!}{r!(n-r)!}$

R.H.S. $= \binom{n}{n-r} = \dfrac{n!}{(n-r)![n-(n-r)]!} = \dfrac{n!}{(n-r)!(r)!} = \dfrac{n!}{r!(n-r)!}$

Thus, $\binom{n}{r} = \binom{n}{n-r}$.

(ii)
$$r\binom{n}{r} = n\binom{n-1}{r-1}$$

L.H.S. $= r\binom{n}{r} = r\dfrac{n!}{r!(n-r)!}$

$= \dfrac{r.n!}{r!(n-r)!}$

$= \dfrac{r.n!}{r(r-1)!(n-r)!}$

$= \dfrac{n!}{(r-1)!(n-r)!}$

R.H.S. $= n\binom{n-1}{r-1}$

$= n\dfrac{(n-1)!}{(r-1)![(n-1)-(r-1)]!}$

$= \dfrac{n(n-1)!}{(r-1)!(n-r)!}$

$= \dfrac{n!}{(r-1)!(n-r)!}$

Thus, $r\binom{n}{r} = n\binom{n-1}{r-1}$.

Binomial Theorem

An expression with two terms, e.g. $a + b$, is called a **binomial**. The Binomial Theorem is used to write down the expansion of a binomial to any power, e.g. $(a + b)^n$. The expansion of $(a + b)^n$ is found as follows:

$$(a+b)^n = \binom{n}{0}a^n b^0 + \binom{n}{1}a^{n-1}b^1 + \binom{n}{2}a^{n-2}b^2 + \cdots + \binom{n}{n-1}a^1 b^{n-1} + \binom{n}{n}a^0 b^n = \sum_{r=0}^{n}\binom{n}{r}a^{n-r}b^r$$

Notes:

1. The expansion contains $(n + 1)$ terms (one more than the power).

2. The powers of a decrease by 1 in each successive term.

3. The powers of b increase by 1 in each successive term.

4. In each term the sum of the indices of a and b is n.

5. The power of b is always the same as the lower number in the combination bracket.

6. If the binomial is a difference, $(a - b)$, the signs will be alternately $+, -, +, -, +, \cdots$

7. The general term is: $u_{r+1} = \binom{n}{r}a^{n-r}b^r$.

Example

Expand, using the Binomial Theorem, $(x - 3y)^4$.

Solution:

The power is 4, thus there are 5 terms.

$(x - 3y)^4$

$= \binom{4}{0}x^4(-3y)^0 + \binom{4}{1}x^3(-3y)^1 + \binom{4}{2}x^2(-3y)^2 + \binom{4}{3}x^1(-3y)^3 + \binom{4}{4}x^0(-3y)^4$

$= 1.x^4.1 + 4x^3(-3y) + 6x^2(9y^2) + 4x(-27y^3) + 1.1.(81y^4)$

$= x^4 - 12x^3y + 54x^2y^2 - 108xy^3 + 81y^4$

Example

Expand and simplify $(\sqrt{x} + \sqrt{y})^6 + (\sqrt{x} - \sqrt{y})^6$.

Verify your answer by letting $x = 4$ and $y = 1$.

Solution:

Let $\sqrt{x} = a$ and $\sqrt{y} = b$.

$(a + b)^6 = a^6 + \binom{6}{1}a^5b + \binom{6}{2}a^4b^2 + \binom{6}{3}a^3b^3 + \binom{6}{4}a^2b^4 + \binom{6}{5}ab^5 + b^6$

$= a^6 + 6a^5b + 15a^4b^2 + 20a^3b^3 + 15a^2b^4 + 6ab^5 + b^6$

Similarly,

$(a - b)^6 = a^6 - 6a^5b + 15a^4b^2 - 20a^3b^3 + 15a^2b^4 - 6ab^5 + b^6$

Thus $(a + b)^6 + (a - b)^6$

$= 2a^6 + 30a^4b^2 + 30a^2b^4 + 2b^6$

$= 2(\sqrt{x})^6 + 30(\sqrt{x})^4(\sqrt{y})^2 + 30(\sqrt{x})^2(\sqrt{y})^4 + 2(\sqrt{y})^6$

$= 2x^3 + 30x^2y + 30xy^2 + 2y^3$

When $x = 4$, $y = 1$:

$(\sqrt{x} + \sqrt{y})^6 + (\sqrt{x} - \sqrt{y})^6 = (\sqrt{4} + \sqrt{1})^6 - (\sqrt{4} - \sqrt{1})^6 = 3^6 + 1^6 = 730$

$2x^3 + 30x^2y + 30xy^2 + 2y^3 = 2(4)^3 + 30(4)^2(1) + 30(4)(1)^2 + 2(1)^3 = 730$

Example

Expand $(2 + \sqrt{3})^5$ by the Binomial Theorem, and write your answer in the form $a + b\sqrt{3}, a, b \in \mathbf{Z}^+$.

Solution:

$$(2 + \sqrt{3})^5$$

$$= 2^5 + \binom{5}{1}2^4(\sqrt{3}) + \binom{5}{2}2^3(\sqrt{3})^2 + \binom{5}{3}2^2(\sqrt{3})^3 + \binom{5}{4}2(\sqrt{3})^4 + (\sqrt{3})^5$$

$$= 32 + 5(16)(\sqrt{3}) + 10(8)(3) + 10(4)(3\sqrt{3}) + 5(2)(9) + 9\sqrt{3}$$

$$= 32 + 80\sqrt{3} + 240 + 120\sqrt{3} + 90 + 9\sqrt{3}$$

$$= 362 + 209\sqrt{3}$$

Example

(i) Write the first three terms in ascending powers of b and the general term in the binomial expansion of $(a + b)^n$ for $n \in \mathbf{Z}^+$.

(ii) If h is a constant and hx^3y^4 is a term in the expansion of $(2x + 5y^2)^n$, find the value of n and the value of h.

Solution:

(i) $$(a + b)^n = a^n + \binom{n}{1}a^{n-1}b + \binom{n}{2}a^{n-2}b^2 + \cdots$$

$$= a^n + na^{n-1}b + \frac{n(n-1)}{2}a^{n-2}b^2 + \cdots$$

General term: $$u_{r+1} = \binom{n}{r}a^{n-r}b^r$$

[3rd term contains y^4]

(ii) $$(2x + 5y^2)^n = (2x)^n + \binom{n}{1}(2x)^{n-1}(5y^2) + \binom{n}{2}(2x)^{n-2}(5y^2)^2 + \cdots$$

$$u_3 = \binom{n}{2}(2x)^{n-2}(5y^2)^2$$

$$= \binom{n}{2}2^{n-2}x^{n-2}25y^4 = hx^3y^4$$

136

Thus, $x^{n-2} = x^3$ ①

$\Rightarrow$ $n - 2 = 3$

$\Rightarrow$ $n = 5$

put this into ②

and $h = \binom{n}{2} . 2^{n-2} . 25$ ②

$$h = \binom{5}{2} . 2^{5-2} . 25$$

$$= \frac{5.4}{2} . 2^3 . 25$$

$$= (10)(8)(25) = 2\ 000$$

Example

Evaluate (i) $\displaystyle\sum_{r=0}^{20} \binom{20}{r} \left(\frac{3}{4}\right)^{20-r} \left(\frac{1}{4}\right)^r$ (ii) $\displaystyle\sum_{r=0}^{12} \binom{12}{r} \left(\frac{5}{9}\right)^{12-r} \left(\frac{13}{9}\right)^r$

Solution:

$$\sum_{r=0}^{n} \binom{n}{r} a^{n-r} b^r = (a + b)^n$$

(i) Thus, $\displaystyle\sum_{r=0}^{20} \binom{20}{r} \left(\frac{3}{4}\right)^{20-r} \left(\frac{1}{4}\right)^r$

$$= \left(\frac{3}{4} + \frac{1}{4}\right)^{20}$$

$$= (1)^{20} = 1$$

(ii) Thus, $\displaystyle\sum_{r=0}^{12} \binom{12}{r} \left(\frac{5}{9}\right)^{12-r} \left(\frac{13}{9}\right)^r$

$$= \left(\frac{5}{9} + \frac{13}{9}\right)^{12}$$

$$= 2^{12} = 4\ 096$$

$$(1 + x)^n = 1 + \binom{n}{1}x + \binom{n}{2}x^2 + \binom{n}{3}x^3 + \binom{n}{4}x^4 + \cdots$$

Example

If x is so small that x^4 and higher powers of x may be neglected, find an expression of the form $a + bx + cx^2 + dx^3$ for $(1 + 2x - x^2)^5$.

Solution:

Let $(1 + 2x - x^2)^5 = [1 + (2x - x^2)]^5$.

Use the expansion of $(1 + x)^n$ with $n = 5$ and $x = (2x - x^2)$

$$= 1 + \binom{5}{1}(2x - x^2) + \binom{5}{2}(2x - x^2)^2 + \binom{5}{3}(2x - x^2)^3 + \cdots$$

$$= 1 + 5(2x - x^2) + 10(4x^2 - 4x^3 + \cdots) + 10(8x^3 + \cdots) + \cdots$$

Expanding and ignoring terms of x^4 and above gives:

$$= 1 + 10x - 5x^2 + 40x^2 - 40x^3 + 80x^3$$

$$= 1 + 10x + 35x^2 + 40x^3$$

Example

Expand $(1 + x + x^2)(1 - x)^7$ in ascending powers of x up to and including the term in x^3.

Solution:

Using the expansion of $(1 + x)^7$ with $n = 7$ and $x = -x$

$$(1 - x)^7 = 1 + \binom{7}{1}(-x) + \binom{7}{2}(-x)^2 + \binom{7}{3}(-x)^3 + \cdots$$

$$= 1 - 7x + 21x^2 - 35x^3$$

$$\therefore \quad (1 + x + x^2)(1 - x)^7 = (1 + x + x^2)(1 - 7x + 21x^2 - 35x^3 + \cdots)$$

Expanding and ignoring terms of order x^4 and above gives:

$$
\begin{aligned}
(1 + x + x^2)(1 - x)^7 &= 1 - 7x + 21x^2 - 35x^3 \\
& + \quad x - 7x^2 + 21x^3 \\
& + \quad\quad\quad\quad x^2 - 7x^3 \\
\hline
\therefore \quad (1 + x + x^2)(1 - x)^7 &= 1 - 6x + 15x^2 - 21x^3
\end{aligned}
$$

Example

The first three terms of the expansion of $\left(p - \dfrac{x}{3}\right)^6$, in ascending powers of x, are $64 + 16bx + \frac{1}{3}bcx^2$, $a, b, c \in \textbf{\textit{R}}$. Find the value of a, of b and of c.

Solution:

$$\left(p - \frac{x}{3}\right)^6 = p^6 + \binom{6}{1}p^5\left(-\frac{x}{3}\right) + \binom{6}{2}p^4\left(-\frac{x}{3}\right)^2 + \cdots$$

$$= p^6 + 6p^5\left(-\frac{x}{3}\right) + 15p^4\left(\frac{x^2}{9}\right)$$

$$= p^6 - 2p^5x + \tfrac{5}{3}p^4x^2$$

$$= 64 + 16bx + \tfrac{1}{3}bcx^2$$

Equating coefficients gives:

$\Rightarrow \quad p^6 = 64$ ①	$16b = -2p^5$ ②	$\frac{1}{3}bc = \frac{5}{3}p^4$ ③
$p = 2$	$16b = -2(2)^5$	
$p = 2$ in ② and ③	$16b = -64$	$\frac{1}{3}(-4)(c) = \frac{5}{3}(2)^4$
	$b = -4$	$-4c = 80$
	put $b = -4$ in ③	$c = -20$

138

Example

Write down the binomial expansion of $(1 + 2x)^n$ in ascending powers of x as far as the term containing x^3.

Given that the coefficient of x^3 is twice the coefficient of x^2 and that both are positive, find the value of n.

Solution:

$$(1 + 2x)^n = 1 + \binom{n}{1}(2x) + \binom{n}{2}(2x)^2 + \binom{n}{3}(2x)^3 \quad [\text{as far as } x^3]$$

$$= 1 + n(2x) + \frac{n(n-1)}{1.2}(4x^2) + \frac{n(n-1)(n-2)}{1.2.3}(8x^3)$$

$$= 1 + 2nx + n(n-1).2x^2 + \frac{n(n-1)(n-2)}{3}.4x^3$$

$$= 1 + 2nx + 2n(n-1)x^2 + \frac{4n(n-1)(n-2)}{3}x^3$$

Given: coefficient of $x^3 = 2$ (coefficient of x^2)

$$\Rightarrow \quad \frac{4n(n-1)(n-2)}{3} = 2[2n(n-1)]$$

$$\Rightarrow \quad \frac{4n(n-1)(n-2)}{3} = 4n(n-1)$$

$$\Rightarrow \quad 4n(n-1)(n-2) = 3.4n(n-1)$$

$$\Rightarrow \quad n-2 = 3$$

$$\Rightarrow \quad n = 5$$

Note: If $n = 0$, $n = 1$, there would be no coefficient of x^3.

Example

Write out the first three terms in the expansion of $\left(x^4 + \dfrac{1}{x^4}\right)^{20}$.

Write down the general term and find the term independent of x.

Solution:

$$\left(x^4 + \frac{1}{x^4}\right)^{20} = (x^4)^{20} + \binom{20}{1}(x^4)^{19}\left(\frac{1}{x^4}\right) + \binom{20}{2}(x^4)^{18}\left(\frac{1}{x^4}\right)^2 \quad [\text{first 3 terms}]$$

$$= x^{80} + 20.x^{76}.\frac{1}{x^4} + 190x^{72}.\frac{1}{x^8}$$

$$= x^{80} + 20x^{72} + 190x^{64}$$

General term $= u_{r+1} = \dbinom{20}{r}(x^4)^{20-r}\left(\dfrac{1}{x^4}\right)^r$

$$= \dbinom{20}{r}x^{80-4r}\cdot\dfrac{1}{x^{4r}}$$

$$= \dbinom{20}{r}x^{80-4r}\cdot x^{-4r} = \dbinom{20}{r}x^{80-8r}$$

$u_{r+1} = \dbinom{20}{r}x^{80-8r}$ independent of x $\Rightarrow$ power of $x = 0$

Let $\qquad\qquad 80 - 8r = 0$

$\Rightarrow \qquad\qquad -8r = -80$

$\Rightarrow \qquad\qquad r = 10$

$u_{r+1} = u_{10+1} = u_{11}$

Thus, $u_{11} = \dbinom{20}{10}x^{80-8(10)}$

$$= \dbinom{20}{10}x^0$$

$$= \dbinom{20}{10} \quad \text{[independent of } x]$$

Thus, the eleventh term $\dbinom{20}{10}$ is independent of x.

Example

(i) Find the fifth term of $\left(x - \dfrac{1}{\sqrt{x}}\right)^{20}$.

(ii) Find, and simplify, the middle term in the expansion of $(3 - 4x)^8$.

(iii) Find the coefficient of x^{10} in the expansion of $(2x - 3)^{14}$.

(iv) Find the term independent of x in the expansion of $\left(2x - \dfrac{1}{x^2}\right)^9$ and simplify.

140

Solution:

(i) $\left(x - \dfrac{1}{\sqrt{x}}\right)^{10}$

General term:

$$u_{r+1} = \binom{20}{r}(x^{20-r})\left(\dfrac{-1}{\sqrt{x}}\right)^4$$

$u_5 = u_{r+1} \implies r = 4$

Thus, $u_5 = \binom{20}{4}(x^{20-4})\left(\dfrac{-1}{\sqrt{x}}\right)^4$

$= 4\,845(x^{16})\left(\dfrac{1}{x^2}\right)$

$= 4\,845x^{14}$

(ii) $(3 - 4x)^8$

General term:

$$u_{r+1} = \binom{8}{r}(3)^{8-r}(-4x)^r$$

There are 9 terms in the expansion. Thus, middle term is u_5.

$u_5 = u_{r+1} \implies r = 4$

$\therefore \quad u_5 = \binom{8}{4}(3^{8-4})(-4x)^4$

$= (70)(81)(256x^4)$

$= 1\,451\,520x^4$

(iii) $(2x - 3)^{14}$

General term:

$$u_{r+1} = \binom{14}{r}(2x)^{14-r}(-3)^r$$

Power of $x = 10 \implies 14 - r = 10 \implies r = 4$
[it is the fifth term]

$u_5 = \binom{14}{4}(2x)^{14-4}(-3)^4$

$= 1\,001(2x)^{10}(81)$

$= 1\,001(2^{10})x^{10}(81)$

$= 81\,081\,(2^{10})x^{10}$

$\therefore$ the coefficient is $81\,081\,(2^{10})$.

(iv) $\left(2x - \dfrac{1}{x^2}\right)^9$

General term:

$$u_{r+1} = \binom{9}{r}(2x)^{9-r}\left(\dfrac{-1}{x^2}\right)^r$$

$= \binom{9}{r}(2^{9-r})(x^{9-r})(x^{-2r})(-1)^r$

$= \binom{9}{r}(2^{9-r})(x^{9-3r})(-1)^r$

Independent of $x \implies$ power of $x = 0$

$\implies \quad 9 - 3r = 0 \implies r = 3$ [4th term]

$u_4 = \binom{9}{3}(2^{9-3})(x^{9-9})(-1)^3$

$= (84)(2^6)(x^0)(-1)$

$= 84(64)(1)(-1)$

$= -5\,376$

Relations between Binomial Coefficients

In the expansion of $(1 + x)^n$, $\binom{n}{0}, \binom{n}{1}, \binom{n}{2}, \ldots, \binom{n}{n}$ are called binomial coefficients.

Example

(i) Prove that $\binom{n}{0} + \binom{n}{1} + \binom{n}{2} + \binom{n}{3} + \cdots + \binom{n}{n} = 2^n$

Hence, prove that $\binom{n}{0} + \binom{n}{2} + \binom{n}{4} + \cdots = \binom{n}{1} + \binom{n}{3} + \binom{n}{5} + \cdots = 2^{n-1}$

(ii) Evaluate $\binom{12}{0} + \binom{12}{1} + \binom{12}{2} + \cdots + \binom{12}{11} + \binom{12}{12}$

(iii) Evaluate the sum of the coefficients in the expansion of $(x + 3)^8$.

Solution:

(i) Consider the expansion of $(1 + x)^n$.

$$(1 + x)^n = \binom{n}{0} + \binom{n}{1}x + \binom{n}{2}x^2 + \binom{n}{3}x^3 + \cdots + \binom{n}{n}x^n$$

This is true for all x. Let $x = 1$ on both sides.

$$\Rightarrow \quad (1 + 1)^n = \binom{n}{0} + \binom{n}{1} + \binom{n}{2} + \binom{n}{3} + \cdots + \binom{n}{n}$$

$$\therefore \quad 2^n = \binom{n}{0} + \binom{n}{1} + \binom{n}{2} + \binom{n}{3} + \cdots + \binom{n}{n}$$

Let $x = -1$ on both sides.

$$\Rightarrow \quad (1 - 1)^n = \binom{n}{0} - \binom{n}{1} + \binom{n}{2} - \binom{n}{3} + \binom{n}{4} - \binom{n}{5} + \cdots$$

$$\therefore \quad 0 = \binom{n}{0} - \binom{n}{1} + \binom{n}{2} - \binom{n}{3} + \binom{n}{4} - \binom{n}{5} + \cdots$$

$$\Rightarrow \quad \binom{n}{0} + \binom{n}{2} + \binom{n}{4} + \cdots = \binom{n}{1} + \binom{n}{3} + \binom{n}{5} + \cdots$$

$$= \frac{1}{2}\left[\binom{n}{0} + \binom{n}{1} + \binom{n}{2} + \binom{n}{3} + \binom{n}{4} + \binom{n}{5} + \cdots\right]$$

$$= \tfrac{1}{2}(2^n) \quad \text{[by result above]}$$

$$= 2^{n-1}$$

(ii) $\dbinom{12}{0} + \dbinom{12}{1} + \dbinom{12}{2} + \cdots + \dbinom{12}{12} = 2^{12} = 4\ 096$

(iii) $(x + 3)^8 = \dbinom{8}{0}x^8 + \dbinom{8}{1}x^7(3) + \dbinom{8}{2}x^6(3)^2 + \cdots + \dbinom{8}{8}(3)^8$

Let $x = 1$ on both sides

$\Rightarrow\ (1 + 3)^8 = \dbinom{8}{0} + \dbinom{8}{1}(3) + \dbinom{8}{2}(3)^2 + \cdots + \dbinom{8}{8}(3)^8 = 4^8$

Thus, the sum of the coefficients is $4^8 = 65\ 536$.

Chapter 5
Differential Calculus

Limits of Functions

Example

Evaluate **(i)** $\lim\limits_{x \to 4} \dfrac{x^2 - 16}{x - 4}$ **(ii)** $\lim\limits_{t \to 2} \dfrac{t^3 - 8}{t^2 - 4}$ **(iii)** $\lim\limits_{x \to 3} \dfrac{x - 3}{1 - \sqrt{4 - x}}$.

Solution:

(i) $\lim\limits_{x \to 4} \dfrac{x^2 - 16}{x - 4} = \dfrac{0}{0}$ [indeterminate]

Thus, factorise top and bottom, simplify and try again.

$$\lim_{x \to 4} \frac{x^2 - 16}{x - 4}$$

$$= \lim_{x \to 4} \frac{(x - 4)(x + 4)}{(x - 4)}$$

$$= \lim_{x \to 4} (x + 4) = 4 + 4 = 8$$

(ii) $\lim\limits_{t \to 2} \dfrac{t^3 - 8}{t^2 - 4} = \dfrac{0}{0}$ [indeterminate]

Thus, factorise top and bottom, simplify and try again.

$$\lim_{t \to 2} \frac{t^3 - 8}{t^2 - 4}$$

$$= \lim_{t \to 2} \frac{(t - 2)(t^2 + 2t + 4)}{(t - 2)(t + 2)}$$

$$= \lim_{t \to 2} \frac{t^2 + 2t + 4}{t + 2} = \frac{4 + 4 + 4}{4} = 3$$

(iii) $\lim\limits_{x \to 3} \dfrac{x - 3}{1 - \sqrt{4 - x}} = \dfrac{0}{0}$ [indeterminate]

What we do here is multiply top and bottom by $(1 + \sqrt{4 - x})$,

the conjugate surd of $(1 - \sqrt{4 - x})$, simplify and try again.

$$\text{Thus, } \lim_{x \to 3} \frac{x - 3}{1 - \sqrt{4 - x}} = \lim_{x \to 3} \frac{(x - 3)}{(1 - \sqrt{4 - x})} \cdot \frac{1 + \sqrt{4 - x}}{1 + \sqrt{4 - x}}$$

$$= \lim_{x \to 3} \frac{(x - 3)(1 + \sqrt{4 - x})}{[1 - (4 - x)]} \quad \leftarrow [\text{do not multiply out top}]$$

$$= \lim_{x \to 3} \frac{(x - 3)(1 + \sqrt{4 - x})}{(x - 3)}$$

$$= \lim_{x \to 3} (1 + \sqrt{4 - x}) = 1 + 1 = 2$$

Trigonometric Functions

$$\lim_{\theta \to 0} \frac{\sin k\theta}{k\theta} = 1 = \lim_{\theta \to 0} \frac{k\theta}{\sin k\theta}, \quad k \in \mathbf{R}$$

Note: $\lim_{\theta \to 0} \cos \theta = 1$

Example

Find
(i) $\lim_{x \to 0} \dfrac{\sin 5x + \sin 3x}{x}$

(ii) $\lim_{\theta \to 0} \dfrac{5\theta}{\sin 4\theta}$

(iii) $\lim_{x \to 0} \dfrac{2x^2}{1 - \cos x}$

(iv) $\lim_{\theta \to 0} \dfrac{\sin 2\theta}{\sin 3\theta}$

(v) $\lim_{\theta \to 0} \dfrac{\tan 4\theta}{5\theta}$

(vi) $\lim_{x \to 0} \dfrac{\cos 5x - \cos 3x}{\cos 4x - \cos 2x}$

Solution:

(i) $\lim_{x \to 0} \dfrac{\sin 5x + \sin 3x}{x}$

$= \lim_{x \to 0} \dfrac{\sin 5x}{x} + \lim_{x \to 0} \dfrac{\sin 3x}{x}$

$= \lim_{x \to 0} \dfrac{\sin 5x}{5x} \cdot 5 + \lim_{x \to 0} \dfrac{\sin 3x}{3x} \cdot 3$

$= (1)(5) + (1)(3) = 5 + 3 = 8$

(ii) $\lim_{\theta \to 0} \dfrac{5\theta}{\sin 4\theta}$

$\lim_{\theta \to 0} \dfrac{\theta}{\sin 4\theta} \cdot \dfrac{5}{1}$

$\lim_{\theta \to 0} \dfrac{4\theta}{\sin 4\theta} \cdot \dfrac{5}{4}$

$= (1)\left(\dfrac{5}{4}\right) = \dfrac{5}{4}$

(iii) $\lim_{x \to 0} \dfrac{2x^2}{1 - \cos x}$

$= \lim_{x \to 0} \dfrac{2x^2}{2 \sin^2 \frac{x}{2}} = \lim_{x \to 0} \dfrac{x}{\sin \frac{x}{2}} \cdot \dfrac{x}{\sin \frac{x}{2}}$

$= \lim_{x \to 0} \dfrac{\frac{x}{2}}{\sin \frac{x}{2}} \cdot \dfrac{\frac{x}{2}}{\sin \frac{x}{2}} \cdot 4$

$= (1)(1)(4) = 4$

$\cos 2x = 1 - 2 \sin^2 x \quad \text{[tables]}$

$\Rightarrow \quad \cos x = 1 - 2 \sin^2 \dfrac{x}{2}$

$\therefore \quad 1 - \cos x$

$= 1 - \left(1 - 2 \sin^2 \dfrac{x}{2}\right)$

$= 2 \sin^2 \dfrac{x}{2}$

(iv) $\displaystyle\lim_{\theta\to0}\frac{\sin2\theta}{\sin3\theta} = \lim_{\theta\to0}\frac{\sin2\theta}{1}\cdot\frac{1}{\sin3\theta}$

$\displaystyle = \lim_{\theta\to0}\frac{\sin2\theta}{2\theta}\cdot\frac{3\theta}{\sin3\theta}\cdot\frac{2}{3}$

$\displaystyle = (1)(1)\left(\frac{2}{3}\right) = \frac{2}{3}$

(v) $\displaystyle\lim_{\theta\to0}\frac{\tan4\theta}{5\theta}$

$\displaystyle = \lim_{\theta\to0}\frac{\sin4\theta}{\cos4\theta}\cdot\frac{1}{5\theta}$

$\displaystyle = \lim_{\theta\to0}\frac{\sin4\theta}{1}\cdot\frac{1}{\cos4\theta}\cdot\frac{1}{5\theta}$

$\displaystyle = \lim_{\theta\to0}\frac{\sin4\theta}{4\theta}\cdot\frac{1}{\cos4\theta}\cdot\frac{4}{5}$

$\displaystyle = (1)(1)\left(\frac{4}{5}\right)$

$\displaystyle = \frac{4}{5}$

(vi) $\displaystyle\lim_{x\to0}\frac{\cos5x - \cos3x}{\cos4x - \cos2x}$

$\displaystyle = \lim_{x\to0}\frac{-2\sin4x\sin x}{-2\sin3x\sin x}$ [tables, page 9]

$\displaystyle = \lim_{x\to0}\frac{\sin4x}{\sin3x}$

$\displaystyle = \lim_{x\to0}\frac{\sin4x}{1}\cdot\frac{1}{\sin3x}$

$\displaystyle = \lim_{x\to0}\frac{\sin4x}{4x}\cdot\frac{3x}{\cos3x}\cdot\frac{4}{3}$

$\displaystyle = (1)(1)\left(\frac{4}{3}\right) = \frac{4}{3}$

Differentiation from First Principles

$$\frac{dy}{dx} = f'(x) = \lim_{h\to0}\frac{f(x+h)-f(x)}{h}$$

Method: Find:

1. $f(x+h)$

2. $f(x+h)-f(x)$

3. $\dfrac{f(x+h)-f(x)}{h}$

4. $\displaystyle\lim_{h\to0}\frac{f(x+h)-f(x)}{h}$

There are six functions on our course that we can be asked to differentiate from first

principles: x^2, x^3, $\sqrt{x}$, $\dfrac{1}{x}$, $\sin x$, $\cos x$.

146

Example

Differentiate from first principles with respect to x:

(i) x^2

(ii) x^3

(iii) $\sqrt{x}$

(iv) $\dfrac{1}{x}$

(v) $\sin x$

(vi) $\cos x$

Solution:

(i)
$$f(x) = x^2$$
$$f(x + h) = (x + h)^2$$
$$f(x + h) - f(x) = (x + h)^2 - x^2$$
$$= x^2 + 2xh + h^2 - x^2$$
$$= 2xh + h^2$$
$$\frac{f(x + h) - f(x)}{h} = 2x + h$$
$$\lim_{h \to 0} \frac{f(x + h) - f(x)}{h} = \lim_{h \to 0} 2x + h$$
$$= 2x$$

Thus, $f'(x) = 2x$.

(ii)
$$f(x) = x^3$$
$$f(x + h) = (x + h)^3$$
$$f(x + h) - f(x) = (x + h)^3 - x^3$$
$$= x^3 + 3x^2h + 3xh^2 + h^3 - x^3$$
$$= 3x^2h + 3xh^2 + h^3$$
$$\frac{f(x + h) - f(x)}{h} = 3x^2 + 3xh + h^2$$
$$\lim_{h \to 0} \frac{f(x + h) - f(x)}{h} = \lim_{h \to 0} (3x^2 + 3xh + h^2)$$
$$= 3x^2$$

Thus, $f'(x) = 3x^2$.

(iii)

$$f(x) = \sqrt{x}$$

$$f(x + h) = \sqrt{x + h}$$

$$f(x + h) - f(x) = \sqrt{x + h} - \sqrt{x} \quad \left[\begin{array}{l}\text{multiply top and bottom by } \sqrt{x + h} + \sqrt{x}, \\ \text{the conjugate surd of } \sqrt{x + h} - \sqrt{x}\end{array}\right]$$

$$= \frac{\sqrt{x + h} - \sqrt{x}}{1} \cdot \frac{\sqrt{x + h} + \sqrt{x}}{\sqrt{x + h} + \sqrt{x}}$$

$$= \frac{x + h - x}{\sqrt{x + h} + \sqrt{x}}$$

$$= \frac{h}{\sqrt{x + h} + \sqrt{x}}$$

$$\frac{f(x + h) - f(x)}{h} = \frac{1}{\sqrt{x + h} + \sqrt{x}}$$

$$\lim_{h \to 0} \frac{f(x + h) - f(x)}{h} = \lim_{h \to 0} \frac{1}{\sqrt{x + h} + \sqrt{x}} = \frac{1}{\sqrt{x} + \sqrt{x}} = \frac{1}{2\sqrt{x}}$$

Thus, $f'(x) = \dfrac{1}{2\sqrt{x}}$.

(iv)

$$f(x) = \frac{1}{x}$$

$$f(x + h) = \frac{1}{x + h}$$

$$f(x + h) - f(x) = \frac{1}{x + h} - \frac{1}{x}$$

$$= \frac{x - (x + h)}{x(x + h)}$$

$$= \frac{-h}{x(x + h)}$$

$$\frac{f(x + h) - f(x)}{h} = \frac{-1}{x(x + h)}$$

$$\lim_{h \to 0} \frac{f(x + h) - f(x)}{h} = \lim_{h \to 0} \frac{-1}{x(x + h)} = -\frac{1}{x^2}$$

Thus, $f'(x) = -\dfrac{1}{x^2}$.

(v)

$$f(x) = \sin x$$

$$f(x + h) = \sin(x + h)$$

$$f(x + h) - f(x) = \sin(x + h) - \sin x$$

$$= 2 \cos\left(\frac{x + h + x}{2}\right) \sin\left(\frac{x + h - x}{2}\right) \quad \text{[tables, page 9]}$$

$$= 2 \cos\left(\frac{2x + h}{2}\right) \sin\left(\frac{h}{2}\right)$$

$$\frac{f(x + h) - f(x)}{h} = 2 \cos\left(\frac{2x + h}{2}\right) \cdot \frac{\sin\left(\frac{h}{2}\right)}{h}$$

$$= \cos\left(\frac{2x + h}{2}\right) \cdot \frac{\sin\frac{h}{2}}{\frac{h}{2}} \quad \text{[divide top and bottom by 2]}$$

$$\lim_{h \to 0} \frac{f(x + h) - f(x)}{h} = \lim_{h \to 0} \cos\left(\frac{2x + h}{2}\right) \cdot \frac{\sin\frac{h}{2}}{\frac{h}{2}}$$

$$= (\cos x)(1) = \cos x$$

Thus, $f'(x) = \cos x$.

(vi)

$$f(x) = \cos x$$

$$f(x + h) = \cos(x + h)$$

$$f(x + h) - f(x) = \cos(x + h) - \cos x$$

$$= -2 \sin\left(\frac{x + h + x}{2}\right) \sin\left(\frac{x+h-x}{2}\right) \quad \text{[tables, page 9]}$$

$$= -2 \sin\left(\frac{2x + h}{2}\right) \sin\left(\frac{h}{2}\right)$$

$$\frac{f(x + h) - f(x)}{h} = -2 \sin\left(\frac{2x + h}{2}\right) \cdot \frac{\sin\left(\frac{h}{2}\right)}{h}$$

$$= -\sin\left(\frac{2x + h}{2}\right) \cdot \frac{\sin\frac{h}{2}}{\frac{h}{2}} \quad \text{[divide top and bottom by 2]}$$

$$\lim_{h \to 0} \frac{f(x + h) - f(x)}{h} = \lim_{h \to 0} -\sin\left(\frac{2x + h}{2}\right) \cdot \frac{\sin\left(\frac{h}{2}\right)}{\frac{h}{2}}$$

$$= (-\sin x)(1) = -\sin x$$

Thus, $f'(x) = -\sin x$.

Differentiation by Rule

Let u and v be functions of x, and n and a are constants.

	$f(x)$	$f'(x)$
Basic Rules	a	0
	x^n	nx^{n-1}
	ax^n	nax^{n-1}
Product Rule	uv	$u\dfrac{dv}{dx} + v\dfrac{du}{dx}$
Quotient Rule	$\dfrac{u}{v}$	$\dfrac{v\dfrac{du}{dx} - u\dfrac{dv}{dx}}{v^2}$
Chain Rule	$y(u)$	$\dfrac{dy}{du} \cdot \dfrac{du}{dx}$
extended	$y[u(v)]$	$\dfrac{dy}{du} \cdot \dfrac{du}{dv} \cdot \dfrac{dv}{dx}$
	u^n	$nu^{n-1}\dfrac{du}{dx}$

The following are in the tables on page 41, but they are shown only for x.
The chain rule is used throughout, assuming u is a function of x. Therefore, if you are using the tables, replace x with u and **always** multiply by $\dfrac{du}{dx}$.

Note: For $\sin^{-1}\dfrac{x}{a}$ and $\tan^{-1}\dfrac{x}{a}$, assume $a = 1$ and continue as above.

$f(x)$	$f'(x)$
cos u	$-\sin u \cdot \dfrac{du}{dx}$
sin u	$\cos u \cdot \dfrac{du}{dx}$
tan u	$\sec^2 u \cdot \dfrac{du}{dx}$
sec u	$\sec u \tan u \cdot \dfrac{du}{dx}$
cosec u	$-\text{cosec}\, u \cot u \cdot \dfrac{du}{dx}$

$f(x)$	$f'(x)$
cot u	$-\text{cosec}^2 u \cdot \dfrac{du}{dx}$
e^u	$e^u \cdot \dfrac{du}{dx}$
ln u	$\dfrac{1}{u} \cdot \dfrac{du}{dx}$
$\sin^{-1} u$	$\dfrac{1}{\sqrt{1-u^2}} \cdot \dfrac{du}{dx}$
$\tan^{-1} u$	$\dfrac{1}{1+u^2} \cdot \dfrac{du}{dx}$

Example

Find the derivatives of the functions:

(i) $\dfrac{x^2 - 1}{x^2 + 1}$

(ii) $(2x + 1)^3$

(iii) $\sqrt{1 + 3x}$

(iv) $\sqrt{\dfrac{1 - x}{1 + x}}$

(v) $\cos(3x - 1)$

(vi) $\tan^2 3\theta$

(vii) $3\sin^5(x^2 - 3x)$

(viii) $\left(x^2 + \dfrac{3}{x}\right)^2$

(ix) $\dfrac{1}{x^2} + \dfrac{1}{x} + \dfrac{1}{\sqrt{x}}$

Solution:

(i) $\quad y = \dfrac{x^2 - 1}{x^2 + 1}$

$$\frac{dy}{dx} = \frac{(x^2 + 1)(2x) - (x^2 - 1)(2x)}{(x^2 + 1)^2}$$

$$= \frac{2x^3 + 2x - 2x^3 + 2x}{(x^2 + 1)^2}$$

$$= \frac{4x}{(x^2 + 1)^2}$$

(ii) $y = (2x + 1)^3$

(power of 3 is dominant, $\therefore$ use chain rule)

$$\frac{dy}{dx} = 3(2x + 1)^2(2) = 6(2x + 1)^2$$

(iii) $y = \sqrt{1 + 3x} = (1 + 3x)^{\frac{1}{2}}$

(power of $\frac{1}{2}$ is dominant, $\therefore$ use chain rule)

$$\frac{dy}{dx} = \frac{1}{2}(1 + 3x)^{-\frac{1}{2}}(3)$$

$$= \frac{3}{2(1 + 3x)^{\frac{1}{2}}} = \frac{3}{2\sqrt{1 + 3x}}$$

(iv) $y = \sqrt{\dfrac{1 - x}{1 + x}} = \left(\dfrac{1 - x}{1 + x}\right)^{\frac{1}{2}}$

(power of $\frac{1}{2}$ is dominant, $\therefore$ use chain rule)

$$\frac{dy}{dx} = \frac{1}{2}\left(\frac{1 - x}{1 + x}\right)^{-\frac{1}{2}}\left[\frac{(1 + x)(-1) - (1 - x)(1)}{(1 + x)^2}\right]$$

$$= \frac{1}{2}\left(\frac{1 + x}{1 - x}\right)^{\frac{1}{2}}\left[\frac{-1 - x - 1 + x}{(1 + x)^2}\right]$$

$$= \frac{(1 + x)^{\frac{1}{2}}}{2(1 - x)^{\frac{1}{2}}} \cdot \frac{-2}{(1 + x)^2}$$

$$= \frac{-1}{(1 - x)^{\frac{1}{2}}(1 + x)^{\frac{3}{2}}}$$

(v) $y = \cos(3x - 1)$

$$\frac{dy}{dx} = -\sin(3x - 1)(3)$$

$$= -3\sin(3x - 1)$$

(vi) $y = \tan^2 3\theta = (\tan 3\theta)^2$

(power of 2 is dominant, $\therefore$ use chain rule)

$$\frac{dy}{dx} = 2(\tan 3\theta)(\sec^2 3\theta)(3)$$

$$= 6\tan 3\theta \sec^2 3\theta$$

(vii) $y = 3 \sin^5(x^2 - 3x)$

$y = 3[\sin(x^2 - 3x)]^5$ (power of 5 is dominant, $\therefore$ use chain rule)

$\dfrac{dy}{dx} = 15[\sin(x^2 - 3x)]^4[\cos(x^2 - 3x)](2x - 3)$

$\qquad = 15(2x - 3) \sin^4(x^2 - 3x) \cos(x^2 - 3x)$

(viii) $y = \left(x^2 + \dfrac{3}{x}\right)^2 = (x^2 + 3x^{-1})^2$

$\dfrac{dy}{dx} = 2(x^2 + 3x^{-1})(2x - 3x^{-2})$

$\qquad = 2\left(x^2 + \dfrac{3}{x}\right)\left(2x - \dfrac{3}{x^2}\right)$

$\qquad = 4x^3 + 6 - \dfrac{18}{x^3}$

(ix) $y = \dfrac{1}{x^2} + \dfrac{1}{x} + \dfrac{1}{\sqrt{x}}$

$y = x^{-2} + x^{-1} + x^{-\frac{1}{2}}$

$\dfrac{dy}{dx} = -2x^{-3} - x^{-2} - \dfrac{1}{2}x^{-\frac{3}{2}}$

$\qquad = -\dfrac{2}{x^3} - \dfrac{1}{x^2} - \dfrac{1}{2x^{\frac{3}{2}}}$

Example

Find the derivatives of the functions:

(i) $\sin^{-1} 3x$

(ii) $(\sin^{-1} 5x)^2$

(iii) $\tan^{-1} \dfrac{x}{1 + x}$

(iv) $\tan^{-1}(2\theta^3)$

Solution:

(i) $y = \sin^{-1} 3x$

$\dfrac{dy}{dx} = \dfrac{1}{\sqrt{1 - (3x)^2}} \cdot 3$

$\qquad = \dfrac{3}{\sqrt{1 - 9x^2}}$

(ii) $y = (\sin^{-1} 5x)^2$

$\dfrac{dy}{dx} = 2(\sin^{-1} 5x)^1 \cdot \dfrac{1}{\sqrt{1 - (5x)^2}} \cdot 5$

$\qquad = \dfrac{10 \sin^{-1} 5x}{\sqrt{1 - 25x^2}}$

(iii) $\quad y = \tan^{-1} \dfrac{x}{1+x}$

$$\dfrac{dy}{dx} = \dfrac{1}{1 + \left(\dfrac{x}{1+x}\right)^2} \cdot \left(\dfrac{(1+x)(1) - (x)(1)}{(1+x)^2}\right)$$

$$= \dfrac{1}{1 + \dfrac{x^2}{(1+x)^2}} \cdot \left(\dfrac{1 + x - x}{(1+x)^2}\right)$$

$$= \dfrac{(1+x)^2}{(1+x)^2 + x^2} \cdot \dfrac{1}{(1+x)^2}$$

$$= \dfrac{1}{(1+x)^2 + x^2}$$

(iv) $\quad y = \tan^{-1}(2\theta^3)$

$$\dfrac{dy}{dx} = \dfrac{1}{1 + (2\theta^3)^2} \cdot 6\theta^2$$

$$= \dfrac{6\theta^2}{1 + 4\theta^6}$$

Laws of Logs

$\ln ab = \ln a + \ln b$	$\ln \dfrac{a}{b} = \ln a - \ln b$	$\ln a^n = n \ln a$

Using the laws of logs before differentiating can simplify the work.

Example

Find the derivatives of the functions:

(i) $\ln (3x^2 + 1)$

(ii) $\ln (\tan x)$

(iii) $e^{\cos 3x}$

(iv) $e^{4x^2 + \sin x}$

(v) $\ln \dfrac{e^x}{1 + e^x}$

(vi) $\ln \sqrt{\sin x}$

(vii) $\ln \left(\dfrac{1 + \sin x}{1 - \sin x}\right)$

Solution:

(i) $\quad y = \ln (3x^2 + 1)$

$$\dfrac{dy}{dx} = \dfrac{1}{3x^2 + 1} \cdot 6x$$

$$= \dfrac{6x}{3x^2 + 1}$$

(ii) $\quad y = \ln (\tan x)$

$$\dfrac{dy}{dx} = \dfrac{1}{\tan x} \cdot \sec^2 x$$

$$= \dfrac{\sec^2 x}{\tan x}$$

(iii) $y = e^{\cos 3x}$

$$\frac{dy}{dx} = e^{\cos 3x}(-\sin 3x)(3)$$

$$= -3 \sin 3x . e^{\cos 3x}$$

(iv) $y = e^{4x^2 + \sin x}$

$$\frac{dy}{dx} = e^{4x^2 + \sin x}(8x + \cos x)$$

$$= (8x + \cos x)e^{4x^2 + \sin x}$$

(v) $y = \ln \dfrac{e^x}{1 + e^x}$

$$y = \ln e^x - \ln(1 + e^x)$$

$$\frac{dy}{dx} = \frac{1}{e^x} \cdot e^x - \frac{1}{1 + e^x} \cdot e^x$$

$$= \frac{e^x}{e^x} - \frac{e^x}{1 + e^x}$$

$$= \frac{1}{1} - \frac{e^x}{1 + e^x}$$

$$= \frac{1 + e^x - e^x}{1 + e^x} = \frac{1}{1 + e^x}$$

Method 1

(vi) $y = \ln \sqrt{\sin x} = \ln [(\sin x)^{\frac{1}{2}}]$

$$\frac{dy}{dx} = \frac{1}{(\sin x)^{\frac{1}{2}}} \cdot \frac{1}{2}(\sin x)^{-\frac{1}{2}}(\cos x)$$

$$= \frac{\cos x}{2(\sin x)^{\frac{1}{2}}(\sin x)^{\frac{1}{2}}} = \frac{\cos x}{2 \sin x} = \frac{1}{2}\cot x$$

Method 2 (using laws of logs)

(vi) $y = \ln [(\sin x)^{\frac{1}{2}}]$

$$y = \tfrac{1}{2}\ln(\sin x)$$

$$\frac{dy}{dx} = \frac{1}{2} \cdot \frac{1}{\sin x} \cdot \cos x$$

$$= \frac{\cos x}{2 \sin x} = \frac{1}{2}\cot x$$

(vii) $y = \ln \dfrac{1 + \sin x}{1 - \sin x} = \ln(1 + \sin x) - \ln(1 - \sin x)$

$$\frac{dy}{dx} = \frac{1}{1 + \sin x} \cdot \cos x - \frac{1}{1 - \sin x} \cdot - \cos x$$

$$= \frac{\cos x}{1 + \sin x} + \frac{\cos x}{1 - \sin x}$$

$$= \frac{\cos x - \cos x \sin x + \cos x + \cos x \sin x}{(1 + \sin x)(1 - \sin x)} = \frac{2 \cos x}{1 - \sin^2 x}$$

$$= \frac{2 \cos x}{\cos^2 x} = 2 \sec x$$

Combinations of the product rule, quotient rule, chain rule.

Example

Find the derivatives of the functions:

(i) $x^2 \ln(2x + 1)$ (ii) $e^{2x} \cos x$ (iii) $\dfrac{3x + 2}{(x + 1)^3}$ (iv) $(x + 1)^4(2x - 1)^3$

Solution:

(i) $y = x^2 \ln(2x + 1)$

$$\frac{dy}{dx} = x^2 \cdot \frac{1}{2x + 1} \cdot 2 + \ln(2x + 1)(2x)$$

$$= \frac{2x^2}{2x + 1} + 2x \ln(2x + 1)$$

(ii) $y = e^{2x} \cos x$

$$\frac{dy}{dx} = e^{2x}(-\sin x) + \cos x(e^{2x})(2)$$

$$= 2e^{2x} \cos x - e^{2x} \sin x$$

$$= e^{2x}(2 \cos x - \sin x)$$

(iii) $y = \dfrac{3x + 2}{(x + 1)^3}$

$$\frac{dy}{dx} = \frac{(x + 1)^3(3) - (3x + 2)3(x + 1)^2(1)}{(x + 1)^6}$$

[now divide each part by $(x + 1)^2$]

$$= \frac{(x + 1)(3) - 3(3x + 2)}{(x + 1)^4}$$

$$= \frac{-6x - 3}{(x + 1)^4} = \frac{-3(2x + 1)}{(x + 1)^4}$$

(iv) $y = (x + 1)^4(2x - 1)^3$

$$\frac{dy}{dx} = (x + 1)^4 3(2x - 1)^2(2) + (2x - 1)^3 4(x + 1)^3(1)$$

$$= 6(x + 1)^4(2x - 1)^2 + 4(x + 1)^3(2x - 1)^3$$

$$= 2(x + 1)^3(2x - 1)^2[3(x + 1) + 2(2x - 1)]$$

$$= 2(x + 1)^3(2x - 1)^2(7x + 1)$$

Evaluating Derivatives

Example

(i)　If $y = 2 \sin x \cos x$, evaluate $\dfrac{dy}{dx}$ at $x = \dfrac{\pi}{8}$.

(ii)　If $y = x^2 \ln x$, evaluate $\dfrac{dy}{dx}$ at $x = e$.

(iii)　If $y = \ln e^{-x} \sqrt{\dfrac{1 + 2x}{1 - 2x}}$, show that $\dfrac{dy}{dx} = \dfrac{1 + 4x^2}{1 - 4x^2}$

　　　and find the value of $\dfrac{dy}{dx}$ at $x = -1$.

Solution:

(i)
$$y = 2 \sin x \cos x = \sin 2x$$

$$\frac{dy}{dx} = 2 \cos 2x$$

$$\left. \frac{dy}{dx} \right|_{x = \frac{\pi}{8}} = 2 \cos \frac{\pi}{4} = 2 \frac{1}{\sqrt{2}} = \sqrt{2}$$

(ii)
$$y = x^2 \ln x$$

$$\frac{dy}{dx} = x^2 \cdot \left(\frac{1}{x} \right) + \ln x \, (2x)$$

$$= x + 2x \ln x$$

$$\left. \frac{dy}{dx} \right|_{x = e} = e + 2e \ln e$$

$$= e + 2e(1) = e + 2e = 3e$$

(iii)
$$y = \ln e^{-x} \sqrt{\frac{1 + 2x}{1 - 2x}} = \ln e^{-x} \frac{\sqrt{1 + 2x}}{\sqrt{1 - 2x}} = \ln e^{-x} \frac{(1 + 2x)^{\frac{1}{2}}}{(1 - 2x)^{\frac{1}{2}}}$$

$$y = \ln e^{-x} + \ln (1 + 2x)^{\frac{1}{2}} - \ln (1 - 2x)^{\frac{1}{2}}$$

$$y = -x \ln e + \tfrac{1}{2} \ln (1 + 2x) - \tfrac{1}{2} \ln (1 - 2x)$$

$$y = -x + \tfrac{1}{2} \ln (1 + 2x) - \tfrac{1}{2} \ln (1 - 2x) \quad [\ln e = 1]$$

$$\frac{dy}{dx} = -1 + \frac{1}{2} \cdot \frac{1}{1 + 2x} \cdot (2) - \frac{1}{2} \cdot \frac{1}{1 - 2x} \cdot (-2)$$

$$= -1 + \frac{1}{1 + 2x} + \frac{1}{1 - 2x}$$

$$= \frac{-(1 + 2x)(1 - 2x) + (1 - 2x) + (1 + 2x)}{(1 + 2x)(1 - 2x)}$$

$$= \frac{-1 + 4x^2 + 1 - 2x + 1 + 2x}{1 - 4x^2} = \frac{1 + 4x^2}{1 - 4x^2}$$

$$\left. \frac{dy}{dx} \right|_{x = -1} = \frac{1 + 4(-1)^2}{1 - 4(-1)^2} = \frac{1 + 4}{1 - 4} = -\frac{5}{3}$$

Implicit Differentiation

An implicit function involving x and y can be differentiated with respect to x as it stands, using the chain rule.

It is useful to remember that, by the chain rule,

$$\frac{d}{dx}(y^2) = 2y\frac{dy}{dx} \quad \text{and} \quad \frac{d}{dx}(y^3) = 3y^2\frac{dy}{dx}$$

as y is considered as a function of x.

Method:

1. Differentiate, term by term, on both sides with respect to x.

2. Bring all terms with $\frac{dy}{dx}$ to the left and bring all other terms to the right.

3. Make $\frac{dy}{dx}$ the subject of the equation.

Example

(i)   Given $2x^2 + y^2 = 4x$, evaluate $\frac{dy}{dx}$ at the point $(1, \sqrt{2})$.

(ii)   Given $2x^3 = 3xy^2 - y^3 + 6 = 0$, evaluate $\frac{dy}{dx}$ at the point $(-1, 1)$.

Solution:

(i) $2x^2 + y^2 = 4x$

$$4x + 2y\frac{dy}{dx} = 4$$

$$2x + y\frac{dy}{dx} = 2$$

$$y\frac{dy}{dx} = 2 - 2x$$

$$\frac{dy}{dx} = \frac{2 - 2x}{y}$$

$$= \frac{2(1 - x)}{y}$$

$$\left.\frac{dy}{dx}\right|_{\substack{x=1 \\ y=\sqrt{2}}} = \frac{2(1 - 1)}{\sqrt{2}} = 0$$

(use product rule here)

(ii)
$$2x^3 + 3xy^2 - y^3 + 6 = 0$$

$$6x^2 + 3\left[x \cdot 2y\frac{dy}{dx} + y^2(1)\right] - 3y^2\frac{dy}{dx} = 0$$

$$6x^2 + 6xy\frac{dy}{dx} + 3y^2 - 3y^2\frac{dy}{dx} = 0$$

$$6xy\frac{dy}{dx} - 3y^2\frac{dy}{dx} = -6x^2 - 3y^2$$

$$\frac{dy}{dx}(6xy - 3y^2) = -6x^2 - 3y^2$$

$$\frac{dy}{dx} = \frac{-6x^2 - 3y^2}{6xy - 3y^2} = \frac{2x^2 + y^2}{y^2 - 2xy} = \frac{2x^2 + y^2}{y(y - 2x)}$$

$$\left.\frac{dy}{dx}\right|_{\substack{x=-1\\y=1}} = \frac{2(-1)^2 + (1)^2}{1(1 + 2)} = \frac{3}{3} = 1$$

Parametric Differentiation

If x and y are each expressed in terms of a third variable, say t (or θ), called the parameter, then $x = f(t)$ and $y = g(t)$ give the parametric form of the equation relating to x and y.

To find $\dfrac{dy}{dx}$, do the following:

1. Find $\dfrac{dx}{dt}$ and $\dfrac{dy}{dt}$, separately.	**2.** Use $\dfrac{dy}{dx} = \dfrac{dy}{dt} \cdot \dfrac{dt}{dx}$.

Example

(i) Given that $x = \dfrac{t - 2}{t + 1}$ and $y = \dfrac{t + 2}{t + 1}$, find the value of $\dfrac{dy}{dx}$.

(ii) If $x = a(\cos\theta + \theta\sin\theta)$ and $y = a(\sin\theta - \theta\cos\theta)$, show that $\dfrac{dy}{dx} = \tan\theta$.

$$\left[a \neq 0,\ -\pi < \theta < \pi \text{ and } \theta \neq \pm\frac{\pi}{2}\right]$$

Solution:

(i) $\quad x = \dfrac{t-2}{t+1}$ $\qquad\qquad\qquad\qquad\qquad\qquad$ $y = \dfrac{t+2}{t+1}$

$\qquad \dfrac{dx}{dt} = \dfrac{(t+1)(1) - (t-2)(1)}{(t+1)^2}$ $\qquad\qquad$ $\dfrac{dy}{dt} = \dfrac{(t+1)(1) - (t+2)(1)}{(t+1)^2}$

$\qquad\qquad = \dfrac{3}{(t+1)^2}$ $\qquad\qquad\qquad\qquad\qquad$ $= \dfrac{-1}{(t+1)^2}$

$\dfrac{dy}{dx} = \dfrac{dy}{dt} \cdot \dfrac{dt}{dx} = \dfrac{-1}{(t+1)^2} \cdot \dfrac{(t+1)^2}{3} = -\dfrac{1}{3}$

(ii) $\quad x = a(\cos\theta + \theta\sin\theta)$ $\qquad\qquad\qquad$ $y = a(\sin\theta - \theta\cos\theta)$

$\qquad \dfrac{dx}{d\theta} = a(-\sin\theta + \theta.\cos\theta + \sin\theta.1)$ $\qquad$ $\dfrac{dy}{d\theta} = a[\cos\theta - (\theta.-\sin\theta + \cos\theta.1)]$

$\qquad\qquad = a(-\sin\theta + \theta\cos\theta + \sin\theta)$ $\qquad\qquad = a(\cos\theta + \theta\sin\theta - \cos\theta)$

$\qquad\qquad = a\,\theta\cos\theta$ $\qquad\qquad\qquad\qquad\qquad\quad = a\,\theta\sin\theta$

$\dfrac{dy}{dx} = \dfrac{dy}{d\theta} \cdot \dfrac{d\theta}{dx} = \dfrac{a\theta\sin\theta}{a\theta\cos\theta} = \dfrac{\sin\theta}{\cos\theta} = \tan\theta$

Example

Given that $x = e^\theta \cos\theta$ and $y = e^\theta \sin\theta$, where $\dfrac{-3\pi}{4} < \theta < \dfrac{\pi}{4}$, show that

(i) $\quad \left(\dfrac{dx}{d\theta}\right)^2 + \left(\dfrac{dy}{d\theta}\right)^2 = 2e^{2\theta}$

(ii) $\quad \dfrac{dy}{dx} = \tan\left(\theta + \dfrac{\pi}{4}\right)$.

Solution:

$\qquad x = e^\theta \cos\theta$ $\qquad\qquad\qquad\qquad\qquad$ $y = e^\theta \sin\theta$

$\qquad \dfrac{dx}{d\theta} = e^\theta(-\sin\theta) + \cos\theta\,(e^\theta)$ $\qquad$ $\dfrac{dy}{d\theta} = e^\theta(\cos\theta) + \sin\theta\,(e^\theta)$

$\qquad\qquad = e^\theta(\cos\theta - \sin\theta)$ $\qquad\qquad\qquad = e^\theta(\cos\theta + \sin\theta)$

(i) $\left(\dfrac{dx}{d\theta}\right)^2 + \left(\dfrac{dy}{d\theta}\right)^2 = [e^\theta(\cos\theta - \sin\theta)]^2 + [e^\theta(\cos\theta + \sin\theta)]^2$

$\qquad\qquad\qquad\qquad\qquad = e^{2\theta}[\cos^2\theta - 2\sin\theta\cos\theta + \sin^2\theta + \cos^2\theta + 2\sin\theta\cos\theta + \sin^2\theta]$

$\qquad\qquad\qquad\qquad\qquad = e^{2\theta}[2(\cos^2\theta + \sin^2\theta)]$

$\qquad\qquad\qquad\qquad\qquad = 2e^{2\theta}$

(ii) $\dfrac{dy}{dx} = \dfrac{dy}{d\theta} \cdot \dfrac{d\theta}{dx}$

$$= \dfrac{e^{\theta}(\cos\theta + \sin\theta)}{e^{\theta}(\cos\theta - \sin\theta)}$$

$$= \dfrac{\cos\theta + \sin\theta}{\cos\theta - \sin\theta}$$

$$= \dfrac{1 + \tan\theta}{1 - \tan\theta}$$

(divide top and bottom by $\cos\theta$)

$\tan\left(\theta + \dfrac{\pi}{4}\right)$

$$= \dfrac{\tan\theta + \tan\dfrac{\pi}{4}}{1 - \tan\theta\tan\dfrac{\pi}{4}}$$

$$= \dfrac{\tan\theta + 1}{1 - \tan\theta}\left(\tan\dfrac{\pi}{4} = 1\right)$$

$$= \dfrac{1 + \tan\theta}{1 - \tan\theta}$$

Thus, $\dfrac{dy}{dx} = \tan\left(\theta + \dfrac{\pi}{4}\right)$, as both are equal to $\dfrac{1 + \tan\theta}{1 - \tan\theta}$.

Finding the Slope and Equation of a Tangent to a Curve at a Point on the Curve

$$\dfrac{dy}{dx} = \text{the slope of a tangent to a curve at any point on the curve}$$

To find the slope and equation of a tangent to a curve at a given point, (x_1, y_1), on the curve, do the following:

Step 1: Find $\dfrac{dy}{dx}$.

Step 2: Evaluate $\left.\dfrac{dy}{dx}\right|_{x=x_1}$ [this gives m, the slope of the tangent].

[If the angle the curve makes with the x-axis is required, use the tan tables or calculator.]

Step 3: Use m (from step 2) and the given point (x_1, y_1) in the equation:

$$(y - y_1) = m(x - x_1)$$

Note: Sometimes only the value of x is given. When this happens, substitute the value of x into the original function to find y for step 3.

Example

Find the equation of the tangent to the curve $y = \dfrac{x-1}{x+2}$ at $x = -1$.

Solution:

$$y = \frac{x-1}{x+2}$$

$$\frac{dy}{dx} = \frac{(x+2)(1) - (x-1)(1)}{(x+2)^2}$$

$$= \frac{3}{(x+2)^2}$$

$$\left.\frac{dy}{dx}\right|_{x=-1} = \frac{3}{(-1+2)^2} = 3$$

$$y = \frac{x-1}{x+2}$$

when $x = -1$, $y = \dfrac{-1-1}{-1+2} = -2$

Thus, the point $(-1, -2)$ is on the curve.
Slope $= 3$ at this point.

$$(y+2) = 3(x+1)$$

$$\Rightarrow \quad y + 2 = 3x + 3$$

$$\Rightarrow \quad 3x - y + 1 = 0$$

Example

(i)   Find the equation of the tangent to the curve $y^3 - xy - 6x^3 = 0$ at the point $(1, 2)$.

(ii)   The slope of the tangent to the curve $2x^2 + y^2 + 3x - 6y + 9 = 0$ at the point (p, q) is $\frac{1}{2}$. Show that $4p + q = 0$.

Solution:

(i)

$$y^3 - xy - 6x^3 = 0$$

$$3y^2 \frac{dy}{dx} - \left[x\frac{dy}{dx} + y(1) \right] - 18x^2 = 0$$

$$3y^2 \frac{dy}{dx} - x\frac{dy}{dx} - y - 18x^2 = 0$$

$$\frac{dy}{dx}(3y^2 - x) = 18x^2 + y$$

$$\frac{dy}{dx} = \frac{18x^2 + y}{3y^2 - x}$$

$$\left.\frac{dy}{dx}\right|_{\substack{x=1 \\ y=2}} = \frac{18(1)^2 + 2}{3(2)^2 - 1} = \frac{20}{11}$$

Point $(1, 2)$, slope $= \dfrac{20}{11}$

$$(y - y_1) = m(x - x_1)$$

$$(y - 2) = \frac{20}{11}(x - 1)$$

$$11y - 22 = 20x - 20$$

$$20x - 11y + 2 = 0$$

162

(ii) $2x^2 + y^2 + 3x - 6y + 9 = 0$

$$4x + 2y\frac{dy}{dx} + 3 - 6\frac{dy}{dx} = 0$$

$$2y\frac{dy}{dx} - 6\frac{dy}{dx} = -4x - 3$$

$$\frac{dy}{dx}(2y - 6) = -4x - 3$$

$$\frac{dy}{dx} = \frac{-4x - 3}{2y - 6}$$

$$\frac{dy}{dx} = \frac{1}{2} \text{ when } x = p \text{ and } y = q$$

$\Rightarrow \quad \dfrac{-4p - 3}{2q - 6} = \dfrac{1}{2}$

$\Rightarrow \quad -8p - 6 = 2q - 6$

$\Rightarrow \quad -8p - 2q = 0$

$\Rightarrow \quad 4p + q = 0$

Example

Find the equation of the tangent to the curve $x = t^2$, $y = t^3$, $t \in R$ at the point $(4, 8)$ on the curve.

Solution:

$$x = t^2 \quad \Rightarrow \quad \frac{dx}{dt} = 2t$$

$$y = t^3 \quad \Rightarrow \quad \frac{dy}{dt} = 3t^2$$

$$\frac{dy}{dx} = \frac{dy}{dt} \cdot \frac{dt}{dx}$$

$$= \frac{3t^2}{2t}$$

$$= \frac{3t}{2}$$

$x = t^2, \quad y = t^3$

At the point $(4, 8)$:

$t^2 = 4$	$t^3 = 8$
$t = \pm 2$	$t = 2$

Thus, $t = 2$

Thus, $\dfrac{dy}{dx} = \dfrac{3t}{2} = \dfrac{3(2)}{2} = 3$

$$(y - 8) = 3(x - 4)$$

$$y - 8 = 3x - 12$$

$\Rightarrow \quad 3x - y - 4 = 0$

Example

Find the equation of the tangent to the curve defined by:

$x = \theta - 2\cos\theta$, $y = 2\sin\theta - 2\cos\theta$ at the point where $\theta = 0$.

Solution:

$$x = \theta - 2\cos\theta$$

$$\frac{dx}{d\theta} = 1 - 2(-\sin\theta)$$

$$= 1 + 2\sin\theta$$

$$\frac{dy}{dx} = \frac{dy}{d\theta} \cdot \frac{d\theta}{dx}$$

$$= \frac{2\cos\theta + 2\sin\theta}{1 + 2\sin\theta}$$

$$\frac{dy}{dx}\bigg|_{\theta=0} = \frac{2\cos 0 + 2\sin 0}{1 + 2\sin 0}$$

$$= \frac{2(1) + 2(0)}{1 + 2(0)}$$

$$= \frac{2}{1} = 2$$

Thus, the slope at $\theta = 0$ is 2.

$$y = 2\sin\theta - 2\cos\theta$$

$$\frac{dy}{d\theta} = 2\cos\theta - 2(-\sin\theta)$$

$$= 2\cos\theta + 2\sin\theta$$

$\theta = 0$	
$x = \theta - 2\cos\theta$	$y = 2\sin\theta - 2\cos\theta$
$= 0 - 2(1)$	$= 2(0) - 2(1)$
$= -2$	$= -2$

Thus, the point $(-2, -2)$ is on the curve at $\theta = 0$.

Equation of the tangent at $\theta = 0$:

$$(y + 2) = 2(x + 2)$$

$$\Rightarrow \quad y + 2 = 2x + 4$$

$$\Rightarrow \quad 2x - y + 2 = 0$$

Given $\dfrac{dy}{dx}$, to find the Coordinates of the Corresponding Points on a Curve

Sometimes the value of $\dfrac{dy}{dx}$ (slope of the curve at any point on it) is given and we need to find the coordinates of the point, or points, corresponding to this slope.

When this hapens do the following:

Step 1: Find $\dfrac{dy}{dx}$.

Step 2: Let $\dfrac{dy}{dx}$ equal the given value of the slope and solve this equation for x.

Step 3: Substitute the x values obtained in step 2 into the original function to get the corresponding values for y (or vice versa).

Example

A curve is given by the equation $x^2 + 4xy = 2y^2 - 8$. Find an equation relating x, y and $\dfrac{dy}{dx}$. Hence, find the coordinates of the points on the curve at which $\dfrac{dy}{dx} = 1$.

Solution:

$$x^2 + 4xy = 2y^2 - 8$$

$$2x + 4\left(x.\frac{dy}{dx} + y.1\right) = 4y\frac{dy}{dx}$$

$$x + 2x\frac{dy}{dx} + 2y = 2y\frac{dy}{dx}$$

$$2x\frac{dy}{dx} - 2y\frac{dy}{dx} = -x - 2y$$

$$\frac{dy}{dx}(2x - 2y) = -x - 2y$$

$$\frac{dy}{dx} = \frac{-x - 2y}{2x - 2y}$$

Given: $\dfrac{dy}{dx} = 1$

$\Rightarrow \qquad \dfrac{-x - 2y}{2x - 2y} = 1$

$\Rightarrow \qquad -x - 2y = 2x - 2y$

$\Rightarrow \qquad -3x = 0$

$\Rightarrow \qquad x = 0$

$x^2 + 4xy = 2y^2 - 8$

$\Rightarrow \qquad (0)^2 + 4(0)(y) = 2y^2 - 8$

$\Rightarrow \qquad 2y^2 = 8$

$\Rightarrow \qquad y^2 = 4$

$\Rightarrow \qquad y = \pm 2$

Thus, the coordinates of the points at which $\dfrac{dy}{dx} = 1$ are $(0, 2)$ and $(0, -2)$.

Sometimes we are given the value of $\dfrac{dy}{dx}$ and asked to find unknown coefficients.

Consider the next two examples.

Example

The slope of the tangent to the curve $f(x) = ax^3 + bx + 4$ is 21 at the point $(2, 14)$ on the curve. Find the value of a and the value of b.

Solution:

Let $\qquad y = ax^3 + bx + 4$

$\qquad \dfrac{dy}{dx} = 3ax^2 + b = 21 \quad$ [when $x = 2$]

$\Rightarrow \qquad 3a(2)^2 + b = 21$

$\Rightarrow \qquad 12a + b = 21 \quad$ ①

Given: $(2, 14)$ is on the curve.

Thus, $\qquad 14 = a(2)^3 + b(2) + 4$

$\Rightarrow \qquad 14 = 8a + 2b + 4$

$\Rightarrow \qquad 8a + 2b = 10 \quad$ ②

Solving the simultaneous equations ① and ② gives $a = 2$ and $b = -3$.

Example

The curve $y = \dfrac{p + qx}{x(x + 2)}$, $p, q \in \mathbf{R}$, $x \neq 0$, $x \neq -2$ has zero slope at the point $(1, -2)$.

Find the value of p and the value of q.

Solution:

$$y = \frac{p + qx}{x(x + 2)} = \frac{p + qx}{x^2 + 2x}$$

$$\frac{dy}{dx} = \frac{(x^2 + 2x)(q) - (p + qx)(2x + 2)}{(x^2 + 2x)^2} = 0 \quad \text{[for } x = 1 \text{ (given)]}$$

$\Rightarrow \qquad\qquad (1 + 2.1)q - (p + q)(2 + 2) = 0$

$\Rightarrow \qquad\qquad\qquad 3q - 4p - 4q = 0$

$\Rightarrow \qquad\qquad\qquad\quad -4p - q = 0$

$\Rightarrow \qquad\qquad\qquad\quad 4p + q = 0 \quad \text{①}$

Given: the point $(1, -2)$ is on the curve $y = \dfrac{p + qx}{x(x + 2)}$

$\Rightarrow \qquad -2 = \dfrac{p + q}{1(3)}$

$\Rightarrow \quad p + q = -6 \quad \text{②}$

Solving the simultaneous equations ① and ② gives $p = 2$ and $q = -8$.

Second Derivatives

The second derivative is denoted by $\dfrac{d^2y}{dx^2}$ or $f''(x)$ (i.e. differentiate twice).

Example

(i) If $y = \tan^{-1} x$, show that $\dfrac{d^2y}{dx^2}(1 + x^2) + 2x\dfrac{dy}{dx} = 0$.

(ii) If $y = \sin(\ln x)$, show that $x^2\dfrac{d^2y}{dx^2} + x\dfrac{dy}{dx} + y = 0$.

(iii) If $y = e^{-2x}(1 + 2x)$, show that $4y + 4\dfrac{dy}{dx} + \dfrac{d^2y}{dx^2} = 0$.

Solution:

(i) $y = \tan^{-1} x$

$$\frac{dy}{dx} = \frac{1}{1 + x^2}$$

$$\frac{d^2y}{dx^2} = \frac{(1 + x^2)(0) - 1(2x)}{(1 + x^2)^2}$$

$$= \frac{-2x}{(1 + x^2)^2}$$

$$\frac{d^2y}{dx^2}(1 + x^2) + 2x\frac{dy}{dx}$$

$$= \frac{-2x}{(1 + x^2)^2} \cdot (1 + x^2) + 2x \cdot \frac{1}{1 + x^2}$$

$$= \frac{-2x}{1 + x^2} + \frac{2x}{1 + x^2}$$

$$= 0$$

(ii) $y = \sin(\ln x)$

$$\frac{dy}{dx} = \cos(\ln x) \cdot \frac{1}{x}$$

$$= \frac{\cos(\ln x)}{x}$$

$$\frac{d^2y}{dx^2} = \frac{x \cdot -\sin(\ln x) \cdot \frac{1}{x} - \cos(\ln x).1}{x^2}$$

$$= \frac{-\sin(\ln x) - \cos(\ln x)}{x^2}$$

$$x^2\frac{d^2y}{dx^2} + x\frac{dy}{dx} + y$$

$$= x^2\left(\frac{-\sin(\ln x) - \cos(\ln x)}{x^2}\right) + x\left(\frac{\cos(\ln x)}{x}\right) + \sin(\ln x)$$

$$= -\sin(\ln x) - \cos(\ln x) + \cos(\ln x) + \sin(\ln x) = 0$$

(iii) $y = e^{-2x}(1 + 2x)$

$$\frac{dy}{dx} = e^{-2x}(2) + (1 + 2x)e^{-2x}(-2)$$

$$= 2e^{-2x} - 2e^{-2x} - 4xe^{-2x}$$

$$= -4xe^{-2x}$$

$$\frac{d^2y}{dx^2} = (-4x)e^{-2x}(-2) + e^{-2x}(-4)$$

$$= 8xe^{-2x} - 4e^{-2x}$$

$$4y + 4\frac{dy}{dx} + \frac{d^2y}{dx^2}$$

$$= 4e^{-2x}(1 + 2x) + 4(-4xe^{-2x}) + (8xe^{-2x} - 4e^{-2x})$$

$$= 4e^{-2x} + 8xe^{-2x} - 16xe^{-2x} + 8xe^{-2x} - 4e^{-2x}$$

$$= 0$$

Maxima and Minima

1.	For a maximum:	$\dfrac{dy}{dx} = 0$ and $\dfrac{d^2y}{dx^2} < 0$
2.	For a minimum:	$\dfrac{dy}{dx} = 0$ and $\dfrac{d^2y}{dx^2} > 0$

Note: If the questions say 'show' or 'verify', then the second derivative must be used, unless otherwise stated.

Example

(i) If $x + y = 15$, calculate the maximum value of $2x + 3y + xy$.

(ii) If $x + y = 10$, calculate the minimum value of $x^2 + y^2$.

Solution:

(i)
$$x + y = 15$$
$$\Rightarrow \qquad y = 15 - x$$

Let $\quad A = 2x + 3y + xy$

$\Rightarrow \quad A = 2x + 3(15 - x) + x(15 - x)$

$\qquad A = 2x + 45 - 3x + 15x - x^2$

$\qquad A = 45 + 14x - x^2$

$\dfrac{dA}{dx} = 14 - 2x = 0$ (max)

$\Rightarrow \qquad 2x = 14$

$\Rightarrow \qquad x = 7$

$\qquad y = 15 - x = 15 - 7 = 8$

$A_{max} = 2(7) + 3(8) + (7)(8) = 94$

$\dfrac{d^2A}{dx^2} = -2 < 0 \quad \therefore \quad$ a max. value.

(ii) $x + y = 10$
$$y = 10 - x$$

Let $\quad A = x^2 + y^2$

$\Rightarrow \quad A = x^2 + (10 - x)^2$

$\qquad A = x^2 + 100 - 20x + x^2$

$\qquad A = 2x^2 - 20x + 100$

$\dfrac{dA}{dx} = 4x - 20 = 0$ (min)

$\Rightarrow \qquad 4x = 20$

$\Rightarrow \qquad x = 5$

$\qquad y = 10 - x = 10 - 5 = 5$

$A_{min} = (5)^2 + (5)^2 = 25 + 25 = 50$

$\dfrac{d^2A}{dx^2} = 4 > 0 \quad \therefore \quad$ a min. value.

Example

Given that $y = e^{2x} \cos 2x$, find $\dfrac{dy}{dx}$ and $\dfrac{d^2y}{dx^2}$.

Verify that $e^{2x} \cos 2x$ has a maximum value at $x = \dfrac{\pi}{8}$ and write down this maximum value.

Solution:

$$y = e^{2x} \cos 2x$$

$$\frac{dy}{dx} = \cos 2x \cdot 2e^{2x} + e^{2x}(-2 \sin 2x)$$

$$= 2e^{2x} \cos 2x - 2e^{2x} \sin 2x$$

$$\left. \frac{dy}{dx} \right|_{x=\frac{\pi}{8}} = 2e^{\frac{\pi}{4}} \cos \frac{\pi}{4} - 2e^{\frac{\pi}{4}} \sin \frac{\pi}{4}$$

$$= 2e^{\frac{\pi}{4}} \cdot \frac{1}{\sqrt{2}} - 2e^{\frac{\pi}{4}} \cdot \frac{1}{\sqrt{2}}$$

$$= 0$$

$$\frac{d^2y}{dx^2} = \cos 2x \cdot 4e^{2x} + 2e^{2x}(-2 \sin 2x) - [\sin 2x \cdot 4e^{2x} + 2e^{2x}.2 \cos 2x]$$

$$= 4e^{2x} \cos 2x - 4e^{2x} \sin 2x - 4e^{2x} \sin 2x - 4e^{2x} \cos 2x$$

$$= -8e^{2x} \sin 2x$$

$$\left. \frac{d^2y}{dx^2} \right|_{x=\frac{\pi}{8}} = -8e^{\frac{\pi}{4}} . \sin \frac{\pi}{4}$$

$$= -8e^{\frac{\pi}{4}} . \frac{1}{\sqrt{2}}$$

$$< 0$$

Note: We are given maximum value of x is $\dfrac{\pi}{8}$.

At $x = \dfrac{\pi}{8}$, $\dfrac{dy}{dx} = 0$ and $\dfrac{d^2y}{dx^2} < 0$; thus the maximum value of $e^{2x} \cos 2x$ is at $x = \dfrac{\pi}{8}$.

$$y = e^{2x} \cos 2x$$

$$y_{max} = e^{2(\frac{\pi}{8})} \cos 2\left(\frac{\pi}{8} \right) = e^{\frac{\pi}{4}} \cos \frac{\pi}{4} = e^{\frac{\pi}{4}} . \frac{1}{\sqrt{2}} = \frac{e^{\frac{\pi}{4}}}{\sqrt{2}}$$

Example

The concentration C of an antibiotic in the bloodstream after a time of t hours is given

by $C = \dfrac{5t}{1 + \left(\dfrac{t}{k}\right)^2}$ units, where $k > 0$.

If the maximum concentration is reached at $t = 6$ hours, find the value of k.

Solution:

$$C = \frac{5t}{1 + \left(\dfrac{t}{k}\right)^2} = \frac{5t}{1 + \dfrac{t^2}{k^2}} = \frac{5k^2 t}{k^2 + t^2} \qquad \text{[multiply top and bottom by } k^2]$$

$$\frac{dC}{dt} = \frac{(k^2 + t^2)(5k^2) - (5k^2 t)(2t)}{(k^2 + t^2)^2} = 0 \qquad \text{[when } t = 6]$$

$\Rightarrow \qquad (k^2 + 36)\,(5k^2) - 5k^2(6)\,(12) = 0 \qquad$ [put in $t = 6$]

$\Rightarrow \qquad\qquad\qquad k^2 + 36 - 72 = 0 \qquad\qquad$ [divide both sides by $5k^2$]

$\Rightarrow \qquad\qquad\qquad\qquad k^2 = 36$

$\Rightarrow \qquad\qquad\qquad\qquad k = \pm 6$

Thus, $k = 6$ (reject $k = -6$ as we are given $k > 0$).

Example

Show that the expression $\sin \theta + 2 \cos \theta$, where $0 \le \theta \le \dfrac{\pi}{2}$, has a maximum value equal

to $\sqrt{5}$.

Solution:

$y = \sin \theta + 2 \cos \theta$

$\dfrac{dy}{dx} = \cos \theta - 2 \sin \theta = 0$ (max)

$\Rightarrow \qquad 2 \sin \theta = \cos \theta$

$\Rightarrow \qquad \dfrac{2 \sin \theta}{\cos \theta} = 1$

$\Rightarrow \qquad 2 \tan \theta = 1$

$\Rightarrow \qquad\quad \tan \theta = \tfrac{1}{2}$

$\Rightarrow \qquad\qquad \theta = \tan^{-1} \tfrac{1}{2}$

$\tan \theta = \dfrac{1}{2}$

$\Rightarrow \quad \sin \theta = \dfrac{1}{\sqrt{5}}$

and $\cos \theta = \dfrac{2}{\sqrt{5}}$

$\dfrac{dy}{dx} = \cos \theta - 2 \sin \theta$

$\dfrac{d^2 y}{dx^2} = -\sin \theta - 2 \cos \theta$

$= -\dfrac{1}{\sqrt{5}} - 2 \cdot \dfrac{2}{\sqrt{5}} < 0 \quad \therefore$ a max. value

$y = \sin \theta + 2 \cos \theta$

$$y_{max} = \frac{1}{\sqrt{5}} + 2 \cdot \frac{2}{\sqrt{5}} = \frac{1}{\sqrt{5}} + \frac{4}{\sqrt{5}} = \frac{5}{\sqrt{5}} = \frac{5\sqrt{5}}{5} = \sqrt{5}$$

Thus, the maximum value of $\sin \theta + 2 \cos \theta$ is $\sqrt{5}$.

Example

Let $f(x) = e^2x - ae^x$, $x \in R$ and a constant, $a > 0$.

Show that $f(x)$ has a local minimum at a point $(b, f(b))$, specifying the value of b in terms of a.

Solution:

$f(x) = e^{2x} - ae^x$

$f'(x) = 2e^{2x} - ae^x = 0$ (min)

$2e^{2x} = ae^x$

$2e^x = a$

$e^x = \left(\dfrac{a}{2}\right)$

$x \ln e = \ln\left(\dfrac{a}{2}\right)$

$x = \ln\left(\dfrac{a}{2}\right)$

$f''(x) = 4e^{2x} - ae^x$

$= 4(e^x)^2 - ae^x$

$= 4\left(\dfrac{a}{2}\right)^2 - a\left(\dfrac{a}{2}\right)$

$= 4\dfrac{a^2}{4} - \dfrac{a^2}{2}$

$= a^2 - \dfrac{a^2}{2}$

$= \dfrac{a^2}{2} > 0$ ∴ a min. value

Thus, a local minimum value of $e^{2x} - ae^x$ occurs at $x = \ln\left(\dfrac{a}{2}\right)$,

∴   minimum point $= (b, f(b)) = \left(\ln\dfrac{a}{2}, f\left(\ln\dfrac{a}{2}\right)\right)$.

Note: $\log_x x = 1$. Thus, $\ln e = \log_e e = 1$.

Related Rates of Change

If we know the rate of change of x with respect to a third variable, say t,

then we know $\dfrac{dx}{dt}$ and we can use the chain rule to find $\dfrac{dy}{dt}$,

$$\text{i.e. } \frac{dy}{dt} = \frac{dx}{dt} \times \frac{dy}{dx}$$

In many rate of change problems we will deal with 3 things:

> **1.** What we want to find. **2.** What we are given.
> **3.** What we need to complete the fraction (look for link).

$$\text{Find} = (\text{Given}) \times \begin{pmatrix} \text{What we need to} \\ \text{complete the fraction} \end{pmatrix}$$

[we simply use the chain rule]

Example

(i) If $y = (x^2 - 3x)^3$, find $\dfrac{dy}{dt}$ when $x = 2$, given $\dfrac{dx}{dt} = \dfrac{1}{2}$.

(ii) If $y = \left(\dfrac{x-1}{x}\right)^2$, find $\dfrac{dx}{dt}$ when $x = 2$, given $\dfrac{dy}{dt} = 4$.

Solution:

(i) Find = Given × Need

$$\dfrac{dy}{dt} = \dfrac{dx}{dt} \cdot \dfrac{dy}{dx}$$

$$= \tfrac{1}{2}[3(x^2 - 3x)^2(2x - 3)]$$

$$= \tfrac{3}{2}(x^2 - 3x)^2(2x - 3)$$

$$\left.\dfrac{dy}{dt}\right|_{x=2} = \tfrac{3}{2}(4 - 6)^2(4 - 3) = \tfrac{3}{2}(4)(1) = 6$$

Link

$$y = (x^2 - 3x)^3$$

$$\dfrac{dy}{dx} = 3(x^2 - 3x)^2(2x - 3)$$

(ii) Find = Given × Need

$$\dfrac{dx}{dt} = \dfrac{dy}{dt} \cdot \dfrac{dx}{dy}$$

$$= 4\left(\dfrac{x^3}{2(x-1)}\right)$$

$$= \dfrac{2x^3}{x - 1}$$

$$\left.\dfrac{dx}{dt}\right|_{x=2} = \dfrac{2(2)^3}{2 - 1} = \dfrac{16}{1} = 16$$

Link

$$y = \left(\dfrac{x-1}{x}\right)^2$$

$$\dfrac{dy}{dx} = 2\left(\dfrac{x-1}{x}\right)\left(\dfrac{x(1) - (x-1)(1)}{x^2}\right)$$

$$= 2\left(\dfrac{x-1}{x}\right) \cdot \left(\dfrac{1}{x^2}\right)$$

$$= \dfrac{2(x-1)}{x^3}$$

Thus, $\dfrac{dx}{dy} = \dfrac{x^3}{2(x-1)}$.

Example

The radius of a circle increases at 8 cm per second. What is the rate of increase of the area when the radius is 10 cm?

Solution:

$$\underset{\downarrow}{\text{Find}} = \underset{\downarrow}{\text{Given}} \times \underset{\nwarrow}{\text{Need}}$$

$$\frac{dA}{dt} = \frac{dr}{dt} \cdot \frac{dA}{dr}$$

$$= 8 \times 2\pi r$$

$$= 16\pi r$$

$$\left.\frac{dA}{dt}\right|_{r=10} = 16\pi(10) = 160\pi \, \text{cm}^2/\text{sec}$$

Link

$$A = \pi r^2$$

$$\frac{dA}{dr} = 2\pi r$$

Example

A spherical snowball melts at the rate of 20 cm³/h.

What is the rate of change of the radius when:

(i) the radius is r?   (ii) the radius is 2 cm?

What is the rate of change of the surface area when the radius is 5 cm?

Solution:

(i) $$\underset{\downarrow}{\text{Find}} = \underset{\downarrow}{\text{Given}} \times \underset{\nwarrow}{\text{Need}}$$

$$\frac{dr}{dt} = \frac{dV}{dt} \cdot \frac{dr}{dV}$$

$$= -20 \times \frac{1}{4\pi r^2}$$

$$\frac{dr}{dt} = \frac{-20}{4\pi r^2} = \frac{-5}{\pi r^2} \, \text{cm/h}$$

(ii) $$\left.\frac{dr}{dt}\right|_{r=2} = \frac{-5}{\pi . 2^2} = \frac{-5}{4\pi} \, \text{cm/h}$$

Link

$$V = \tfrac{4}{3}\pi r^3$$

$$\frac{dV}{dr} = 3 \times \frac{4}{3}\pi r^2$$

$$\frac{dV}{dr} = 4\pi r^2$$

$$\Rightarrow \quad \frac{dr}{dV} = \frac{1}{4\pi r^2}$$

Let the surface area $= S$

$$\text{Find} = \text{Given} \times \text{Need}$$

$$\frac{dS}{dt} = \frac{dr}{dt} \cdot \frac{dS}{dr}$$

$$= \frac{-5}{\pi r^2} \times 8\pi r$$

$$= \frac{-40\pi r}{\pi r^2} = \frac{-40}{r}$$

$$\left.\frac{dS}{dt}\right|_{r=5} = \frac{-40}{5} = -8 \ \text{cm}^2/\text{h}$$

Link

$$S = 4\pi r^2$$

$$\frac{dS}{dr} = 8\pi r$$

Example

The path of a football is given by the equation

$$y = x - \frac{x^2}{40}, \ x \geq 0.$$

If $\dfrac{dx}{dt} = 10\sqrt{2}$ for all t, find $\dfrac{dy}{dt}$ when $x = 10$.

Solution:

$$\text{Find} = \text{Given} \times \text{Need}$$

$$\frac{dy}{dt} = \frac{dx}{dt} \cdot \frac{dy}{dx}$$

$$= 10\sqrt{2}\left(1 - \frac{x}{20}\right)$$

$$\left.\frac{dy}{dt}\right|_{x=10} = 10\sqrt{2}\left(1 - \frac{10}{20}\right) = 10\sqrt{2}\left(1 - \frac{1}{2}\right) = 10\sqrt{2}\left(\frac{1}{2}\right) = 5\sqrt{2}$$

Link

$$y = x - \frac{1}{40}x^2$$

$$\frac{dy}{dx} = 1 - \frac{1}{20}x = 1 - \frac{x}{20}$$

Example

A point $p(x, y)$ travels along the curve $y^2 = 8x^3$, $x, y > 0$. If the rate of change of the x-coordinate is $\frac{1}{3}$ m/s, find the corresponding rate of change of the y-coordinate when $x = 2$.

Solution:

We are given the rate of change of the x-coordinate is $\frac{1}{3}$ m/s, i.e. $\dfrac{dx}{dt} = \dfrac{1}{3}$.

Find = Given × Need

$$\frac{dy}{dt} = \frac{dx}{dt} \cdot \frac{dy}{dx}$$

$$= \frac{1}{3}\left(\frac{12x^2}{y}\right)$$

$$= \frac{4x^2}{y}$$

$$\left.\frac{dy}{dt}\right|_{\substack{x=2 \\ y=8}} = \frac{4(2)^2}{8} = \frac{16}{8} = 2\,\text{m/s}$$

Link

$$y^2 = 8x^3$$

$$2y\frac{dy}{dx} = 24x^2$$

$$\frac{dy}{dx} = \frac{24x^2}{2y} = \frac{12x^2}{y}$$

Given: $\qquad x = 2$

$\qquad\qquad y^2 = 8x^3 = 8(2)^3$

$\Rightarrow \qquad y^2 = 64$

$\Rightarrow \qquad y = 8$ (as $y > 0$)

Thus, when $\qquad x = 2, y = 8$.

Some questions involve velocity and acceleration of particles.

Suppose s represents the distance an object travelled and t represents the time.

Then $\dfrac{ds}{dt}$ represents the velocity at any time (rate of change of distance)

and $\dfrac{d^2s}{dt^2}$ represents the acceleration at any time (rate of change of speed).

Example

A particle is moving in a straight line. Its distance, s metres, from a fixed point o after t seconds is given by $s = t^3 - 9t^2 + 15t + 2$.

Calculate:

(i) its velocity at any time t **(ii)** its velocity after 6 seconds

(iii) the distances of the particle from o when it is instantly at rest

(iv) its acceleration after 4 seconds.

Solution:

(i) $\qquad\qquad s = t^3 - 9t^2 + 15t + 2$

velocity $= \dfrac{ds}{dt} = 3t^2 - 18t + 15$

(velocity at any time t)

(ii) Velocity after 6 seconds

$\left.\dfrac{ds}{dt}\right|_{t=6} = 3(6)^2 - 18(6) + 15 = 15\,\text{m/s}$

175

(iii) The particle is at rest when its velocity $\dfrac{ds}{dt}$ is zero.

$$\frac{ds}{dt} = 3t^2 - 18t + 15 = 0$$

$$\Rightarrow \qquad t^2 - 6t + 5 = 0$$

$$\Rightarrow \qquad (t-5)(t-1) = 0$$

$$\Rightarrow \qquad t = 1 \quad \text{or} \quad t = 5$$

Thus, the particle is stopped after 1 second and again after 5 seconds.

Distance $= s = t^3 - 9t^2 + 15t + 2$

$t = 1$: $s = (1)^3 - 9(1)^2 + 15(1) + 2 = 9$ m

$t = 5$: $s = (5)^3 - 9(5)^2 + 15(5) + 2 = -23$ m

Thus, after 1 second, the particle is 9 m from 0
and, after 5 seconds, the particle is 23 m from 0 (distance cannot be negative).

(iv)
$$\frac{ds}{dt} = 3t^2 - 18t + 15$$

$$\text{acceleration} = \frac{d^2s}{dt^2} = 6t - 18$$

$$\left.\frac{d^2s}{dt^2}\right|_{t=4} = 6(4) - 18 = 6 \text{ m/s}^2$$

The Newton–Raphson Formula

If x_n is an approximate solution of the equation $f(x) = 0$, then x_{n+1} is a better approximation where:

$$x_{n+1} = x_n - \frac{f(x_n)}{f'(x_n)}$$

It is an iterative (repetitive) procedure and is continued until the required degree of accuracy is achieved.

Example

Given that $f(x) = x^3 - 3x^2 - 1$, show that the equation $f(x) = 0$ has only one real root and that this real root lies in the interval $3 < x < 4$.

Use three iterations of the Newton–Raphson formula applied to $f(x) = 0$, with $x_1 = 3$, to find an approximation to the real root, giving your answer correct to three decimal places.

Solution:

$$f(x) = x^3 - 3x^2 - 1$$

$$f'(x) = 3x^2 - 6x = 0 \quad \text{(max/min)}$$

$$\Rightarrow \qquad x^2 - 2x = 0$$

$$\Rightarrow \qquad x(x - 2) = 0$$

$$\Rightarrow \qquad x = 0 \quad \text{or} \quad x = 2$$

$$f(x) = x^3 - 3x^2 - 1$$

$$f(3) = 27 - 27 - 1 = -1 < 0$$

$$f(4) = 64 - 48 - 1 = 15 > 0$$

$$f(x) = x^3 - 3x^2 - 1 \quad \Rightarrow \quad f'(x) = 3x^2 - 6x$$

When $x = 0$, $y = -1$ and when $x = 2$, $y = -5$.

Thus, the turning points are $(0, -1)$ and $(2, -5)$.

As both turning points are on the same side of the x-axis, $f(x)$ has only one real root.

Thus, there is a root between 3 and 4 and the root is nearer 3 than 4, as -1 is closer to 0 than 15 is.

Iteration 1:

$$x_1 = 3: x_2 = x_1 - \frac{f(x_1)}{f'(x_1)}$$

$$= 3 - \frac{f(3)}{f'(3)} = 3 - \left(\frac{-1}{9}\right) = 3 \cdot 1111111$$

Iteration 2:

$$x_2 = 3 \cdot 1111111: \quad x_3 = x_2 - \frac{f(x_2)}{f'(x_2)}$$

$$= 3 \cdot 1111111 - \frac{f(3 \cdot 1111111)}{f'(3 \cdot 1111111)} = 3 \cdot 1111111 - \left(\frac{0 \cdot 0754458}{10 \cdot 37037}\right) = 3 \cdot 103836$$

Iteration 3:

$$x_3 = 3 \cdot 103836: \quad x_4 = x_3 - \frac{f(x_3)}{f'(x_3)}$$

$$= 3 \cdot 103836 - \frac{f(3 \cdot 103836)}{f'(3 \cdot 103836)} = 3 \cdot 103836 - \left(\frac{0 \cdot 0003350}{10 \cdot 278377}\right) = 3 \cdot 1038034$$

Thus, correct to 3 decimal places, the real root of $f(x) = 0$ is $3 \cdot 104$, as x_3 and x_4 agree, correct to 3 decimal places.

Note: If the turning points of the graph of a cubic function are on opposite sides of the x-axis, then the associated cubic equation will have 3 real roots.

Example

Show that the equation $x^3 = 7x - 1$ has a root between 2 and 3.

Taking 2·5 as a first approximation, apply the Newton–Raphson formula twice to obtain a better approximation, giving your answer correct to 3 significant figures.

Solution:

$$x^3 = 7x - 1 \quad \Rightarrow \quad x^3 - 7x + 1 = 0$$

Let $f(x) = x^3 - 7x + 1$

$$f(2) = 8 - 14 + 1 = -5 < 0$$

$$f(3) = 27 - 21 + 1 = 7 > 0$$

Thus, $x^3 = 7x - 1$ has a root between 2 and 3.

$$f(x) = x^3 - 7x + 1 \quad \Rightarrow \quad f'(x) = 3x^2 - 7$$

Iteration 1:

$$x_1 = 2 \cdot 5 \colon \ x_2 = x_1 - \frac{f(x_1)}{f'(x_1)}$$

$$= 2 \cdot 5 - \frac{f(2 \cdot 5)}{f'(2 \cdot 5)}$$

$$= 2 \cdot 5 - \left(\frac{-0 \cdot 875}{11 \cdot 75} \right)$$

$$= 2 \cdot 5744681$$

Iteration 2:

$$x_2 = 2 \cdot 5744681 \colon \ x_3 = x_2 - \frac{f(x_2)}{f'(x_2)}$$

$$= 2 \cdot 5744681 - \frac{f(2 \cdot 5744681)}{f'(2 \cdot 5744681)}$$

$$= 2 \cdot 5744681 - \left(\frac{0 \cdot 0420044}{12 \cdot 883658} \right)$$

$$= 2 \cdot 5712078$$

Thus, a root of $x^3 = 7x - 1$ is 2·57, correct to three significant figures, as x_1 and x_2 agree, correct to three significant figures.

Example

Show that the Newton–Raphson formula for approximating a root of the equation

$x^3 + x - 6 = 0$, is given by $x_{n+1} = \dfrac{2x_n^3 + 6}{3x_n^2 + 1}$.

Taking $x_1 = 1.5$, approximate a root of this equation, corret to two decimal places.

Solution:

$$f(x) = x^3 + x - 6 \qquad\qquad f'(x) = 3x^2 + 1$$

$$f(x_n) = x_n^3 + x_n - 6 \qquad\quad f'(x_n) = 3x_n^2 + 1$$

$$x_{n+1} = x_n - \frac{f(x_n)}{f'(x_n)}$$

$$= x_n - \frac{x_n^3 + x_n - 6}{3x_n^2 + 1}$$

$$= \frac{x_n(3x_n^2 + 1) - (x_n^3 + x_n - 6)}{3x_n^2 + 1}$$

$$= \frac{2x_n^3 + 6}{3x_n^2 + 1}$$

We can now use this formula to estimate the root correct to two decimal places.

$x_1 = 1.5$ (given)

$$x_2 = \frac{2x_1^3 + 6}{3x_1^2 + 1} = \frac{2(1.5)^3 + 6}{3(1.5)^2 + 1} = \frac{12.75}{7.75} = 1.6451613$$

$$x_3 = \frac{2x_2^3 + 6}{3x_2^2 + 1} = \frac{2(1.6451613)^3 + 6}{3(1.6451613)^2 + 1} = \frac{14.905441}{9.119667} = 1.6344282$$

$$x_4 = \frac{2x_3^3 + 6}{2x_3^2 + 1} = \frac{2(1.6344282)^3 + 6}{3(1.6344282)^2 + 1} = \frac{14.732278}{9.0140666} = 1.6343653$$

As x_3 and x_4 agree to two decimal places, a root is 1.63.

Example

The equation $x^3 + ax - 1 = 0$ is known to have a root close to $x = \frac{1}{2}$. When $x = \frac{1}{2}$ is used as the first approximation in the Newton–Raphson formula, the second approximation is $\frac{5}{11}$. Find the value of a.

Solution:

$$f(x) = x^3 + ax - 1 \qquad f'(x) = 3x^2 + a$$

$$x_{n+1} = x_n - \frac{f(x_n)}{f'(x_n)}$$

$$x_1 = \tfrac{1}{2} \quad \text{[given]}$$

$$x_2 = x_1 - \frac{f(x_1)}{f'(x_1)}$$

$$\Rightarrow \quad \frac{5}{11} = \frac{1}{2} - \frac{f(\frac{1}{2})}{f'(\frac{1}{2})}$$

$$\Rightarrow \quad \frac{5}{11} = \frac{1}{2} - \frac{\dfrac{4a-7}{8}}{\dfrac{6+8a}{8}}$$

$$\Rightarrow \quad \frac{5}{11} = \frac{1}{2} - \frac{4a-7}{6+8a}$$

$$\Rightarrow \quad \frac{5 \cdot 2(6+8a) = 11(6+8a) - 22(4a-7)}{22(6+8a)}$$

$$\Rightarrow \quad 60 + 80a = 66 + 88a - 88a + 154$$

$$\Rightarrow \qquad 80a = 160$$

$$\Rightarrow \qquad a = 2$$

$$f(\tfrac{1}{2}) = (\tfrac{1}{2})^3 + a(\tfrac{1}{2}) - 1$$

$$= \frac{1}{8} + \frac{a}{2} - 1$$

$$= \frac{1 + 4a - 8}{8}$$

$$= \frac{4a - 7}{8}$$

$$f'(\tfrac{1}{2}) = 3(\tfrac{1}{2})^2 + a$$

$$= \frac{3}{4} + a$$

$$= \frac{3 + 4a}{4}$$

$$= \frac{6 + 8a}{8}$$

Curve Sketching

The following information is used when asked to sketch a curve:

1.	Given Points	If $f(-3) = 5$, then the point $(-3, 5)$ is on the curve.
2.	Intercepts	On the x-axis, $y = 0$. On the y-axis, $x = 0$.
3.	Increasing	$\dfrac{dy}{dx} > 0$
4.	Decreasing	$\dfrac{dy}{dx} < 0$
5.	Local Maximum Point	$\dfrac{dy}{dx} = 0$ and $\dfrac{d^2 y}{dx^2} < 0$
6.	Local Minimum Point	$\dfrac{dy}{dx} = 0$ and $\dfrac{d^2 y}{dx^2} > 0$
7.	Point of Inflection	$\dfrac{d^2 y}{dx^2} = 0$ and $\dfrac{d^3 y}{dx^3} \neq 0$

Note: Only use $\dfrac{d^3 y}{dx^3} \neq 0$ when asked to 'verify' that a curve has a point of inflection.

Rational Functions

We may be asked to find asymptotes for rational functions of the form $\dfrac{a}{x + b}$ or $\dfrac{x}{x + b}$.

8. Vertical Asymptote: Bottom $= 0$ i.e. $x + b = 0$	**9.** Horizontal Asymptote: $y = \lim\limits_{x \to \infty} f(x)$

Example

$$y = f(x) = x^3 - 6x^2 + 9x, \qquad x \in \mathbf{R}.$$

(i) Find the coordinates of the points on the curve $y = f(x)$ at which $f'(x) = 0$. Determine the nature of these points.

(ii) Verify that the curve $y = f(x)$ has a point of inflection and find its coordinates.

(iii) Find where the curve $y = f(x)$ intersects the axes.

(iv) Draw a rough sketch of the curve $y = f(x)$.

Solution:

(i) $f(x) = x^3 - 6x^2 + 9x$

$f'(x) = 3x^2 - 12x + 9 = 0$ (max/min) $\qquad\qquad$ $f''(x) = 6x - 12$

$\Rightarrow \qquad x^2 - 4x + 3 = 0 \qquad\qquad\qquad$ $f''(1) = 6 - 12 = -6 < 0$ (max)

$\Rightarrow \quad (x-1)(x-3) = 0 \qquad\qquad\qquad$ $f''(3) = 18 - 12 = 6 > 0$ (min)

$\Rightarrow \qquad x = 1 \quad$ or $\quad x = 3$

When $x = 1$, $y = 4$ and when $x = 3$, $y = 0$ and $f'''(x) \neq 0$.

Thus, $(1, 4)$ is a local maximum and $(3, 0)$ is a local minimum.

(ii) For a point of inflection $f''(x) = 0$.

$\qquad\qquad f'(x) = 3x^2 - 12x + 9 \qquad\qquad$ When $x = 2$, $y = 2$.

$\qquad\qquad f''(x) = 6x - 12 = 0 \qquad\qquad\quad$ $(2, 2)$ is the point of inflection

$\Rightarrow \qquad\qquad 6x = 12$

$\Rightarrow \qquad\qquad x = 2$

$f'''(x) = 6 \neq 0$; thus, there is a point of inflection at $x = 2$.

(iii) <u>On the x-axis, $y = 0$</u>

$\qquad y = x^3 - 6x^2 + 9x$

$\qquad y = 0 \Rightarrow x^3 - 6x^2 + 9x = 0$

$\qquad\quad x(x^2 - 6x + 9) = 0$

$\qquad\quad x(x - 3)(x - 3) = 0$

$\Rightarrow \quad x = 0 \quad$ or $\quad x = 3$

Thus, the curve intersects the x-axis at $x = 0$ and $x = 3$.

<u>On the y-axis, $x = 0$</u>

$\qquad y = x^3 - 6x^2 + 9x$

$\qquad x = 0 \quad \Rightarrow \quad y = 0$

Thus, the curve intersects the y-axis at $y = 0$.

(iv) Sketch of $y = f(x)$.

Using the information from (i), (ii) and (iii), we sketch the graph of $y = f(x)$.

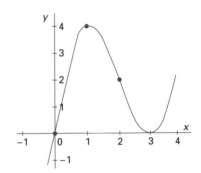

182

Example

Show that the curve $y = x^4 - 4x^3 + 6x^2 - 4x + 8$ has no point of inflection.

Solution:

For a point of inflection to exist, $\dfrac{d^2y}{dx^2} = 0$ and $\dfrac{d^3y}{dx^3} \neq 0$.

$y = x^4 - 4x^3 + 6x^2 - 4x + 8$

$\dfrac{dy}{dx} = 4x^3 - 12x^2 + 12x - 4$

$\dfrac{d^2y}{dx^2} = 12x^2 - 24x + 12$

$\dfrac{d^3y}{dx^3} = 24x - 24$

$\dfrac{d^2y}{dx^2} = 0$

$\Rightarrow \qquad 12x^2 - 24x + 12 = 0$

$\Rightarrow \qquad x^2 - 2x + 1 = 0$

$\Rightarrow \qquad (x - 1)(x - 1) = 0$

$\Rightarrow \qquad x = 1$

$\dfrac{d^3y}{dx^3}\bigg|_{x=1} = 24(1) - 24 = 24 - 24 = 0$

As $\dfrac{d^3y}{dx^3} = 0$ at $x = 1$, there is no point of inflection.

Example

Draw a rough graph of a function $y = f(x)$ which satisfies the following conditions:

(a) $y = -4$ at $x = -1$

$y = 5$ at $x = 3$.

(b) $\dfrac{dy}{dx} = 0$ at $x = -1$ and $x = 3$.

(c) $\dfrac{dy}{dx} > 0$ for $-1 < x < 3$.

(d) $\dfrac{dy}{dx} < 0$ for $x < -1$ and $x > 3$.

Solution:

The information can be reduced to the following:

(a) Given two points on the curve $(-1, -4)$ and $(3, 5)$.

(b) These two points are turning points.

(c) The curve is increasing between $x = -1$ and $x = 3$.

(d) The curve is decreasing before $x = -1$ and after $x = 3$.

Below is a rough sketch of the graph.

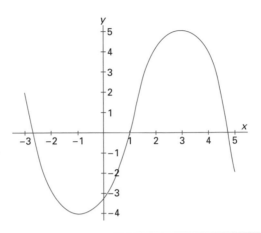

Example

Let $f(x) = \dfrac{x}{x-3}$, $x \ne 3$ and $x \in R$.

(i)   Show that $f(x)$ has no turning points and that it is decreasing for all $x \ne 3$, in its domain.

(ii)   Show that the curve $f(x)$ has no points of inflection.

(iii)   Find the equations of the asymptotes of the curve $f(x)$.

(iv)   Draw a sketch of the curve $f(x)$.

(v)   Find how x_1 and x_2 are related if the tangents at $(x_1, f(x_1))$ and $(x_2, f(x_2))$ are parallel and $x_1 \ne x_2$.

Solution:

$$f(x) = \frac{x}{x-3}$$

(i) $f'(x) = \dfrac{(x-3)(1) - (x)(1)}{(x-3)^2}$

$$= \frac{x-3-x}{(x-3)^2}$$

$$= \frac{-3}{(x-3)^2} = -3(x-3)^{-2}$$

$\dfrac{-3}{(x-3)^2} < 0$ for all $x \ne 3$

(as top is always negative and bottom is always positive).

Thus, the curve has no stationary points and is decreasing for all $x \ne 3$.

184

(ii)

$$f''(x) = (-2)(-3)(x-3)^{-3}(1)$$

$$= 6(x-3)^{-3}$$

$$= \frac{6}{(x-3)^3}$$

$$f''(x) = 0 \quad \text{[for a point of inflection]}$$

$$\Rightarrow \quad \frac{6}{(x-3)^3} = 0$$

$$\Rightarrow \quad 6 = 0 \quad \text{[not true]}$$

Thus, $f''(x) \neq 0$

∴   No points of inflection.

(iii) $f(x) = \dfrac{x}{x-3}$

Vertical asymptote:

Bottom = 0

$$\Rightarrow \quad x - 3 = 0$$

$$\Rightarrow \quad x = 3$$

Horizontal asymptote:

$$y = \lim_{x \to \infty} f(x)$$

$$= \lim_{x \to \infty} \frac{x}{x-3}$$

$$= \lim_{x \to \infty} \frac{1}{1 - \dfrac{3}{x}}$$

$$= \frac{1}{1-0}$$

$$\Rightarrow \quad y = 1$$

(iv) For the graph, $y = f(x)$.

When $x = 0$, $y = 0$;

thus, the point $(0, 0)$ is on the curve.

Sketch:

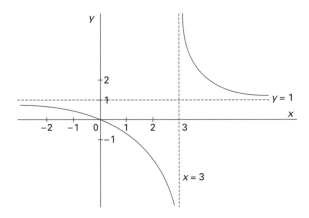

The asymptotes are shown by the broken lines

(v)

$$\frac{dy}{dx} = \frac{-3}{(x-3)^2}$$

$$\left.\frac{dy}{dx}\right|_{x=x_1} = \frac{-3}{(x_1-3)^2}$$

$$\left.\frac{dy}{dx}\right|_{x=x_2} = \frac{-3}{(x_2-3)^2}$$

Parallel tangents

$$\Rightarrow \quad \frac{-3}{(x_1-3)^2} = \frac{-3}{(x_2-3)^2}$$

$$\Rightarrow \quad (x_1-3)^2 = (x_2-3)^2$$

$$\Rightarrow \quad (x_1-3) = \pm(x_2-3)$$

$$\Rightarrow \quad x_1 - 3 = x_2 - 3 \quad \text{or} \quad x_1 - 3 = -x_2 + 3$$

$$\Rightarrow \quad x_1 = x_2 \quad \text{or} \quad x_1 + x_2 = 6$$

Thus, $x_1 + x_2 = 6$ $\quad$[as $x_1 \neq x_2$].

Chapter 6
Integration

Basics

The derivative of $f(x)$ is written $f'(x)$.

As integration reverses the process of differentiation, for a function $f(x)$ we have:

$$\int f'(x)\,dx = f(x) + c$$

where c is called the constant of integration.

The basic rule is:

$$\int x^n\,dx = \frac{x^{n+1}}{n+1} + c \quad (n \neq -1)$$

In words: Increase the power by 1 and divide by the new power.

Example

Find   (i) $\displaystyle\int (x-1)(2x+3)\,dx$ (ii) $\displaystyle\int (1+x^2)^3\,dx$ (iii) $\displaystyle\int \left(x^2 + \frac{1}{x}\right)^2 dx$

(iv) $\displaystyle\int \sqrt{x}(1+x^2)\,dx$ (v) $\displaystyle\int \left(\frac{x^4 + 2x^2 + 1}{x^2}\right)dx$ (vi) $\displaystyle\int \left(\frac{x+1}{\sqrt{x}}\right)dx$

Solution:

(i) $\displaystyle\int (x-1)(2x+3)\,dx$

$= \displaystyle\int (2x^2 + 3x - 2x - 3)\,dx$

$= \displaystyle\int (2x^2 + x - 3)\,dx$

$= \frac{2}{3}x^3 + \frac{1}{2}x^2 - 3x + c$

(ii) $\displaystyle\int (1+x^2)^3\,dx$

$= \displaystyle\int (1 + 3x^2 + 3x^4 + x^6)\,dx$

$= x + \frac{3x^3}{3} + \frac{3x^5}{5} + \frac{x^7}{7} + c$

$= x + x^3 + \frac{3}{5}x^5 + \frac{1}{7}x^7 + c$

(iii)
$$\int \left(x^2 + \frac{1}{x}\right)^2 dx$$

$$= \int \left(x^4 + 2x^2 \cdot \frac{1}{x} + \frac{1}{x^2}\right) dx$$

$$= \int (x^4 + 2x + x^{-2}) \, dx$$

$$= \frac{x^5}{5} + \frac{2x^2}{2} + \frac{x^{-2+1}}{-2+1} + c$$

$$= \frac{1}{5}x^5 + x^2 + \frac{x^{-1}}{-1} + c$$

$$= \frac{1}{5}x^5 + x^2 - \frac{1}{x} + c$$

(iv)
$$\int \sqrt{x}\,(1 + x^2) \, dx$$

$$= \int x^{\frac{1}{2}}(1 + x^2) \, dx$$

$$= \int (x^{\frac{1}{2}} + x^{\frac{5}{2}}) \, dx$$

$$= \frac{x^{\frac{1}{2}+1}}{\frac{1}{2}+1} + \frac{x^{\frac{5}{2}+1}}{\frac{5}{2}+1} + c$$

$$= \frac{x^{\frac{3}{2}}}{\frac{3}{2}} + \frac{x^{\frac{7}{2}}}{\frac{7}{2}} + c$$

$$= \frac{2}{3}x^{\frac{3}{2}} + \frac{2}{7}x^{\frac{7}{2}} + c$$

(v)
$$\int \left(\frac{x^4 + 2x^2 + 1}{x^2}\right) dx$$

$$= \int \left(\frac{x^4}{x^2} + \frac{2x^2}{x^2} + \frac{1}{x^2}\right) dx$$

$$= \int (x^2 + 2 + x^{-2}) \, dx$$

$$= \frac{x^3}{3} + 2x + \frac{x^{-1}}{-1} + c$$

$$= \frac{1}{3}x^3 + 2x - \frac{1}{x} + c$$

(vi)
$$\int \left(\frac{x+1}{\sqrt{x}}\right) dx$$

$$= \int \left(\frac{x^1}{x^{\frac{1}{2}}} + \frac{1}{x^{\frac{1}{2}}}\right) dx$$

$$= \int (x^{\frac{1}{2}} + x^{-\frac{1}{2}}) \, dx$$

$$= \frac{x^{\frac{3}{2}}}{\frac{3}{2}} + \frac{x^{\frac{1}{2}}}{\frac{1}{2}} + c$$

$$= \frac{2}{3}x^{\frac{3}{2}} + 2x^{\frac{1}{2}} + c$$

Sometimes if we are given some extra information we may be asked to find the constant of integration or an expression for $f(x)$.

Example

(i) Find the constant of integration given that $\int (6t^2 + 12t + 1) \, dt = 5$, when $t = -2$.

(ii) Find the function of $y = f(x)$, given that $f'(x) = 3x^2 - 2$ and that the graph of $y = f(x)$ passes through the point $(-2, 6)$.

187

Solution:

(i)
$$\int (6t^2 + 12t + 1)\,dt$$

$$= 2t^3 + 6t^2 + t + c$$

Given: This is $= 5$ when $t = -2$.

$$\therefore \quad 2(-2)^3 + 6(-2)^2 + (-2) + c = 5$$

$$\Rightarrow \quad -16 + 24 - 2 + c = 5$$

$$\Rightarrow \quad 6 + c = 5$$

$$c = -1$$

Thus, the constant of integration is –1.

(ii) Given: $f'(x) = 3x^2 - 2$

$$\Rightarrow \quad \int f'(x)\,dx = \int (3x^2 - 2)\,dx$$

[integrate both sides with respect to x]

$$\Rightarrow \quad f(x) = x^3 - 2x + c$$

or $\quad\quad y = x^3 - 2x + c$

Given: A point of the curve is (–2, 6).

Thus, when $x = -2$, $y = 6$

$$\Rightarrow \quad 6 = (-2)^3 - 2(-2) + c$$

$$\Rightarrow \quad 6 = -8 + 4 + c$$

$$\Rightarrow \quad c = 10$$

$$\therefore \quad \text{Thus, } f(x) = x^3 - 2x + 10.$$

The Definite Integral

$$\int_a^b f'(x)\,dx = [f(x)]_a^b = f(b) - f(a)$$

There is no constant of integration.

Example

Evaluate **(i)** $\displaystyle\int_1^3 (5x^2 + 3x)\,dx$

(ii) $\displaystyle\int_1^4 \left(\sqrt{x} - \frac{3}{x}\right)^2 dx$

(iii) $\displaystyle\int_0^2 \left(\frac{x^3 - 8}{x - 2}\right)dx$

(iv) $\displaystyle\int_1^4 \left(\frac{x^4 - x^3 + \sqrt{x} - 1}{x^2}\right)dx.$

Solution:

(i) $\displaystyle\int_1^3 (5x^2 + 3x)\,dx$

$$= \left[\frac{5x^3}{3} + \frac{3x^2}{2}\right]_1^3$$

$$= \left[\frac{5(3)^3}{3} + \frac{3(3)^2}{2}\right] - \left[\frac{5(1)^3}{3} + \frac{3(1)^2}{2}\right]$$

$$= \left(45 + \frac{27}{2}\right) - \left(\frac{5}{3} + \frac{3}{2}\right)$$

$$= 58\tfrac{1}{2} - 3\tfrac{1}{6}$$

$$= 55\tfrac{1}{3}$$

(ii) $\displaystyle\int_1^4 \left(\sqrt{x} - \frac{3}{x}\right)^2 dx = \int_1^4 \left(x - \frac{6}{\sqrt{x}} + \frac{9}{x^2}\right) dx$

$$= \int_1^4 (x - 6x^{-\frac{1}{2}} + 9x^{-2})\,dx$$

$$= \left[\frac{x^2}{2} - \frac{6x^{\frac{1}{2}}}{\frac{1}{2}} + \frac{9x^{-1}}{-1}\right]_1^4$$

$$= \left[\frac{x^2}{2} - 12\sqrt{x} - \frac{9}{x}\right]_1^4$$

$$= \left(\frac{4^2}{2} - 12\sqrt{4} - \frac{9}{4}\right) - \left(\frac{1^2}{2} - 12\sqrt{1} - \frac{9}{1}\right)$$

$$= (8 - 24 - 2\tfrac{1}{4}) - (\tfrac{1}{2} - 12 - 9)$$

$$= -18\tfrac{1}{4} + 20\tfrac{1}{2} = 2\tfrac{1}{4}$$

(iii) $\displaystyle\int_0^2 \left(\frac{x^3 - 8}{x - 2}\right) dx$

$$= \int_0^2 (x^2 + 2x + 4)\,dx$$

[using long division or factors]

$$= \left[\frac{x^3}{3} + \frac{2x^2}{2} + 4x\right]_0^2$$

$$= \left[\frac{x^3}{3} + x^2 + 4x\right]_0^2$$

$$= \left[\frac{2^3}{3} + 2^2 + 4(2)\right] - [0]$$

$$= \tfrac{8}{3} + 4 + 8$$

$$= 14\tfrac{2}{3}$$

(iv) $\displaystyle\int_1^4 \left(\frac{x^4 - x^3 + \sqrt{x} - 1}{x^2} \right) dx$

$\displaystyle = \int_1^4 \left(\frac{x^4}{x^2} - \frac{x^3}{x^2} + \frac{x^{\frac{1}{2}}}{x^2} - \frac{1}{x^2} \right) dx$

$\displaystyle = \int_1^4 \left(x^2 - x + x^{-\frac{3}{2}} - x^{-2} \right) dx$

$\displaystyle = \left[\frac{x^3}{3} - \frac{x^2}{2} + \frac{x^{-\frac{1}{2}}}{-\frac{1}{2}} - \frac{x^{-1}}{-1} \right]_1^4$

$\displaystyle = \left[\frac{x^3}{3} - \frac{x^2}{2} - \frac{2}{\sqrt{x}} + \frac{1}{x} \right]_1^4$

$\displaystyle = \left(\frac{64}{3} - \frac{16}{2} - \frac{2}{\sqrt{4}} + \frac{1}{4} \right) - \left(\frac{1}{3} - \frac{1}{2} - \frac{2}{\sqrt{1}} + \frac{1}{1} \right)$

$\displaystyle = (12\tfrac{7}{12}) - (-1\tfrac{1}{6}) = 13\tfrac{3}{4}$

Integration by Substitution

Some integrals may be found more easily by using substitution. When evaluating an indefinite integral by substitution the answer must be transformed back to a function of the original variable.

Example

Find **(i)** $\displaystyle\int (4x - 3)^4 \, dx$ **(ii)** $\displaystyle\int 2x(x^2 + 3)^5 \, dx$ **(iii)** $\displaystyle\int x\sqrt{1 - x^2} \, dx$.

Solution:

(i) $\displaystyle\int (4x - 3)^4 \, dx$

$\displaystyle = \int u^4 \cdot \frac{1}{4} \, du$

$\displaystyle = \frac{1}{4} \int u^4 \, du$

$\displaystyle = \frac{1}{4} \cdot \frac{u^5}{5} + c$

$\displaystyle = \frac{u^5}{20} + c$

$\displaystyle = \frac{(4x - 3)^5}{20} + c$

Substitution

let	$u = 4x - 3$
	$du = 4 \, dx$
	$\frac{1}{4} du = dx$

190

(ii) $\displaystyle\int 2x(x^2 + 3)^5\,dx$

<table>
<tr><td colspan="2">Substitution</td></tr>
<tr><td>Let</td><td>$u = x^2 + 3$</td></tr>
<tr><td></td><td>$du = 2x\,dx$</td></tr>
</table>

$\displaystyle = \int u^5\,du$

$\displaystyle = \frac{u^6}{6} + c$

$\displaystyle = \frac{(x^2 + 3)^6}{6} + c$

(iii) $\displaystyle\int x\sqrt{1 - x^2}\,dx$

<table>
<tr><td colspan="2">Substitution</td></tr>
<tr><td colspan="2">$u = 1 - x^2$</td></tr>
<tr><td colspan="2">$du = -2x\,dx$</td></tr>
<tr><td colspan="2">$-\frac{1}{2}du = x\,dx$</td></tr>
</table>

$\displaystyle = -\frac{1}{2}\int u^{\frac{1}{2}}\,du$

$\displaystyle = -\frac{1}{2}\cdot\frac{u^{\frac{3}{2}}}{\frac{3}{2}} + c$

$\displaystyle = -\frac{1}{2}\cdot\frac{2}{3}u^{\frac{3}{2}} + c$

$\displaystyle = -\frac{1}{3}u^{\frac{3}{2}} + c = -\frac{1}{3}(1 - x^2)^{\frac{3}{2}} + c$

Sometimes we have to rearrange as well as substitute.

Example

Find $\displaystyle\int \frac{x}{\sqrt{x - 3}}\,dx$.

Solution:

$\displaystyle\int \frac{x}{\sqrt{x - 3}}\,dx = \int \frac{u + 3}{u^{\frac{1}{2}}}\,du$

<table>
<tr><td colspan="2">Substitution</td></tr>
<tr><td>Let</td><td>$u = x - 3$</td></tr>
<tr><td></td><td>$du = dx$</td></tr>
<tr><td colspan="2">We must also do some rearranging:</td></tr>
<tr><td></td><td>$u = x - 3$</td></tr>
<tr><td>$\Rightarrow$</td><td>$x = u + 3$</td></tr>
</table>

$\displaystyle = \int (u^{\frac{1}{2}} + 3u^{-\frac{1}{2}})\,du$

$\displaystyle = \frac{u^{\frac{3}{2}}}{\frac{3}{2}} + 3\frac{u^{\frac{1}{2}}}{\frac{1}{2}} + c$

$\displaystyle = \frac{2}{3}u^{\frac{3}{2}} + 6u^{\frac{1}{2}} + c$

$\displaystyle = \frac{2}{3}(x - 3)^{\frac{3}{2}} + 6\sqrt{x - 3} + c$

Example

Evaluate (i) $\displaystyle\int_0^1 x(1+x^2)^5\,dx$ (ii) $\displaystyle\int_1^{\sqrt{6}} \frac{2x}{\sqrt{x^2+3}}\,dx$

Solution:

(i) $\displaystyle\int_0^1 x(1+x^2)^5\,dx$

Substitution

$$u = 1 + x^2$$
$$du = 2x\,dx$$
$$\tfrac{1}{2}\,du = x\,dx$$

$$\int x(1+x^2)^5\,dx$$

$$= \frac{1}{2}\int u^5\,du$$

$$= \frac{1}{2}\cdot\frac{u^6}{6} = \frac{1}{12}u^6 = \frac{1}{12}(1+x^2)^6$$

$$\therefore \int_0^1 x(1+x^2)^5\,dx$$

$$= \tfrac{1}{12}[(1+x^2)^6]_0^1$$

$$= \tfrac{1}{12}(2^6 - 1^6)$$

$$= \tfrac{1}{12}(64 - 1)$$

$$= \tfrac{1}{12}(63) = \tfrac{63}{12}$$

(ii) $\displaystyle\int_1^{\sqrt{6}} \frac{2x}{\sqrt{x^2+3}}\,dx$

Substitution

$$u = x^2 + 3$$
$$du = 2x\,dx$$

$$\int \frac{2x}{\sqrt{x^2+3}}\,dx$$

$$= \int \frac{1}{\sqrt{u}}\,du = \int \frac{1}{u^{\frac{1}{2}}}\,du$$

$$= \int u^{-\frac{1}{2}}\,du$$

$$= \frac{u^{\frac{1}{2}}}{\frac{1}{2}}$$

$$= 2u^{\frac{1}{2}} = 2\sqrt{u} = 2\sqrt{x^2+3}$$

$$\therefore \int_1^{\sqrt{6}} \frac{2x}{\sqrt{x^2+3}}\,dx$$

$$= 2[\sqrt{x^2+3}]_1^{\sqrt{6}}$$

$$= 2(3 - 2) = 2(1) = 2$$

Two Special Integrals

1. $\displaystyle\int e^{ax}\,dx = \frac{1}{a}e^{ax} + c$	or	$\displaystyle\int e^{ax+b}\,dx = \frac{1}{a}e^{ax+b} + c$
2. $\displaystyle\int \frac{1}{x}\,dx = \ln x + c$	or	$\displaystyle\int \frac{1}{ax+b}\,dx = \frac{1}{a}\ln(ax+b) + c$

Example

(i) Find $\int e^{5x-2}\,dx$.

(ii) Evaluate $\int_0^1 6xe^{x^2}\,dx$.

Solution:

(i) $\int e^{5x-2}\,dx = \frac{1}{5}e^{5x-2} + c$

(ii) $\int_0^1 6xe^{x^2}\,dx$

Substitution
$u = x^2$ (power of e)
$du = 2x\,dx$
$3\,du = 6x\,dx$

$\int 6x\, e^{x^2}\,dx = 3\int e^u\,du$

$= 3e^u$

$= 3e^{x^2}$

$\therefore \quad \int_0^1 6xe^{x^2}\,dx = 3[e^{x^2}]_0^1$

$= 3(e^1 - e^0) = 3(e - 1)$

Example

Find (i) $\int \dfrac{2\,dx}{3x + 1}$ (ii) $\int \dfrac{2x\,dx}{x^2 + 1}$.

Solution:

(i) $\int \dfrac{2\,dx}{3x + 1}$

Substitution
$u = 3x + 1$
$du = 3\,dx$
$\frac{1}{3}\,du = dx$

$\therefore \quad \int \dfrac{2\,dx}{3x + 1} = 2\int \dfrac{dx}{3x + 1}$

$= 2\cdot\dfrac{1}{3}\int \dfrac{du}{u}$

$= \frac{2}{3}\ln u + c$

$= \frac{2}{3}\ln(3x + 1) + c$

(ii) $\int \dfrac{2x\,dx}{x^2 + 1}$

Substitution
$u = x^2 - 1$
$du = 2x\,dx$

$\therefore \quad \int \dfrac{2x\,dx}{x^2 + 1}$

$= \int \dfrac{du}{u}$

$= \ln u$

$= \ln(x^2 + 1) + c$

Example

Evaluate $\int_0^6 \dfrac{x}{x+3}\,dx$.

Solution:

$$\int \frac{x}{x+3}\,dx = \int \frac{u-3}{u}\,du$$

$$= \int \left(1 - \frac{3}{u}\right)du$$

$$= \int \left(1 - 3\frac{1}{u}\right)du$$

$$= u - 3\ln u$$

$$= (x+3) - 3\ln(x+3)$$

$$\therefore \quad \int_0^6 \frac{x}{x+3} = [(x+3) - 3\ln(x+3)]_0^6$$

$$= (9 - 3\ln 9) - (3 - 3\ln 3)$$

$$= 9 - 3\ln 9 - 3 + 3\ln 3$$

$$= 6 - 3(\ln 9 - \ln 3)$$

$$= 6 - 3\ln\tfrac{9}{3}$$

$$= 6 - 3\ln 3$$

Substitution

$$u = x + 3$$
$$du = dx$$

rearranging is also required:

$$u = x + 3$$
$$u - 3 = x$$

Example

Evaluate **(i)** $\int_0^1 \dfrac{e^{\sqrt{x}}}{\sqrt{x}}\,dx$ **(ii)** $\int_0^{\ln 2} \dfrac{e^x}{e^x + 3}\,dx$ **(iii)** $\int_0^1 \dfrac{dx}{1 + e^{-x}}$.

Solution:

(i) $\displaystyle\int_0^1 \frac{e^{\sqrt{x}}}{\sqrt{x}}\,dx = \int_0^1 \frac{1}{\sqrt{x}} \cdot e^{\sqrt{x}}\,dx$

$$\int \frac{1}{\sqrt{x}} \cdot e^{\sqrt{x}}\,dx = 2\int e^u\,dx$$

$$= 2e^u = 2e^{\sqrt{x}}$$

$$\therefore \quad \int_0^1 \frac{e^{\sqrt{x}}}{\sqrt{x}}\,dx = 2[e^{\sqrt{x}}]_0^1$$

$$= 2(e^1 - e^0) = 2(e - 1)$$

Substitution

$$u = \sqrt{x}$$
$$u = x^{\frac{1}{2}}$$
$$du = \frac{1}{2\sqrt{x}}\,dx$$
$$2\,du = \frac{1}{\sqrt{x}}\,dx$$

(ii) $\displaystyle\int_0^{\ln 2} \frac{e^x}{e^x + 3}\,dx$

Substitution

$$u = e^x + 3$$
$$du = e^x\,dx$$

$$\int \frac{e^x}{e^x + 3}\,dx = \int \frac{du}{u}$$

$$= \ln u$$
$$= \ln (e^x + 3)$$

$$\therefore \int_0^{\ln 2} \frac{e^x}{e^x + 3}\,dx = [\ln (e^x + 3)]_0^{\ln 2}$$

Note:

$$a^{\log_a b} = b$$
$$\therefore \quad e^{\ln 2} = e^{\log_e 2} = 2$$

$$= \ln (e^{\ln 2} + 3) - \ln(e^0 + 3)$$
$$= \ln (2 + 3) - \ln(1 + 3)$$
$$= \ln 5 - \ln 4 = \ln\tfrac{5}{4}$$

(iii) Avoid e^{-x} if possible.

$$\frac{1}{1 + e^{-x}} = \frac{1}{1 + \dfrac{1}{e^x}} = \frac{e^x}{e^x + 1} \qquad \text{[multiply each part of the fraction by } e^x]$$

$$\therefore \quad \int_0^1 \frac{1}{1 + e^{-x}}\,dx = \int_0^1 \frac{e^x}{e^x + 1}\,dx$$

Substitution

$$u = e^x + 1$$
$$du = e^x\,dx$$

$$\int \frac{e^x}{e^x + 1}\,dx = \int \frac{du}{u}$$

$$= \ln u = \ln(e^x + 1)$$

$$\therefore \quad \int_0^1 \frac{dx}{1 + e^{-x}} = [\ln (e^x + 1)]_0^1$$

$$= \ln(e^1 + 1) - \ln(e^0 + 1)$$
$$= \ln(e + 1) - \ln(2) = \ln\left(\frac{e + 1}{2}\right)$$

Trigonometric Integrals

$$\int \cos(nx + k) = \frac{1}{n} \sin(nx + k) + c \quad \text{and} \quad \int \sin(nx + k) = -\frac{1}{n} \cos(nx + k) + c$$

Example

Find (i) $\displaystyle\int \cos 5x\, dx$ (ii) $\displaystyle\int \sin(3x - 2)\, dx$ (iii) $\displaystyle\int (\cos 3\theta + \sin(2\theta - 3))\, d\theta$.

Solution:

(i) $\displaystyle\int \cos 5x\, dx = \frac{1}{5} \sin 5x + c$

(ii) $\displaystyle\int \sin(3x - 2)dx = -\frac{1}{3}\cos(3x - 2) + c$

(iii) $\displaystyle\int (\cos 3\theta + \sin(2\theta - 3))d\theta = \frac{1}{3}\sin 3\theta - \frac{1}{2}\cos(2\theta - 3) + c$

Products $\displaystyle\int \sin mx .\cos nx$

Always write the bigger angle first and then use the formulae on page 9 of the tables to change the product into a sum or difference.

Example

(i) Find $\displaystyle\int \sin 5x \cos 9x\, dx$ (ii) Evaluate $\displaystyle\int_0^{\frac{\pi}{6}} \cos 2\theta \sin 4\theta\, d\theta$.

Solution:

(i) $\displaystyle\int \sin 5x \cos 9x\, dx$

$\displaystyle = \int \cos 9x \sin 5x\, dx$ [put bigger angle first]

$\displaystyle = \int \frac{1}{2}[\sin(9x + 5x) - \sin(9x - 5x)]dx$ [using tables, page 9]

$\displaystyle = \frac{1}{2} \int (\sin 14x - \sin 4x)dx$

$\displaystyle = \frac{1}{2}\left(-\frac{\cos 14x}{14} + \frac{\cos 4x}{4}\right) + c$

$$= -\frac{\cos 14x}{28} + \frac{\cos 4x}{8} + c$$

$$= \frac{\cos 4x}{8} - \frac{\cos 14x}{28} + c$$

(ii) $\displaystyle\int_0^{\frac{\pi}{6}} \cos 2\theta \sin 4\theta \, d\theta$

$$= \int_0^{\frac{\pi}{6}} \sin 4\theta \cos 2\theta \, d\theta \qquad\qquad \text{[put bigger angle first]}$$

$$= \int_0^{\frac{\pi}{6}} \frac{1}{2}[\sin(4\theta + 2\theta) + \sin(4\theta - 2\theta)] \, d\theta \quad \text{[using tables, page 9]}$$

$$= \frac{1}{2} \int_0^{\frac{\pi}{6}} \sin 6\theta + \sin 2\theta) \, d\theta$$

$$= \frac{1}{2} \left[-\frac{\cos 6\theta}{6} - \frac{\cos 2\theta}{2} \right]_0^{\frac{\pi}{6}}$$

$$= -\frac{1}{2} \left[\frac{\cos 6\theta}{6} + \frac{\cos 2\theta}{2} \right]_0^{\frac{\pi}{6}}$$

$$= -\frac{1}{2} \left[\left(\frac{\cos \pi}{6} + \frac{\cos \dfrac{\pi}{3}}{2} \right) - \left(\frac{\cos 0}{6} + \frac{\cos 0}{2} \right) \right]$$

$$= -\frac{1}{2} \left[\left(-\frac{1}{6} + \frac{1}{4} \right) - \left(\frac{1}{6} + \frac{1}{2} \right) \right]$$

$$= -\frac{1}{2} \left(-\frac{7}{12} \right) = \frac{7}{24}$$

$$\int \cos^2 x \, dx \quad \text{or} \quad \int \sin^2 x \, dx$$

Rewrite the integrand using the double angle formulae on page 9 of the tables.

$$\cos^2 x = \tfrac{1}{2}(1 + \cos 2x) \quad \text{and} \quad \sin^2 = \tfrac{1}{2}(1 - \cos 2x)$$

Example

Evaluate (i) $\displaystyle\int_0^{\frac{\pi}{4}} \cos^2 x \, dx$ (ii) $\displaystyle\int_{\frac{\pi}{8}}^{\frac{\pi}{4}} 2 \sin^2 4\theta \, d\theta.$

Solution:

(i) $\displaystyle\int_0^{\frac{\pi}{4}} \cos^2 x \, dx$

$$= \int_0^{\frac{\pi}{4}} \frac{1}{2}(1 + \cos 2x) \, dx$$

$$= \frac{1}{2} \int_0^{\frac{\pi}{4}} (1 + \cos 2x) \, dx$$

$$= \frac{1}{2}\left[x + \frac{\sin 2x}{2} \right]_0^{\frac{\pi}{4}}$$

$$= \frac{1}{2}\left[\left(\frac{\pi}{4} + \frac{\sin \frac{\pi}{2}}{2} \right) - \left(0 + \frac{\sin 0}{2} \right) \right]$$

$$= \frac{1}{2}\left[\left(\frac{\pi}{4} + \frac{1}{2} \right) - (0 + 0) \right]$$

$$= \frac{\pi}{8} + \frac{1}{4}$$

(ii) $\displaystyle\int_{\frac{\pi}{8}}^{\frac{\pi}{4}} 2 \sin^2 4\theta \, d\theta$

$$= \int_{\frac{\pi}{8}}^{\frac{\pi}{4}} 2 \cdot \frac{1}{2}(1 - \cos 8\theta) \, d\theta$$

$$= \int_{\frac{\pi}{8}}^{\frac{\pi}{4}} (1 - \cos 8\theta) \, d\theta$$

$$= \left[\theta - \frac{\sin 8\theta}{8} \right]_{\frac{\pi}{8}}^{\frac{\pi}{4}}$$

$$= \left(\frac{\pi}{4} - \frac{\sin 2\pi}{8} \right) - \left(\frac{\pi}{8} - \frac{\sin \pi}{8} \right)$$

$$= \left(\frac{\pi}{4} - 0 \right) - \left(\frac{\pi}{8} - 0 \right)$$

$$= \frac{\pi}{4} - \frac{\pi}{8} = \frac{\pi}{8}$$

$$\int \cos^2 x \sin x \, dx \quad \text{or} \quad \int \sin^2 x \cos x \, dx$$

The substitution required is to let u = (trigonometric function with the even power).

Example

(i) Find $\displaystyle\int \cos \theta (2 + 3 \sin^2 \theta) \, d\theta$ (ii) Evaluate $\displaystyle\int_0^{\frac{\pi}{2}} \sin x \cos^2 x \, dx.$

Solution:

(i) $\displaystyle\int \cos\theta(2 + 3\sin^2\theta)\,d\theta$

Substitution
$u = \sin\theta$
$du = \cos\theta\,d\theta$

$\displaystyle= \int (2 + 3u^2)\,du$

$= 2u + u^3 + c$

$= 2\sin\theta + \sin^3\theta + c$

(ii) $\displaystyle\int_0^{\frac{\pi}{2}} \sin x \cos^2 x\,dx$

Substitution
$u = \cos x$
$du = -\sin x\,dx$
$-du = \sin x\,dx$

$\displaystyle\int \sin x \cos^2 x\,dx = -\int u^2\,du$

$= -\tfrac{1}{3}u^3$

$= -\tfrac{1}{3}\cos^3 x$

$\therefore \displaystyle\int_0^{\frac{\pi}{2}} \sin x \cos^2 x\,dx = -\tfrac{1}{3}[\cos^3 x]_0^{\frac{\pi}{2}} = -\tfrac{1}{3}(0 - 1) = \tfrac{1}{3}$

Example

Evaluate $\displaystyle\int_0^{\frac{\pi}{2}} \sin 2x\, e^{\sin^2 x}\,dx$.

Solution:

$\displaystyle\int_0^{\frac{\pi}{2}} \sin 2x\, e^{\sin^2 x}\,dx$

$\displaystyle\int \sin 2x\, e^{\sin^2 x}\,dx$

$u = \sin^2 x$ (power of e)
$du = 2\sin x \cos x\,dx$
$du = \sin 2x\,dx$

$\displaystyle= \int e^u\,du = e^u = e^{\sin^2 x}$

$\therefore \displaystyle\int_0^{\frac{\pi}{2}} \sin 2x\, e^{\sin^2 x}\,dx = [e^{\sin^2 x}]_0^{\frac{\pi}{2}}$

$\displaystyle= e^1 + e^0 \left[\sin^2\frac{\pi}{2} = \left(\sin\frac{\pi}{2}\right)^2 = 1^2 = 1 \right]$

$= e - 1$

Example

Simplify $\dfrac{\cos^3 x}{1 + \sin x}$ and, hence, evaluate $\displaystyle\int_0^{\frac{\pi}{2}} \dfrac{\cos^3 x \, dx}{1 + \sin x}$.

Solution:

$$\dfrac{\cos^3 x}{1 + \sin x} = \dfrac{\cos^2 x \cdot \cos x}{1 + \sin x}$$

$$= \dfrac{(1 - \sin^2 x)\cos x}{(1 + \sin x)} = \dfrac{(1 - \sin x)(1 + \sin x)\cos x}{(1 + \sin x)} = (1 - \sin x)\cos x$$

Thus, $\displaystyle\int_0^{\frac{\pi}{2}} \dfrac{\cos^3 x \, dx}{1 + \sin x} = \int_0^{\frac{\pi}{2}} (1 - \sin x)\cos x \, dx$

$$\int (1 - \sin x)\cos x \, dx = -\int u \, du$$

$$= -\dfrac{u^2}{2} = \dfrac{-(1 - \sin x)^2}{2}$$

$$\therefore \int_0^{\frac{\pi}{2}} (1 - \sin x)\cos x \, dx = -\dfrac{1}{2}[(1 - \sin x)^2]_0^{\frac{\pi}{2}}$$

$$= -\tfrac{1}{2}[(1 - 1)^2 - (1 - 0)^2]$$

$$= -\tfrac{1}{2}(0 - 1) = \tfrac{1}{2}$$

Substitution

$u = 1 - \sin x$
$du = -\cos x \, dx$
$-du = \cos x \, dx$

One of the limits missing

Example

(i)   Given that $a > 0$ and $\displaystyle\int_1^a (3x^2 - 2x - 4) \, dx = 10$, find a.

(ii)   If $\displaystyle\int_e^{e^t} \dfrac{dx}{x \ln x} = \ln 2$, find t.

Solution:

(i) $\displaystyle\int_1^a (3x^2 - 2x - 4) \, dx = 10$

$\Rightarrow \qquad\qquad [x^3 - x^2 - 4x]_1^a = 10$

$\Rightarrow \quad (a^3 - a^2 - 4a) - (1 - 1 - 4) = 10$

$\Rightarrow \qquad\qquad a^3 - a^2 - 4a - 6 = 0$

$\qquad\qquad f(3) = 3^3 - 3^2 - 4(3) - 6 = 27 - 9 - 12 - 6 = 0$

Thus, $a = 3$ ($a = 3$ is the only real solution of $a^3 - a^2 - 4a - 6 = 0$).

(ii) $\displaystyle\int_{e}^{e^{t}} \frac{dx}{x \ln x} = \ln 2$

$$\int \frac{dx}{x \ln x} = \int \frac{1}{x} \cdot \frac{1}{\ln x} \, dx$$

Substitution

$u = \ln x$
$du = \dfrac{1}{x} dx$

$$= \int \frac{1}{u} \, du$$

$$= \ln u$$

$$= \ln(\ln x)$$

$\therefore \displaystyle\int_{e}^{e^{t}} \frac{dx}{x \ln x} = [\ln(\ln x)]_{e}^{e^{t}}$

Notes:

$\ln e = \log_{e} e = 1$

$\ln e^{t} = \log_{e} e^{t} = t \log_{e} e = t(1) = t$

$\ln 1 = 0$

$$= \ln(\ln e^{t}) - \ln(\ln e)$$

$$= \ln t - \ln 1$$

$$= \ln t$$

Given: $\ln t = \ln 2$

$\Rightarrow \quad t = 2$

Further Special Integrals

$$\boxed{\int \frac{dx}{a^{2} + x^{2}} = \frac{1}{a} \tan^{-1} \frac{x}{a} + c}$$

Example

Find **(i)** $\displaystyle\int \frac{dx}{16 + x^{2}}$ **(ii)** $\displaystyle\int \frac{dx}{25 + x^{2}}$.

Solution:

(i)

$$\int \frac{dx}{16 + x^{2}}$$

$$= \int \frac{dx}{4^{2} + x^{2}}$$

$$= \frac{1}{4} \tan^{-1} \frac{x}{4} + c$$

(ii)

$$\int \frac{dx}{25 + x^{2}}$$

$$= \int \frac{dx}{5^{2} + x^{2}}$$

$$= \frac{1}{5} \tan^{-1} \frac{x}{5} + c$$

Sometimes a substitution is required.

Example

Evaluate $\displaystyle\int_{\frac{2}{3}}^{\frac{2\sqrt{3}}{3}} \frac{dx}{4 + 9x^2}$.

Solution:

$\displaystyle\int_{\frac{2}{3}}^{\frac{2\sqrt{3}}{3}} \frac{dx}{4 + 9x^2}$

$$\int \frac{dx}{4 + 9x^2} = \int \frac{dx}{2^2 + (3x)^2}$$

Substitution

$u = 3x$
$du = 3\,dx$
$\frac{1}{3}du = dx$

$$= \frac{1}{3} \int \frac{du}{2^2 + u^2}$$

$$= \frac{1}{3} \cdot \frac{1}{2} \tan^{-1} \frac{u}{2}$$

$$= \frac{1}{6} \tan^{-1} \frac{3x}{2}$$

$$\therefore \int_{\frac{2}{3}}^{\frac{2\sqrt{3}}{3}} \frac{dx}{4 + 9x^2} = \frac{1}{6} \left[\tan^{-1} \frac{3x}{2} \right]_{\frac{2}{3}}^{\frac{2\sqrt{3}}{3}}$$

$$= \tfrac{1}{6}(\tan^{-1}\sqrt{3} - \tan^{-1} 1)$$

$$= \frac{1}{6}\left(\frac{\pi}{3} - \frac{\pi}{4} \right) = \frac{1}{6}\left(\frac{\pi}{12} \right) = \frac{\pi}{72}$$

A more difficult variation on the above involves completing the square.

Example

Find the values of p and q such that $x^2 - 4x + 13 \equiv (x - p)^2 + q^2$.

Hence, evaluate $\displaystyle\int_2^3 \frac{dx}{x^2 - 4x + 13}$, giving your answer in the form $k \tan^{-1} k$.

Write down the value of k.

Solution:

$$x^2 - 4x + 13 = x^2 - 4x + 4 + 9 = (x-2)^2 + 3^2 = (x-p)^2 + q^2$$

$$\Rightarrow \quad p = 2 \quad \text{and} \quad q = 3$$

$$\int \frac{dx}{x^2 - 4x + 13} = \int \frac{dx}{(x-2)^2 + 3^2}$$

Substitution

$$\boxed{\begin{array}{l} u = x - 2 \\ du = dx \end{array}}$$

$$= \int \frac{du}{u^2 + 3^2}$$

$$= \frac{1}{3} \tan^{-1} \frac{u}{3}$$

$$= \frac{1}{3} \tan^{-1} \frac{x-2}{3}$$

$$\therefore \quad \int_2^3 \frac{dx}{x^2 - 4x + 13} = \frac{1}{3}\left[\tan^{-1} \frac{x-2}{3} \right]_2^3$$

$$= \frac{1}{3}(\tan^{-1} \tfrac{1}{3} - \tan^{-1} 0) = \frac{1}{3} \tan^{-1} \tfrac{1}{3} = k \tan^{-1} k$$

Thus, $k = \frac{1}{3}$.

$$\boxed{\int \frac{dx}{\sqrt{a^2 - x^2}} = \sin^{-1} \frac{x}{a} + c}$$

Example

(i) Find $\displaystyle\int \frac{dx}{\sqrt{16 - x^2}}$.

(ii) Evaluate $\displaystyle\int_0^{\sqrt{3}} \frac{dx}{\sqrt{4 - x^2}}$.

Solution:

(i)
$$\int \frac{dx}{\sqrt{16 - x^2}}$$

$$= \int \frac{dx}{\sqrt{4^2 - x^2}}$$

$$= \sin^{-1} \frac{x}{4} + c$$

(ii)
$$\int_0^{\sqrt{3}} \frac{dx}{\sqrt{4 - x^2}}$$

$$= \int_0^{\sqrt{3}} \frac{dx}{\sqrt{2^2 - x^2}}$$

$$= \left[\sin^{-1} \frac{x}{2} \right]_0^{\sqrt{3}}$$

$$= \sin^{-1} \frac{\sqrt{3}}{2} - \sin^{-1} 0 = \frac{\pi}{3} - 0 = \frac{\pi}{3}$$

Sometimes a substitution is required.

Example

Evaluate $= \displaystyle\int_0^{\frac{3}{4}} \frac{dx}{\sqrt{9 - 4x^2}}$.

Solution:

$$\int_0^{\frac{3}{4}} \frac{dx}{\sqrt{9 - 4x^2}} = \int_0^{\frac{3}{4}} \frac{dx}{\sqrt{3^2 - (2x)^2}}$$

$$\int \frac{dx}{\sqrt{9 - 4x^2}} = \frac{1}{2} \int \frac{du}{\sqrt{3^2 - u^2}}$$

Substitution

$$u = 2x$$

$$du = 2\,dx$$

$$\tfrac{1}{2}\,du = dx$$

$$= \frac{1}{2} \sin^{-1} \frac{u}{3}$$

$$= \frac{1}{2} \sin^{-1} \frac{2x}{3}$$

$$\therefore \quad \int_0^{\frac{3}{4}} \frac{dx}{\sqrt{9 - 4x^2}} = \frac{1}{2}\left[\sin^{-1} \frac{2x}{3} \right]_0^{\frac{3}{4}}$$

$$= \tfrac{1}{2}(\sin^{-1}\tfrac{1}{2} - \sin^{-1}0)$$

$$= \tfrac{1}{2}\sin^{-1}\tfrac{1}{2}$$

$$= \frac{1}{2}\left(\frac{\pi}{6} \right) = \frac{\pi}{12}$$

A more difficult variation on the above involves completing the square.

Example

Find $\displaystyle\int \frac{dx}{\sqrt{8 - 2x - x^2}}$.

Solution:

First of all we must write $8 - 2x - x^2$ in the form $p^2 - (x + q)^2$.

$$8 - 2x - x^2 = 8 - (x^2 + 2x) = 8 + 1 - (x^2 + 2x + 1) = 9 - (x + 1)^2 = 3^2 - (x + 1)^2$$

         ↑   ↑

     add 1   subtract 1

Thus, $\displaystyle\int \frac{dx}{\sqrt{8 - 2x - x^2}} = \int \frac{dx}{\sqrt{3^2 - (x + 1)^2}}$

Substitution

$u = x + 1$
$du = dx$

$$= \int \frac{du}{\sqrt{3^2 - u^2}}$$

$$= \sin^{-1} \frac{u}{3} + c$$

$$= \sin^{-1} \frac{x + 1}{3} + c$$

Integrals of the form $\displaystyle\int \sqrt{a^2 - x^2}\ dx$ (not in the tables)

Method: Use the substitution $x = a \sin \theta$.

Note: It is simpler to change the limits to the corresponding limits for θ.

Example

Evaluate $\displaystyle\int_0^4 \sqrt{16 - x^2}\ dx$.

Solution:

$$\int \sqrt{16 - x^2}\ dx = \int \sqrt{4^2 - x^2}\ dx$$

Substitution

$x = 4 \sin \theta$
$dx = 4 \cos \theta\ d\theta$

$16 - x^2 = 16 - 16 \sin^2 \theta = 16(1 - \sin^2 \theta) = 16 \cos^2 \theta$

$\therefore \quad \sqrt{16 - x^2} = \sqrt{16 \cos^2 \theta} = 4 \cos \theta$

$\therefore \quad \displaystyle\int_0^4 \sqrt{16 - x^2}\ dx$

$$= \int_0^{\frac{\pi}{2}} 4 \cos \theta .4 \cos \theta\ d\theta$$

$$= 16 \int_0^{\frac{\pi}{2}} \cos^2 \theta\ d\theta = 16 \int_0^{\frac{\pi}{2}} \frac{1}{2}(1 + \cos 2\theta)\ d\theta = 8 \int_0^{\frac{\pi}{2}} (1 + \cos 2\theta)\ d\theta$$

$$= 8[\theta + \tfrac{1}{2} \sin 2\theta]_0^{\frac{\pi}{2}}$$

$$= 8\left[\left(\frac{\pi}{2} + 0\right) - (0 - 0)\right] = 8\left(\frac{\pi}{2}\right) = 4\pi$$

Limits

$x = 4$	$x = 0$
$4 \sin \theta = 4$	$4 \sin \theta = 0$
$\sin \theta = 1$	$\sin \theta = 0$
$\theta = \dfrac{\pi}{2}$	$\theta = 0$

Example

Evaluate $\displaystyle\int_0^{\frac{2}{3}} \sqrt{4 - 9x^2}\, dx$.

Solution:

$$\int_0^{\frac{2}{3}} \sqrt{4 - 9x^2}\, dx = \int_0^{\frac{2}{3}} \sqrt{2^2 - (3x)^2}\, dx \quad \text{[write in the form } \sqrt{a^2 - x^2}\text{]}$$

$4 - 9x^2 = 4 - 4\sin^2\theta = 4(1 - \sin^2\theta) = 4\cos^2\theta$ \qquad Substitution

$\therefore\ \sqrt{4 - 9x^2} = \sqrt{4\cos^2\theta} = 2\cos\theta$

Substitution
$3x = 2\sin\theta$
$3\,dx = 2\cos\theta\,d\theta$
$dx = \frac{2}{3}\cos\theta\,d\theta$

$\therefore\quad \displaystyle\int_0^{\frac{2}{3}} \sqrt{4 - 9x^2}\, dx$

$$= \int_0^{\frac{\pi}{2}} 2\cos\theta \cdot \frac{2}{3}\cos\theta\,d\theta$$

Limits

$$= \frac{4}{3}\int_0^{\frac{\pi}{2}} \cos^2\theta\,d\theta$$

$$= \frac{4}{3}\int_0^{\frac{\pi}{2}} \frac{1}{2}(1 + \cos 2\theta)\,d\theta$$

$$= \frac{2}{3}\int_0^{\frac{\pi}{2}} (1 + \cos 2\theta)\,d\theta$$

$x = \frac{2}{3}$	$x = 0$
$2\sin\theta = 3x$	$2\sin\theta = 3x$
$2\sin\theta = 2$	$2\sin\theta = 0$
$\sin\theta = 1$	$\sin\theta = 0$
$\theta = \frac{\pi}{2}$	$\theta = 0$

$$= \frac{2}{3}[\theta + \tfrac{1}{2}\sin 2\theta]_0^{\frac{\pi}{2}}$$

$$= \frac{2}{3}\left[\left(\frac{\pi}{2} + \frac{1}{2}\sin\pi\right) - \left(0 - \frac{1}{2}\sin 0\right)\right] = \frac{2}{3}\left(\frac{\pi}{2}\right) = \frac{\pi}{3}$$

Example

Evaluate $\displaystyle\int_{-3}^{-1} \sqrt{7 - 6x - x^2}\, dx$.

Solution:
First write $7 - 6x - x^2$ in the form $a^2 - (x + b)^2$.

$$7 - 6x - x^2 = 7 - (x^2 + 6x) = 7 + 9 - (x^2 + 6x + 9) = 16 - (x + 3)^2 = 4^2 - (x + 3)^2$$

$\qquad\qquad\qquad\qquad\uparrow\qquad\qquad\qquad\qquad\uparrow$

$\qquad\qquad\qquad\quad$ add 9 $\qquad\quad$ subtract 9

$$\int_{-3}^{-1} \sqrt{7 - 6x - x^2}\, dx = \int_{-3}^{-1} \sqrt{4^2 - (x + 3)^2}\, dx$$

Substitution

$4^2 - (x + 3)^2 = 16 - 16\sin^2\theta = 16(1 - \sin^2\theta) = 16\cos^2\theta$

Substitution
$x + 3 = 4\sin\theta$
$dx = 4\cos\theta\,d\theta$

$\therefore\quad \sqrt{4^2 - (x + 3)^2} = \sqrt{16\cos^2\theta} = 4\cos\theta$

206

$$\therefore \quad \int_{-3}^{-1} \sqrt{4 - (x+3)^2}\, dx$$

$$= \int_{0}^{\frac{\pi}{6}} 4\cos\theta.4\cos\theta\, d\theta = 16 \int_{0}^{\frac{\pi}{6}} \cos^2\theta\, d\theta = 16 \int_{0}^{\frac{\pi}{6}} \frac{1}{2}(1 + \cos 2\theta)$$

$$= 8 \int_{0}^{\frac{\pi}{6}} (1 + \cos 2\theta)\, d\theta$$

$$= 8\left[\theta + \tfrac{1}{2}\sin 2\theta\right]_{0}^{\frac{\pi}{6}}$$

$$= 8\left[\left(\frac{\pi}{6} + \frac{1}{2}\sin\frac{\pi}{3}\right) - \left(0 - \frac{1}{2}\sin 0\right)\right]$$

$$= 8\left(\frac{\pi}{6} + \frac{\sqrt{3}}{4}\right)$$

Limits

x = −1	x = −3
$4\sin\theta = x + 3$	$4\sin\theta = x + 3$
$4\sin\theta = 2$	$4\sin\theta = 0$
$\sin\theta = \tfrac{1}{2}$	$\sin\theta = 0$
$\theta = \dfrac{\pi}{6}$	$\theta = 0$

Applications of Integration: Areas and Volumes

Area

Area between a curve and the x-axis:

The area, A, bounded by the curve $y = f(x)$, the x-axis, and the lines $x = a$ and $x = b$ is given by:

$$A = \int_{a}^{b} y\, dx$$

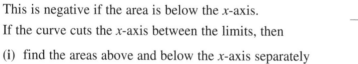

This is positive if the area is above the x-axis.

This is negative if the area is below the x-axis.

If the curve cuts the x-axis between the limits, then

(i) find the areas above and below the x-axis separately

(ii) add these two values together.

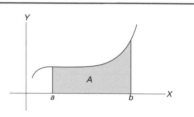

Area between a curve and the y-axis:

The area, A, bounded by the curve $y = f(x)$, the y-axis and the lines $y = a$ and $y = b$ is given by:

$$A = \int_{a}^{b} x\, dy$$

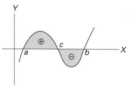

This is positive if the area is to the right of the y-axis.

This is negative if the area is to the left of the y-axis.

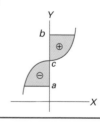

Example

Find the area bounded by the curve $y = x^2 - 7x + 10$, the x-axis and the lines $x = 1$ to $x = 4$.

Solution:

First make a sketch of the curve $y = x^2 - 7x + 10$.

It cuts the x-axis at $y = 0$, i.e.

$$x^2 - 7x + 10 = 0$$
$$\Rightarrow \quad (x - 2)(x - 5) = 0$$
$$\Rightarrow \quad x = 2 \quad \text{or} \quad x = 5$$

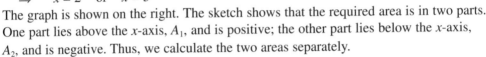

The graph is shown on the right. The sketch shows that the required area is in two parts. One part lies above the x-axis, A_1, and is positive; the other part lies below the x-axis, A_2, and is negative. Thus, we calculate the two areas separately.

$$A_1 = \int_1^2 (x^2 - 7x + 10) \, dx$$

$$= \left[\frac{x^3}{3} - \frac{7x^2}{2} + 10x \right]_1^2$$

$$= (\tfrac{8}{3} - 14 + 20) - (\tfrac{1}{3} - \tfrac{7}{2} + 10)$$

$$= \frac{11}{6}$$

$$A_2 = \int_2^4 (x^2 - 7x + 10) \, dx$$

$$= \left[\frac{x^3}{3} - \frac{7x^2}{2} + 10x \right]_2^4$$

$$= \left(\frac{64}{3} - 56 + 40 \right) - \left(\frac{8}{3} - 14 + 20 \right)$$

$$= -\frac{10}{3}$$

Thus, $A = A_1 + A_2 = \dfrac{11}{6} + \dfrac{10}{3} = \dfrac{31}{6} = 5\tfrac{1}{6}.$

Example

Find the area of the bounded region enclosed by the curve $y = \dfrac{2x}{x^2 + 1}$, the x-axis, the line $x = 1$ and the line $x = 2\sqrt{2}$.

Solution:

$$y = \frac{2x}{x^2 + 1}$$

The graph is always above the x-axis for $x > 0$,

as $\dfrac{2x}{x^2 + 1} > 0$ for $x > 0$.

$$A = \int_1^{2\sqrt{2}} y \, dx = \int_1^{2\sqrt{2}} \frac{2x}{x^2 + 1} \, dx$$

$$= \int \frac{1}{u} \, du$$

$$= \ln u$$

$$= [\ln(x^2 + 1)]_1^{2\sqrt{2}}$$

$$= \ln 9 - \ln 2 = \ln \tfrac{9}{2}$$

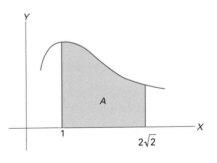

Substitution

$$u = x^2 + 1$$
$$du = 2x \, dx$$

Area between two curves

> 1. We need to find where the curves intersect.
> 2. Subtract the areas under the curves between the points of intersection.

This can be done by the evaluation of one integral using the *x*-coordinates of the point of intersection as the limits.

Example

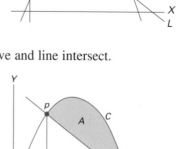

The diagram shows part of the curve

$C: y = 3 + 6x - x^2$ and the line $L: y = 15 - 2x$.

(i) Find the *x*-coordinates of *p* and *q*.

(ii) Calculate the area bounded by *C* and *L*.

Solution:

(i) We need to find the *x*-coordinates where the curve and line intersect.

$$C: y = 3 + 6x - x^2 \quad L: y = 15 - 2x$$

Thus, $\qquad 3 + 6x - x^2 = 15 - 2x$

$\Rightarrow \qquad -x^2 + 8x - 12 = 0$

$\Rightarrow \qquad x^2 - 8x + 12 = 0$

$\Rightarrow \qquad (x - 2)(x - 6) = 0$

$\Rightarrow \qquad x = 2 \quad \text{or} \quad x = 6$

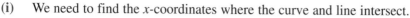

(ii) The shaded region represents the area bounded by the curve, *C*, and the line, *L*, i.e. the area under the curve *less* the area under the line, between the limits $x = 2$ and $x = 6$.

$$\text{Shaded area} = A = \int_2^6 (3 + 6x - x^2)\,dx - \int_2^6 (15 - 2x)\,dx$$

$$= \int_2^6 (3 + 6x - x^2 - 15 + 2x)\,dx$$

$$= \int_2^6 (8x - x^2 - 12)\,dx$$

$$= \left[4x^2 - \frac{x^3}{3} - 12x \right]_2^6$$

$$= (144 - 72 - 72) - (16 - \tfrac{8}{3} - 24)$$

$$= 10\tfrac{2}{3}$$

In the next example we are asked to find the area enclosed by a curve and a line parallel to the *y*-axis. Two methods will be used.

Example

Find the area enclosed by the curve $y = x^2 + 1$ and the line $y = 5$.

Solution:

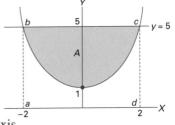

$y = x^2 + 1$

$x = 0: y = 1$ ∴ curve cuts the *y*-axis at $y = 1$

$y = 5: 5 = x^2 + 1 \Rightarrow x^2 = 4 \Rightarrow x = \pm 2$

Method 1: Using subtraction between areas and the *x*-axis

$A = $ (Area of rectangle *abcd*)

$\qquad\qquad\qquad$ $-$ (Area between curve, the *x*-axis and the lines $x = -2$, $x = 2$)

$$= 5 \times 4 - \int_{-2}^{2} y\,dx$$

$$= 20 - \int_{-2}^{2} (x^2 + 1)\,dx$$

$$= 20 - \left[\frac{x^3}{3} + x \right]_{-2}^{2}$$

$$= 20 - [(\tfrac{8}{3} + 2) - (-\tfrac{8}{3} - 2)]$$

$$= 20 - 9\tfrac{1}{3} = 10\tfrac{2}{3}$$

Method 2: Area between curve and the *y*-axis (area to the left of the *y*-axis is negative)

$$A = 2\int_{1}^{5} x\,dy$$

$$= 2\int_{1}^{5} (y - 1)^{\frac{1}{2}}\,dy$$

$$= 2\int_{0}^{4} u^{\frac{1}{2}}\,du$$

$$= 2\left[\frac{u^{\frac{3}{2}}}{\frac{3}{2}} \right]_{0}^{4}$$

$$= \tfrac{4}{3}[u^{\frac{3}{2}}]_{0}^{4} = \tfrac{4}{3}[8 - 0] = 10\tfrac{2}{3}$$

$y = x^2 + 1$

$x = \sqrt{y - 1}$

$x = (y - 1)^{\frac{1}{2}}$

$u = y - 1$
$du = dy$

Limits

x	u
5	4
1	0

Example

The diagram on the right shows a sketch of the function $f: x \rightarrow x^2 - 9$.

If area of $0ax$ = area of aby, find the value of b.

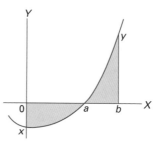

Solution:

Given: Area of $0ax$ = Area of aby

Thus, $\displaystyle\int_0^b (x^2 - 9)\,dx = 0$ (as area below cancels area above)

$\Rightarrow \left[\dfrac{x^3}{3} - 9x \right]_0^b = 0$

$\Rightarrow \dfrac{b^3}{3} - 9b = 0$

$\Rightarrow b^3 - 27b = 0$

$\Rightarrow b(b^2 - 27) = 0$

$\Rightarrow b = 0$ or $b^2 = 27$

$\Rightarrow b = 0$ or $b = \pm \sqrt{27} = \pm 3\sqrt{3}$

As $b > 0$, $b = 3\sqrt{3}$.

Volume

Rotation about the x-axis:
The volume, V, generated by rotating, once, the area bounded by the curve $y = f(x)$, the x-axis and the lines $x = a$ and $x = b$ is given by:

$$V = \pi \int_a^b y^2\,dx$$

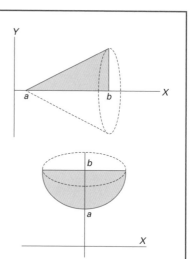

Rotation about the y-axis:
The volume, V, generated by rotating, once, the area bounded by the curve $y = f(x)$, the y-axis and the lines $y = a$ and $y = b$ is given by:

$$V = \pi \int_a^b x^2\,dy$$

Example

Find the volume of the solid generated by rotating about the x-axis the area bounded by the x-axis, the y-axis and the line $2x - 3y - 12 = 0$.

Solution:

We need to find where the line cuts the x- and y-axes.

$$2x - 3y - 12 = 0$$

$$y = 0, x = 6 \quad (6, 0)$$

$$x = 0, y = -4 \quad (0, -4)$$

The diagram below represents the situation.

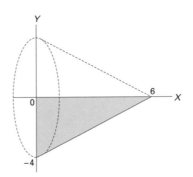

$$V = \pi \int_0^6 y^2\, dx$$

$$= \pi \int_0^6 \left[\frac{2}{3}(x - 6) \right]^2 dx$$

$$= \pi \int_0^6 \frac{4}{9}(x^2 - 12x + 36)\, dx$$

$$= \frac{4\pi}{9} \int_0^6 (x^2 - 12x + 36)\, dx$$

$$= \frac{4\pi}{9} \left[\frac{x^3}{3} - 6x^2 + 36x \right]_0^6$$

$$= \frac{4\pi}{9} [(72 - 216 + 216) - (0 - 0 + 0)]$$

$$= \frac{4\pi}{9} (72) = 32\,\pi$$

Generates a cone:

$$2x - 3y - 12 = 0$$

$$-3y = -2x + 12$$

$$3y = 2x - 12$$

$$y = \left(\frac{2x - 12}{3} \right)$$

$$y = \tfrac{2}{3}(x - 6)$$

Example

Find the volume of the solid generated by rotating about the y-axis the area bounded by the y-axis, the line $2x - y - 2 = 0$ and the lines $y = 2$ and $y = 6$.

Solution:

The diagram on the right represents the situation.

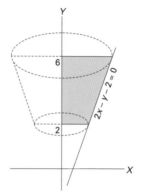

$$V = \pi \int_2^6 x^2 \, dy$$

$$= \pi \int_2^6 \frac{1}{4}(y^2 + 4y + 4) \, dy$$

$$= \frac{\pi}{4} \int_2^6 (y^2 + 4y + 4) \, dy$$

$$= \frac{\pi}{4} \left[\frac{y^3}{3} + 2y^2 + 4y \right]_2^6$$

$$= \frac{\pi}{4} [(72 + 72 + 24) - (\tfrac{8}{3} + 8 + 8)]$$

$$= \frac{\pi}{4} \left(168 - 18\tfrac{2}{3} \right)$$

$$= \frac{\pi}{4} \left(\frac{448}{3} \right)$$

$$= \frac{112}{3} \pi$$

Generates a frustrum:

$$2x - y - 2 = 0$$
$$2x = y + 2$$
$$x = \tfrac{1}{2}(y + 2)$$
$$x^2 = \tfrac{1}{4}(y + 2)^2$$
$$x^2 = \tfrac{1}{4}(y^2 + 4y + 4)$$

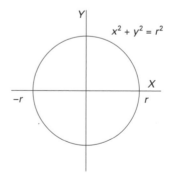

Example

Show that the volume generated by rotating the circle $x^2 + y^2 = r^2$ about the x-axis is $\frac{4}{3}\pi r^3$.

Solution:

$$V = \pi \int_{-r}^{r} y^2 \, dx$$

$$= \pi \int_{-r}^{r} (r^2 - x^2) \, dx$$

$$= \pi \left[r^2 x - \frac{x^3}{3} \right]_{-r}^{r}$$

$$= \pi \left[\left(r^3 - \frac{r^3}{3} \right) - \left(-r^3 + \frac{r^3}{3} \right) \right]$$

$$= \pi \left(r^3 - \frac{r^3}{3} + r^3 - \frac{r^3}{3} \right)$$

$$= \pi \left(\tfrac{4}{3} r^3 \right)$$

$$= \tfrac{4}{3} \pi r^3$$

The circle cuts the x-axis at $-r$ and r.

Thus, the limits of integration are $-r$ and r.

$$x^2 + y^2 = r^2$$
$$\Rightarrow \qquad y^2 = (r^2 - x^2)$$

Example

Find the volume of the solid generated by rotating about the x-axis the area bounded by the x-axis, the circle $(x-2)^2 + y^2 = 9$ and the lines $x = 3$ and $x = 4$.

Solution:

$$V = \pi \int_3^4 y^2 \, dx$$

$$= \pi \int_3^4 (5 + 4x - x^2) \, dx$$

$$= \pi \left[5x + 2x^2 - \frac{x^3}{3} \right]_3^4$$

$$= \pi[(20 + 32 - \tfrac{64}{3}) - (15 + 18 - 9)]$$

$$= \pi[30\tfrac{2}{3} - 24]$$

$$= \pi(6\tfrac{2}{3})$$

$$= \frac{20}{3}\pi$$

$(x-2)^2 + y^2 = 9$

centre = (2, 0), radius = 3

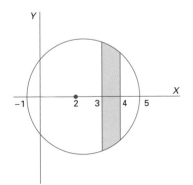

Generates a slice of a sphere:

$$(x-2)^2 + y^2 = 9$$
$$y^2 = 9 - (x-2)^2$$
$$y^2 = 9 - x^2 + 4x - 4$$
$$y^2 = 5 + 4x - x^2$$

Chapter 7
Proofs

Factor Theorem

> For a polynomial $f(x)$, if $f(a) = 0$, then $(x - a)$ is a factor of $f(x)$.

Proof:

Let

$$f(x) = a_0 + a_1x + a_2x^2 + a_3x^3$$

then

$$f(a) = a_0 + a_1a + a_2a^2 + a_3a^3$$

and

$$f(x) - f(a) = a_1(x - a) + a_2(x^2 - a^2) + a_3(x^3 - a^3)$$
$$= a_1(x - a) + a_2(x - a)(x + a) + a_3(x - a)(x^2 + ax + a^2)$$
$$= (x - a)[a_1 + a_2(x + a) + a_3(x^2 + ax + a^2)]$$

$\therefore \quad (x - a)$ is a factor of $f(x) - f(a)$

but $f(a) = 0$,

$\therefore \quad (x - a)$ is a factor of $f(x)$.

De Moivre's Theorem

> $(\cos\theta + i\sin\theta)^n = \cos n\theta + i\sin n\theta$

Proof: (for $n \in N$)

$$P(n): (\cos\theta + i\sin\theta)^n = \cos n\theta + i\sin n\theta, \quad n \in N$$

Step 1: $P(0): (\cos\theta + i\sin\theta)^0 = \cos 0(\theta) + i\sin 0\,(\theta)$

$$1 = \cos 0 + i\sin 0$$
$$1 = 1 \quad \text{which is true}$$

$\therefore \quad P(0)$ is true.

Step 2: Assume $P(k)$ is true, i.e. $(\cos\theta + i\sin\theta)^k = \cos k\theta + i\sin k\theta$

Test $P(k + 1)$:

Multiply both sides by $(\cos\theta + i\sin\theta)$

$$(\cos\theta + i\sin\theta)^k (\cos\theta + i\sin\theta) = (\cos k\theta + i\sin k\theta)(\cos\theta + i\sin\theta)$$

$\Rightarrow \qquad (\cos\theta + i\sin\theta)^{k+1} = (\cos k\theta \cos\theta - \sin k\theta \sin\theta)$
$$+ i(\sin k\theta \cos\theta + \cos k\theta \sin\theta)$$
$$= \cos(k\theta + \theta) + i\sin(k\theta + \theta)$$
$$= \cos(k + 1)\theta + i\sin(k + 1)\theta$$

i.e. $P(k + 1)$ is true if $P(k)$ is true.

Hence, by the principle of mathematical induction $P(n)$ is true.

Proof for $n \in \mathbf{Z}$. Consider the case when n is negative.

Proof:

Consider $(\cos \theta + i \sin \theta)^{-n}$, $n \in \mathbf{N}_0$

$(\cos \theta + i \sin \theta)^{-n}$

$= \dfrac{1}{(\cos \theta + i \sin \theta)^n}$

$= \dfrac{1}{\cos n\theta + i \sin n\theta}$ [as $n \in \mathbf{N}_0$]

$= \dfrac{1}{\cos n\theta + i \sin n\theta} \cdot \dfrac{\cos n\theta - i \sin n\theta}{\cos n\theta - i \sin n\theta}$ $\begin{bmatrix} \text{multiply top and bottom by} \\ \text{the conjugate of the bottom} \end{bmatrix}$

$= \dfrac{\cos n\theta - i \sin n\theta}{\cos^2 n\theta + \sin^2 n\theta}$

$= \cos n\theta - i \sin n\theta$ [$\cos^2 n\theta + \sin^2 n\theta = 1$]

$= \cos(-n\theta) + i \sin(-n\theta)$

$\therefore$ $(\cos \theta + i \sin n\theta)^{-n} = \cos(-n\theta) + i \sin(-n\theta)$

Therefore De Moivre's Theorem is true for all $n \in \mathbf{Z}$.

Proofs from first principles of the rules for differentiation.
Sum Rule

If $u = u(x)$ and $v = v(x)$, then:

$$\frac{d}{dx}(u + v) = \frac{du}{dx} + \frac{dv}{dx}$$

Proof:

Let $f(x) = u(x) + v(x)$

$f(x + h) = u(x + h) + v(x + h)$

$f(x + h) - f(x) = u(x + h) + v(x + h) - u(x) - v(x)$

$= u(x + h) - u(x) + v(x + h) - v(x)$

$\dfrac{f(x + h) - f(x)}{h} = \dfrac{u(x + h) - u(x)}{h} + \dfrac{v(x + h) - v(x)}{h}$

$\lim\limits_{h \to 0} \dfrac{f(x + h) - f(x)}{h} = \lim\limits_{h \to 0} \dfrac{u(x + h) - u(x)}{h} + \lim\limits_{h \to 0} \dfrac{v(x + h) - v(x)}{h}$

$= \dfrac{du}{dx} + \dfrac{dv}{dx}$

Thus, $f'(x) = \dfrac{du}{dx} + \dfrac{dv}{dx} = \dfrac{d}{dx}(u + v)$

Product Rule

If $u = u(x)$ and $v = v(x)$, then:

$$\frac{d}{dx}(uv) = u\frac{dv}{dx} + v\frac{du}{dx}$$

Proof:

Let

$$f(x) = u(x).v(x)$$

$$f(x + h) = u(x + h).v(x + h)$$

$$f(x + h) - f(x) = u(x + h).v(x + h) - u(x).v(x)$$

$$= u(x + h).v(x + h) - u(x + h).v(x) + u(x + h).v(x) - u(x).v(x)$$

$$= u(x + h)[v(x + h) - v(x)] + v(x)[u(x + h) - u(x)]$$

$$\frac{f(x + h) - f(x)}{h} = u(x + h)\left[\frac{v(x + h) - v(x)}{h}\right] + v(x)\left[\frac{u(x + h) - u(x)}{h}\right]$$

$$\lim_{h\to 0}\frac{f(x + h) - f(x)}{h} = \lim_{h\to 0}u(x+h)\left[\frac{v(x + h) - v(x)}{h}\right] + \lim_{h\to 0}v(x)\left[\frac{u(x+h) - u(x)}{h}\right]$$

$$= u\frac{dv}{dx} + v\frac{du}{dx}$$

Thus, $f'(x) = u\dfrac{dv}{dx} + v\dfrac{du}{dx} = \dfrac{d}{dx}(uv).$

Quotient Rule

If $u = u(x)$ and $v = v(x)$, then:

$$\frac{d}{dx}\left(\frac{u}{v}\right) = \frac{v\dfrac{du}{dx} - u\dfrac{dv}{dx}}{v^2}$$

Proof:

Let

$$f(x) = \frac{u(x)}{v(x)}$$

$$f(x + h) = \frac{u(x + h)}{v(x + h)}$$

$$f(x + h) - f(x) = \frac{u(x + h)}{v(x + h)} - \frac{u(x)}{v(x)}$$

$$= \frac{u(x + h) \cdot v(x) - u(x) \cdot v(x + h)}{v(x + h)v(x)}$$

$$= \frac{u(x + h)v(x) - u(x)v(x) + u(x)v(x) - u(x)v(x + h)}{v(x + h)v(x)}$$

$$= \frac{v(x)[u(x + h) - u(x)] - u(x)[v(x + h) - v(x)]}{v(x + h)v(x)}$$

$$\frac{f(x + h) - f(x)}{h} = \frac{v(x)\left[\dfrac{u(x + h) - u(x)}{h}\right] - u(x)\left[\dfrac{v(x + h) - v(x)}{h}\right]}{v(x + h)v(x)}$$

$$\lim_{h \to 0}\frac{f(x + h) - f(x)}{h} = \lim_{h \to 0}\frac{v(x)\left[\dfrac{u(x + h) - u(x)}{h}\right] - u(x)\left[\dfrac{v(x + h) - v(x)}{h}\right]}{v(x + h)v(x)}$$

$$= \frac{v\dfrac{du}{dx} - u\dfrac{dv}{dx}}{v^2}$$

Thus, $f'(x) = \dfrac{v\dfrac{du}{dx} - u\dfrac{dv}{dx}}{v^2} = \dfrac{d}{dx}\left(\dfrac{u}{v}\right)$.

Differential Rule

$$\frac{d}{dx}(x^n) = nx^{n-1}, \, n \in \mathbf{N}_0$$

Proof:

$$P(n): \frac{d}{dx}(x^n) = nx^{n-1}, \, n \in \mathbf{N}_0$$

Step 1: $P(1): \dfrac{dx}{dx} = 1$

Let $f(x) = x$

$$\lim_{h \to 0} \frac{f(x+h) - f(x)}{h} = \lim_{h \to 0}\left(\frac{x+h-x}{h}\right) = \lim_{h \to 0} 1 = 1$$

$\therefore$ $P(1)$ is true.

Step 2:   Assume $P(k)$ is true, i.e. $\dfrac{d}{dx}(x^k) = kx^{k-1}$

Test $p(k+1)$:

$$\frac{d}{dx}(x^{k+1}) = \frac{d}{dx}(x \cdot x^k)$$

$$= x\frac{d}{dx}(x^k) + x^k\frac{d}{dx}(x) \qquad \text{[using the product rule]}$$

$$= x \cdot kx^{k-1} + x^k(1) \qquad\qquad \text{[using our assumption and } P(1) \text{ is true]}$$

$$= kx^k + x^k$$

$$= (k+1)x^k$$

Thus, $P(k+1)$ is true if $P(k)$ is true.

Hence, by the principle of mathematical induction $P(n)$ is true.

MATHEMATICS – HIGHER LEVEL PAPER 1 (300 marks)

9:30 to 12:00

Attempt **SIX QUESTIONS** (50 marks each)

Warning: Marks will be lost if all necessary work is not clearly shown.

Answers should include the appropriate units of measurement, where relevant.

_____

1. (a) Simplify fully $\dfrac{x^2+4}{x^2-4} - \dfrac{x}{x+2}$.

    (b) Given that one of the roots is an integer, solve the equation

    $$6x^3 - 29x^2 + 36x - 9 = 0.$$

    (c) Two of the roots of the equation $ax^3 + bx^2 + cx + d = 0$ are p and $-p$.
    Show that $bc = ad$.

2. (a) Express $x^2 + 10x + 32$ in the form $(x+a)^2 + b$.

    (b) α and β are the roots of the equation $x^2 - 7x + 1 = 0$.

        (i) Find the value of $\alpha^2 + \beta^2$.

        (ii) Find the value of $\dfrac{1}{\alpha^3} + \dfrac{1}{\beta^3}$.

    (c) Show that if a and b are non-zero real numbers, then the value of

    $\dfrac{a}{b} + \dfrac{b}{a}$ can never lie between -2 and 2.

    Hint: consider the case where a and b have the same sign separately from the case where a and b have opposite sign.

3. **(a)** Let A be the matrix $\begin{pmatrix} 3 & 5 \\ 1 & 2 \end{pmatrix}$

Find the matrix B, such that $AB = \begin{pmatrix} 4 & 6 \\ 3 & 2 \end{pmatrix}$.

(b) **(i)** Let $z = \dfrac{5}{2+i} - 1$, where $i^2 = -1$.

Express z in the form $a + bi$ and plot it on an Argand diagram.

(ii) Use De Moivre's theorem to evaluate z^6.

(c) Prove, by induction, that

$$(\cos \theta + i \sin \theta)^n = \cos n\theta + i \sin n\theta \text{ for } n \in \mathbf{N}.$$

,

4. **(a)** $2 + \dfrac{2}{3} + \dfrac{2}{9} + \ ....\ $ is a geometric series.

Find the sum to infinity of the series.

(b) Given that $u_n = 2\left(-\dfrac{1}{2}\right)^n - 2$ for all $n \in \mathbf{N}$,

(i) write down u_{n+1} and u_{n+2}

(ii) show that $2u_{n+2} - u_{n+1} - u_n = 0$.

(c) **(i)** Write down an expression in n for the sum $1 + 2 + 3 + \ ....\ + n$ and an expression in n for the sum $1^2 + 2^2 + 3^2 + \ ....\ + n^2$.

(ii) Find, in terms of n, the sum $\displaystyle\sum_{r=1}^{n} (6r^2 + 2r + 5 + 2^r)$.

5. **(a)** Find the range of values of x that satisfy the inequality

$$x^2 - 3x - 10 \leq 0.$$

(b) **(i)** Solve the equation

$$2^{x^2} = 8^{2x+9}.$$

(ii) Solve the equation

$$\log_e (2x + 3) + \log_e (x - 2) = 2 \log_e (x + 4).$$

(c) Show that there are no natural numbers n and r for which

$$\binom{n}{r-1}, \binom{n}{r} \text{ and } \binom{n}{r+1}$$ are consecutive terms in a geometric sequence.

6. **(a)** Differentiate $\sqrt{x^3}$ with respect to x.

(b) Let $y = \dfrac{e^x - e^{-x}}{e^x + e^{-x}}$.

Show that $\dfrac{dy}{dx} = \dfrac{4}{(e^x + e^{-x})^2}$.

(c) The function $f(x) = 2x^3 + 3x^2 + bx + c$ has a local maximum at $x = -2$.

(i) Find the value of b.

(ii) Find the range of values of c for which $f(x) = 0$ has three distinct real roots.

7. **(a)** Differentiate $2x + \sin 2x$ with respect to x.

(b) The equation of a curve is $5x^2 + 5y^2 + 6xy = 16$.

(i) Find $\dfrac{dy}{dx}$ in terms of x and y.

(ii) $(1, 1)$ and $(2, -2)$ are two points on the curve.
Show that the tangents at these points are perpendicular to each other.

(c) Let $y = \sin^{-1}\left(\dfrac{x}{\sqrt{1+x^2}}\right)$.

Find $\dfrac{dy}{dx}$ and express it in the form $\dfrac{a}{a+x^b}$, where $a, b \in \mathbf{N}$.

8. **(a)** Find $\displaystyle\int (2x + \cos 3x)\, dx$.

(b) Evaluate

(i) $\displaystyle\int_0^1 3x^2 e^{x^3}\, dx$

(ii) $\displaystyle\int_2^4 \dfrac{2x^3}{x^2 - 1}\, dx$.

(c) The diagram shows the curve $y = 4 - x^2$ and the line $2x + y - 1 = 0$.

Calculate the area of the shaded region enclosed by the curve and the line.

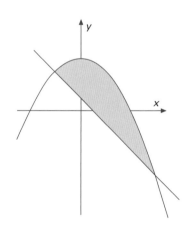

Answers

2008 Paper 1

1. (a) $\dfrac{2}{x-2}$

   (b) $\dfrac{1}{3}$; $\dfrac{3}{2}$; 3

2. (a) $(x+5)^2 + 7$

   (b) (i) 47

       (ii) 322

3. (a) $\begin{pmatrix} -7 & 2 \\ 5 & 0 \end{pmatrix}$

   (b) (i) $1 - i$

       (ii) $8i$

4. (a) 3

   (b) (i) $-\left(-\dfrac{1}{2}\right)^n - 2$; $\dfrac{1}{2}\left(-\dfrac{1}{2}\right)^n - 2$

   (c) (i) $\dfrac{n}{2}(n+1)$; $\dfrac{n}{6}(n+1)(2n+1)$

       (ii) $n(n+1)(2n+1) + n(n+1) + 5n + 2^{n+1} - 2$ or $n[2(n+1)^2 + 5] + 2(2^n - 1)$

5. (a) $-2 \le x \le 5$

   (b) (i) 9; -3

       (ii) 11

6. (a) $\dfrac{3}{2}x^{\frac{1}{2}}$ or $\dfrac{3}{2}\sqrt{x}$

   (c) (i) -12

       (ii) $-20 < c < 7$

7. (a) $2 + 2\cos 2x$

   (b) (i) $\dfrac{-5x - 3y}{3x + 5y}$

   (c) $\dfrac{1}{1 + x^2}$

8. (a) $x^2 + \dfrac{1}{3}\sin 3x + c$

   (b) (i) $e - i$

       (ii) $12 + \ln 5$

   (c) $\dfrac{32}{3}$

MATHEMATICS – HIGHER LEVEL PAPER 1 (300 marks)

9.30 to 12.00

Attempt **SIX QUESTIONS** (50 marks each)

Warning: Marks will be lost if all necessary work is not clearly shown.

Answers should include the appropriate units of measurement, where relevant.

_____

1. **(a)** Find the value of $\dfrac{x}{y}$ when $\dfrac{2x + 3y}{x + 6y} = \dfrac{4}{5}$.

   (b) Let $f(x) = x^2 - 7x + 12$.

      (i) Show that if $f(x + 1) \neq 0$, then $\dfrac{f(x)}{f(x+1)}$ simplifies to $\dfrac{x - 4}{x - 2}$.

      (ii) Find the range of values of x for which $\dfrac{f(x)}{f(x+1)} > 3$.

   (c) Given that $x - c + 1$ is a factor of $x^2 - 5x + 5cx - 6b^2$, express c in terms of b.

2. **(a)** Solve the simultaneous equations
$$x - y + 8 = 0$$
$$x^2 + xy + 8 = 0.$$

   (b) **(i)** The graphs of three quadratic functions, f, g and h, are shown.

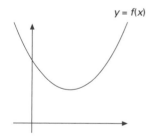

$y = f(x)$

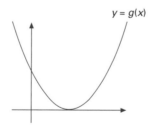

$y = g(x)$

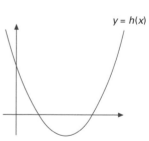

$y = h(x)$

   In each case, state the nature of the roots of the function.

      (ii) The equation $kx^2 + (1 - k) x + k = 0$ has equal real roots.
      Find the possible values of k.

   (c) **(i)** One of the roots of $px^2 + qx + r = 0$ is n times the other root.
      Express r in terms of p, q and n.

      (ii) One of the roots of $x^2 + qx + r = 0$ is five times the other.
      If q and r are positive integers, determine the set of possible values of q.

225

3. (a) $z_1 = a + bi$ and $z_2 = c + di$, where $i^2 = -1$.

Show that $\overline{z_1 + z_2} = \overline{z_1} + \overline{z_2}$, where $\overline{z}$ is the complex conjugate of z.

(b) Let $A = \dfrac{1}{2}\begin{pmatrix} 1 & -\sqrt{3} \\ \sqrt{3} & 1 \end{pmatrix}$.

(i) Express A^3 in the form $\begin{pmatrix} a & 0 \\ 0 & b \end{pmatrix}$, where $a, b \in \mathbf{Z}$.

(ii) Hence, or otherwise, find A^{17}.

(c) (i) Use De Moivre's theorem to prove that $\sin 3\theta = 3\sin\theta - 4\sin^3\theta$.

(ii) Hence, find $\int \sin^3\theta \, d\theta$.

4. (a) Three consecutive terms of an arithmetic series are $4x + 11$, $2x + 11$, and $3x + 17$. Find the value of x.

(b) (i) Show that $\dfrac{2}{r^2 - 1} = \dfrac{1}{r - 1} - \dfrac{1}{r + 1}$, where $r \neq \pm 1$.

(ii) Hence, find $\displaystyle\sum_{r=2}^{n} \dfrac{2}{r^2 - 1}$.

(iii) Hence, evaluate $\displaystyle\sum_{r=2}^{\infty} \dfrac{2}{r^2 - 1}$.

(c) A finite geometric sequence has first term a and common ratio r.
The sequence has $2m + 1$ terms, where $m \in \mathbf{N}$.

(i) Write down the last term, in terms of a, r, and m.

(ii) Write down the middle term, in terms of a, r, and m.

(iii) Show that the product of all of the terms of the sequence is equal to the middle term raised to the power of the number of terms.

5. **(a)** Solve for x: $x - 2 = \sqrt{3x - 2}$.

(b) Prove by induction that, for all positive integers n, 5 is a factor of $n^5 - n$.

(c) Solve the simultaneous equations
$$\log_3 x + \log_3 y = 2$$
$$\log_3 (2y - 3) - 2\log_9 x = 1.$$

6. **(a)** Differentiate $\sin(3x^2 - x)$ with respect to x.

(b) **(i)** Differentiate $\sqrt{x}$ with respect to x, from first principles.

(ii) An object moves in a straight line such that its distance from a fixed point is given by $s = \sqrt{t^2 + 1}$, where s is in metres and t is in seconds. Find the speed of the object when $t = 5$ seconds.

(c) The equation of a curve is $y = \dfrac{2}{x - 3}$.

(i) Write down the equations of the asymptotes and hence sketch the curve.

(ii) Prove that no two tangents to the curve are perpendicular to each other.

7. **(a)** The equation of a curve is $x^2 - y^2 = 25$. Find $\dfrac{dy}{dx}$ in terms of x and y.

(b) A curve is defined by the parametric equations

$$x = \frac{3t}{t^2 - 2} \text{ and } y = \frac{6}{t^2 - 2}, \text{ where } t \neq \pm \sqrt{2}.$$

(i) Find $\dfrac{dy}{dx}$ in terms of t.

(ii) Find the equation of the tangent to the curve at the point given by $t = 2$.

(c) The function $f(x) = x^3 - 3x^2 + 3x - 4$ has only one real root.

(i) Show that the root lies between 2 and 3.

Anne and Barry are each using the Newton-Raphson method to approximate the root. Anne is starting with 2 as a first approximation and Barry is starting with 3.

(ii) Show that Anne's starting approximation is closer to the root than Barry's. (That is, show that the root is less than 2.5.)

(iii) Show, however, that Barry's next approximation is closer to the root than Anne's.

8. **(a)** Find $\displaystyle \int \left(6x + 3 + \frac{1}{x^2} \right) dx$.

(b) Evaluate **(i)** $\displaystyle \int_{-\frac{\pi}{4}}^{\frac{\pi}{4}} \sin 3x \, \sin x \, dx$ **(ii)** $\displaystyle \int_{\ln 3}^{\ln 8} e^x \sqrt{1 + e^x} \, dx$.

(c) Use integration methods to establish the standard formula for the volume of a cone.

Answers

2009 Paper 1

1. (a) $\dfrac{3}{2}$

     (b)   (ii) $1 < x < 2$

     (c) $c = 1 \pm b$

2. (a) $x = -2$ and $y = 6$

     (b)   (i)   Complex roots (non–real roots); two equal real roots (repeated real roots); two distinct (different) real roots

             (ii) $k = -1$ or $k = \dfrac{1}{3}$

     (c)   (i) $r = \dfrac{nq^2}{(n+1)^2 q}$

             (ii) $q = 6, 12, 18, 24, \ldots$

3. (b)   (i) $\begin{pmatrix} -1 & 0 \\ 0 & -1 \end{pmatrix}$

             (ii) $\dfrac{1}{2}\begin{pmatrix} 1 & \sqrt{3} \\ -\sqrt{3} & 1 \end{pmatrix}$

     (c)   (ii) $-\dfrac{3}{4}\cos\theta + \dfrac{1}{12}\cos 3\theta + c$

4. (a) $x = -2$

     (b)   (ii) $\dfrac{3}{2} - \dfrac{1}{n} - \dfrac{1}{n+1}$

             (iii) $\dfrac{3}{2}$

     (c)   (i) ar^{2m}

             (ii) ar^m

5. (a) $x = 6$

     (c) $x = 2$ and $y = \dfrac{9}{2}$

6. **(a)** $(6x - 1) \cos (3x^2 - x)$

  (b) **(ii)** $\dfrac{5}{\sqrt{26}} \, m/s$

  (c) **(i)** $x = 3$ and $y = 0$

7. **(a)** $\dfrac{x}{y}$

  (b) **(i)** $\dfrac{4t}{t^2 + 2}$

  (ii) $4x - 3y - 3 = 0$

8. **(a)** $3x^2 + 3x - \dfrac{1}{x} + c$

  (b) **(i)** $\dfrac{1}{2}$

  (ii) $\dfrac{38}{3}$